BROTHER and LOVER

SCOTIA

DUNKELD

AELRED'S
BRITAIN

RIEVAULX AND DAUGHTER HOUSES

OTHER CISTERCIAN ABBEYS

OTHER MONASTIC HOUSES

OTHER PLACES

BATTLE OF THE STANDARD 1138

MILES

0   100

0   80   160

KILOMETERS

MELROSE 1136
ROXBURGH
LINDISFARNE
Benedictine

NEWMINSTER
1138

DUNDRENNAN
1142
KIRKCUDBRIGHT
WHITHORN
CUMBRIA
NORTHUMBRIA
HEXHAM
Augustinian
JARROW
Benedictine
DURHAM
Benedictine

HOLMCULTRAM
1150

FOUNTAINS
1132
FURNESS 1147
NEWBURGH
Augustinian
BYLAND 1147
KIRKHAM
Augustinian
YORK
WATTON
Gilbertine

RIEVAULX 1132

R. HUMBER

RUFFORD 1146
KIRKSTEAD
1139
REVESBY 1142

WARDEN 1136

LONDON

WAVERLEY 1128
CANTERBURY

BROTHER and LOVER

AELRED *of* RIEVAULX

Brian Patrick McGuire

CROSSROAD • NEW YORK

1994

The Crossroad Publishing Company
370 Lexington Avenue, New York, NY 10017

Copyright © 1994 by Brian Patrick McGuire

All rights reserved. No part of this book may be reproduced, stored in a
retrieval system, or transmitted, in any form or by any means, electronic,
mechanical, photocopying, recording, or otherwise, without the written
permission of The Crossroad Publishing Company.

Printed in the United States of America

Library of Congress Cataloging-in-Publication Data
McGuire, Brian Patrick.
    Brother and lover : Aelred of Rievaulx / Brian Patrick McGuire.
      p. cm.
    Includes bibliographical references and index.
    ISBN 0-8245-1405-X
    1. Aelred, of Rievaulx, Saint, 1110–1167. 2. Christian saints—
England—Biography. I. Title.
BX4700.E7M34   1994
271'.1202—dc20
[B]   93-49884
                                           CIP

to my cistercian friends
in the u.s.a.

who will give you to me, my brother,
sucking the breasts of my mother,
so that i might find you outside
and kiss you?
—songs of songs 8:1

contents

preface

ELRED OF RIEVAULX (1110–67) defies definition. Perhaps the most attractive of monastic figures in twelfth-century Europe, Aelred has become the subject of innumerable controversies. He has been called "the Bernard of the North," the "gay abbot of Rievaulx," and "Saint Aelred." He was not a Bernard, even though the pages that follow will provide some parallels. His sexual identity, however intriguing, will probably always be a matter for controversy. He was never canonized as a saint, except by the Cistercian Order, which even today follows its own observance and holds his feast day on January 12.

I got to know Aelred more than a quarter of a century ago, in the lost world of Berkeley in the 1960s. At Oxford in England and in Copenhagen in Denmark, I have returned time and again to him. In the 1970s I used the medieval biography of Aelred by his contemporary Walter Daniel as a text for students in medieval history. In the 1980s when I prepared a book on friendship, Aelred was my guide to the special quality of the twelfth century. Aelred introduced me to the theory and practice of friendship among people living in monastic community.

In the 1990s I have frequently returned to him. Much of my research now centers on the later Middle Ages, but I continue looking back to the twelfth century and Aelred. I think Aelred deserves new attention in the face of neo-conservative apologists in the Christian churches. Their triumphalism would win Aelred back from the gay historians who, for better and worse, have made use of him.

The more I have read Aelred, the less I have felt able to categorize him in one way or another. He was, as we all are, unique, a human person with talents and limitations. But he is especially worthwhile to study because he left so much that speaks of his person and his period.

In what follows I make no attempt to write a "definitive biography" of Aelred. The definitive biography, thankfully, can never be written of any historical figure. Historians regularly tear up their predecessors' results in finding new approaches and insights. As I write these very lines, there are, I hope, researchers at work who one day will demolish much of what I claim. What follows here is merely a sketch of Aelred, an introduction for the curious, a provocation for the learned, and an experiment for myself.

My purpose is to look at Aelred as a whole person: child, monk, friend, politician, diplomat, writer. I largely leave out, however, one aspect of Aelred: his contributions as theologian. I include Aelred's theological insights only insofar as they illustrate his mind or his milieu. Otherwise I leave their interpretation to experts who are better equipped to interpret them. Names such as Aelred Squire, Charles Dumont, Gaetano Raciti, James McEvoy, and Amédée Hallier immediately come to mind here.

It has become fashionable today either to fictionalize biography or to overlay it with so much learning that the reader gets little sense of the person being described. In the face of this situation, I have asked some of my students for advice. They suggested that I write about Aelred as a person who can be understood. In practically every statement I make about Aelred, my training as a historian warns me that there can be second opinions, contrary interpretations, and other possibilities. At times I let the reader know how difficult it is to judge. But often I prefer that the reader continue reading, instead of stopping short in uncertainty — or turning to footnotes.

I have banned footnotes from this book. They have gotten out of control in academia. Nowadays many books are two books: the text, which is thin and dull, and the footnotes, which are feasts of polemic and opinion. I have kept as much as possible in the text itself and have replaced footnotes with a bibliographical essay at the end. My references in the text are only to the materials taken directly from Aelred or his contemporaries.

As I have written this book, quotations have required more space than I had originally intended. Often Aelred or his medieval biographer Walter Daniel express themselves so well that it would be a shame to try to paraphrase their language. When there are good English translations, I have used them, sometimes updating their language or changing a word or two in order to fit the Latin better. I have consistently spelled Aelred's name with an "e," and so the generation of English scholars who wrote "Ailred" has had to yield to my emendation.

How can I relate in two hundred pages the experiences and insights of Aelred's life and the special qualities of his contribution to the twelfth century? Like many other medieval writers, Aelred was attentive to a literary tradition. His models go back to the Romans, especially to Cicero, and sometimes to church fathers, especially Augustine, Jerome, and Ambrose. At times I have pointed to Aelred's borrowings. For the most part, however, I have assumed that in Aelred the whole is greater than the sum of the literary parts. Aelred cannot be understood merely in terms of the sources that he used and that influenced him.

Another concern of mine has been to present in a fair way the question of Aelred's sexuality. I have decided to leave out any attempt to "prove" that Aelred was physically more attracted to men than to women. The evidence for Aelred's sexual concerns I have dealt with in detail in an article, "Sexual Awareness and Identity in Aelred of Rievaulx," appearing in 1994 in the *American Benedictine Review.* Those interested — and I think it is a legitimate concern for anyone interested in history — can there find the references that I deal with more superficially in this book.

If it ever should be possible to provide a sketch of a whole person in the Middle Ages, this is the case with Aelred. He is available to his readers as a historian, theologian, philosopher, writer of monastic spirituality, and politician. In no single area was he revolutionary or even greatly innovative. But his personal impact and message express the essence of twelfth-century Christian humanism in its approach to God, neighbor, and friend. In our time of academic arrogance and polemics on the one hand and religious fads on the other, Aelred is an oasis of spiritual experience.

No one can put a claim on Aelred, except perhaps the monks and nuns of the Cistercian Order today, who read him in a concentrated manner and help make possible translations of his works. The Cistercians, especially those of the so-called Strict Observance (known popularly as Trappists), have in the past years shown me the realities of monastic commitment in the midst of modern life. In visiting their houses and in speaking to them as individuals and as groups, I have gained from them new inspiration in my work as a medieval historian. As an offspring of the generation of "relevance," I have found in the Cistercians a grateful and a critical audience. To them I dedicate this book.

A few of my Cistercian friends deserve special mention for the guidance and encouragement they have provided in the last year: John-Baptist Porter of New Clairvaux Abbey in California, editor of *Cistercian Studies Quarterly,* helped me through a period of discouragement and insisted on the worth of what I was doing. His abbot, Thomas X. Davis, made possible regular trans-Atlantic telephone calls that sometimes turned into invaluable seminars on subjects such as Aelred's missing mother. At the other end of America, John Albert and other monks of Holy Spirit Abbey in Conyers, Georgia, the monks of Mepkin Abbey in South Carolina, as well as the monks of Gethsemani Abbey, especially Chrysogonus Waddell and his abbot, Timothy Kelly, provided guidance and inspiration on a visit there in 1992.

At Gethsemani, I met Michael Downey, the first lay Catholic theologian of my acquaintance, who was kind enough to make contact for me with Crossroad Publishing Co. Downey's editor at Crossroad, Frank Oveis, encouraged me to turn my thoughts first into a book proposal and then into a manuscript. In this time of economic slowdown, it has been courageous of him to back the idea with his colleagues. John Eagleson at Crossroad deserves thanks for his efficient copy editing of my manuscript.

My colleagues John Baldwin at Johns Hopkins University and Norman Cantor at New York University have both offered good advice. Kevin Long of Saint Thomas More College in Western Australia supplied me with invaluable bibliography, and James France of Oxfordshire kindly obtained articles in Oxford unavailable to me in Denmark. He also helped with proofreading, as did Dorrit Einersen of the English Institute, Copenhagen University.

As I write these lines, a war rages not so far away from Denmark in another corner of Europe. The states of the former Soviet Union disintegrate into ever-greater anarchy. My own adopted country, Denmark, struggles with the asylum applicants who come to its borders to ask for protection. My fellow Danes are torn apart by arguments about cultural pluralism and racism. In America a new administration promises change in the face of poverty and crime — but hardly has the funds to do so.

Where does Aelred belong in this scenario of pain and sorrow? He too experienced a period of anarchy in his world and lived to see the situation improve. In his perennial optimism, he made what has been called a kind of Noah's ark, in which there was room for all different kinds of people. Aelred believed in love, both "tough love" and "gentle love." He lived out his loves and sometimes had to pay dearly for them. Brother and lover, he reaches out to us across the centuries.

Skamstrup, Denmark
The Cistercian feast of Saint Aelred,
January 12, 1993

abbreviations

AS   *Acta Sanctorum*, the Bollandist Lives of the Saints, whose third edition was published in Paris from 1863, with month of the year for saint's feast day and appropriate volume.

CCCM   Corpus Christianorum series, Continuatio Mediævalis. Turnhout, Belgium, 1971– , providing a new Latin edition of Aelred.

CF   Cistercian Fathers series, Spencer, Massachusetts. Kalamazoo, Michigan, 1970– , providing translations of Aelred.

CP   Cistercian Publications. Shannon, Ireland; then Washington D.C.; since 1975: Kalamazoo, Michigan, and Spencer, Massachusetts.

Cuthbert *Reginaldi Monachi Dunelmensis Libellus de Admirandis Beati Cuthberti Virtutibus* (Reginald of Durham on Cuthbert), James Raine, ed., Surtees Society 1 (London, 1835).

Godric   *De Vita et Miraculis S. Godrici, Heremitae de Finchale* (Reginald of Durham on Godric), James Raine, ed., Surtees Society 20 (London, 1845).

PL   J.-P. Migne, Patrologiae cursus completus, series latina, 221 volumes. Paris, 1844–64. PL 195 contains much of Aelred.

Song   The Song of Songs in the Old Testament

WD   Walter Daniel, *The Life of Ailred of Rievaulx*, translated with introduction by Maurice Powicke. Edinburgh: Thomas Nelson, 1950; reprinted Oxford Medieval Texts, Clarendon Press, 1978.

Works of Aelred of Rievaulx

[Note that page numbers given in the internal references to Aelred's works normally refer to the translations, when these are available]

Am Sp
: *De spiritali amicitia,* CCCM 1:287–360. *Spiritual Friendship,* translated by Mary Eugenia Laker, introduction by Douglas Roby, CF 5 (1974).

Anima
: *De Anima,* CCCM 1:685–754. *Dialogue on the Soul,* translated and introduction by C. H. Talbot, CF 22 (1981).

Eulog
: *Eulogium Davidis Regis Scotorum,* Eulogy of King David of Scotland, in *Pinkerton's Lives of Scottish Saints,* revised W. M. Metcalfe, vol. 2 (Paisley: Alexander Gardner, 1889).

Gen Angl
: *Genealogia Regum Anglorum,* the Genealogy of the Kings of the English, available only in Latin in PL 195:711–38.

Hexham
: *De Sanctis Ecclesiae Haugustaldensis* (On the Saints of Hexham), in *The Priory of Hexham* 1, ed. James Raine, Surtees Society 44 (Durham, 1863–64). No translation.

Iesu
: *De Iesu puero duodenni,* CCCM 1:249–78. *Jesus at the Age of Twelve,* in *Treatises: The Pastoral Prayer,* translated by Theodore Berkeley, CF 2 (1971).

Inst Incl
: *De Institutione Inclusarum,* CCCM 1:637–82. *A Rule of Life for a Recluse,* translated by Mary Paul Macpherson, CF 2 (1971).

Oner
: *Sermones de Oneribus,* Aelred's sermons commenting on Isaiah 13ff, in PL 195:361–500, not translated.

Orat past
: *Oratio pastoralis,* CCCM 1:757–63. Translated by R. Penelope Lawson in *Treatises,* CF 2 (1971).

Serm
: *Sermones I–XLVI: Collectio Claraevallensis Prima et Secunda,* rec. Gaetano Raciti, CCCM 2A (1989). Aelred's sermons for the church year, most of which are not translated.

Spec Car
: *De Speculo Caritatis,* CCCM 1:3–161. *The Mirror of Charity,* translated by Elizabeth Connor, introduction by Charles Dumont, CF 17 (1990).

Stand
: *De Bello Standardii,* PL 195:701–12. Aelred's account of the Battle of the Standard in 1138. No translation.

V Edw   *Vita Edwardi*, PL 195:737–90. *The Life of Saint Ed-
             ward King and Confessor*, translated by Jerome Bertram
             (Guildford, Surrey: St. Edward's Press, 1990).

V Nin   *Vita Niniani. Lives of St. Ninian and St. Kentigern*, edited
             by A. P. Forbes (Edinburgh: Edmonston and Douglas,
             1874); Latin text pp. 137–57; English text pp. 3–26.

Watt   *De Sanctimoniali de Wattun*, PL 195:789–96. The Nun
             of Watton, not available in English.

A Note on Translations

Cistercian Publications has kindly given permission to cite from its
available translations of Aelred. Translations of Aelred's historical
works by Jane Patricia Freeland are scheduled for publication by CP in
1994. I am also grateful to Oxford University Press for permission to
use Sir Maurice Powicke's translation of Walter Daniel's *Life of Ailred
of Rievaulx*.

chronology of aelred's background, life, and works

1110   Aelred born at Hexham, son of Eilaf junior, priest.

1113   Death of archbishop of York, Thomas II. The new arch-
            bishop, Thurstan, places Augustinian canons at Hexham
            and so reduces Eilaf junior's authority.

1115/16   Aelred may have gone at this early date to the Scottish
            court.

1124–53   David king of Scots.

1130   Durham cathedral completed.

1130–33   Aelred may have written *The Life of St Ninian* at
            this time.

1132   Monastery of Rievaulx founded in Yorkshire by monks
            of Clairvaux under abbot William, formerly Bernard's
            secretary.

1134   On a trip south for King David of Scotland, Aelred joins
            Rievaulx.

1135–53   The Anarchy, period of intermittent civil war in England.

1138   Eilaf junior surrenders his claims to Hexham and be-
            comes a monk of Durham, in the presence of Aelred and
            his two brothers.

1138   The Battle of the Standard, at Northallerton. Aelred later
            wrote an account of it.

1141–42   Aelred, on mission to Rome for Abbot William of Rie-
            vaulx, probably meets Bernard, perhaps at Clairvaux.

1142–43   Aelred on his return becomes novicemaster at Rievaulx
            and starts work on his *Mirror of Charity*, his central
            theological work.

1143–47   Aelred elected abbot of Rievaulx's daughterhouse
            Revesby in Lincolnshire.

1145–47   On the death of Abbot William, Maurice elected abbot at
            Rievaulx.

1147–67   Aelred abbot of Rievaulx. Probably makes frequent trips
            to Rievaulx's daughterhouses, perhaps as late as 1165 to
            Dundrennan in Galloway.

c. 1148   Draft of the first book of *Spiritual Friendship*.

1153   Deaths of Bernard and of King David. Aelred writes
              the *Eulogy* for David and completes his *Genealogy of
              the Kings of the English* before Henry II becomes king
              in 1154.

c. 1153–57   Aelred writes *On Jesus at the Age of Twelve* for his
              friend Ivo, monk of Wardon, daughterhouse of Rievaulx
              in Bedfordshire.

1155   March 3. Aelred preaches on the translation of the relics
              of the saints of Hexham. This becomes his treatise *On
              the Saints of the Church of Hexham and Their Miracles*.

1163   In connection with the translation of the relics of Saint
              Edward the Confessor at Westminster, Aelred writes his
              Life of the king-saint.

1163–64   *Sermones de Oneribus*, Aelred's sermons based on Isa-
              iah, sent to Gilbert Foliot, bishop of London.

1165–66   Aelred works on his treatise *On the Soul* and completes
              his *On Spiritual Friendship*. Other works cannot be dated
              precisely but are traditionally placed in the last decade of
              his abbacy: *A Rule of Life for a Recluse* and *The Nun
              of Watton*. Aelred's sermons based on the feast of the
              church would have been given all through his abbacy and
              are for the most part impossible to date individually.

1167   January 12. Death of Aelred. Silvain elected abbot.

1184   Ernald abbot of Rievaulx.

1

enòs anò Beginnings

IS REAL NAME WAS ETHELRED. But like everything else in his life, he adapted his name to the new times and their Norman rulers. So he became Ailred — or Aelred. Walter Daniel played with his name in its English form: "The great counsellor had a fitting name, for the English [word] *Aelred* is in Latin *Totum consilium* [all counsel] or *omne consilium* [every counsel]" (WD, p. 8). In the generation living after the Norman Conquest of England in 1066, good counsel was much in demand.

Aelred was born in 1110 in Hexham in the north of England. His England had for decades been torn apart by political and social change. After Danish hegemony under King Canute and his sons, Anglo-Saxon kingship had been reestablished under Edward the Confessor (1042–66). Edward's saintly reputation was probably not acquired until well after his death, thanks partly to the monastic community at Westminster Abbey, whose church he built. We can see Edward and his world on the Bayeux Tapestry, with its edges full of raw doings. These activities balance off the pious gestures in the central section and prepare the way for the battle at Hastings between Earl Godwin, who made himself king on Edward's death, and the duke of Normandy, William.

The events of 1066 did not mean a smooth transfer of power to the new rulers. Anglo-Saxon resistance to the Norman conquerors concentrated especially in the North and rallied around Prince Edgar. William felt obliged to make an expedition to Yorkshire and other northern cities in 1068–69. His scorched-earth policy is recorded in the Anglo-Saxon Chronicle:

Prince Edgar came to York with all the Northumbrians and the citizens made peace with him. And King William came on them by surprise from the south with an overwhelming army and routed them and killed those who could not escape, which was many hundreds of men, and ravaged the city and made St Peter's minster an object of scorn, and ravaged and humiliated all the others. And the prince went back to Scotland.

The Prince Edgar mentioned here is Edgar the Atheling, grandson of the Anglo-Saxon king Edmund Ironside. His escape to Scotland was

1

of great importance for the future of the island, because Edgar's sister, Margaret, married the king of Scotland, Malcolm Canmore. The Scottish line eventually was married into the Norman one and thus united the three royal houses.

This mid-twelfth-century reconciliation was a long way off in the early part of the century when Aelred was born. His world was the same Northumbria whose inhabitants killed King William's representative at Durham, Earl Robert. The Humber River, further south, formed the boundary between the south of England, which for the most part had given way to the new rulers, and the North, whose people still hoped to throw them out. In 1070 relief seemed to be on the way from King Svend of Denmark. On his arrival in the Humber, "the local people came to meet him and made a truce with him — they expected that he was going to conquer the country." The Danes had come in order to plunder, not to stay, as the monks of Ely cathedral soon found out: "They took so much gold and silver, and so many treasures in money and vestments and books that no man can reckon it up to another. They said they did it out of loyalty to the monastery."

Like the legendary American general in Vietnam who destroyed a village "in order to save it," the Danes came to destroy the place in order to save it. For centuries they had been making expeditions across the North Sea to the east coast of England. As early as the 790s they had raided the great monastic center at Lindisfarne (Holy Island) on the Northumbrian Coast. Even though Danish historians today claim that the Vikings should be seen more as merchants than marauders, any self-respecting fisherman or monk who grew up in Northumbria from the ninth to the twelfth centuries knew what to expect from the Vikings.

One Anglo-Saxon family would play a special role in Aelred's life, that of Earl Waldef, who in 1066 was count of Northampton and Huntingdon. Waldef, or Waltheof (his Anglo-Saxon name before he became Normanized), came from a distinguished northern line: his father, Siward, had been earl of Northumbria. Waldef fought at Hastings and later defended home ground at the siege of York. William the Conqueror showed generosity and political acuteness in subsequently pardoning Waldef and arranging that his niece Judith marry Waldef. Their daughter Maud would in 1114 marry the future king of Scotland, David. This alliance added Anglo-Saxon blood to the Scottish line.

In 1075 Count Waldef rebelled a second time again against William the Conqueror, who imprisoned him for a year and finally beheaded him for treason. That should have been the end of his story, but the monks of Croyland in Lincolnshire provided for his burial in their church and the site became a place of pilgrimage. Sir Richard Southern has shown in an outstanding essay, "England's First Entry into Europe," how the cult of Waldef at first was an expression of Anglo-Saxon resistance to the Normans:

His body was cared for by Englishmen; Englishmen flocked to his tomb and were cured by his miraculous intervention. The Normans took no part at all in this; they mocked and doubted, and told their tale of treachery. As late as 1120, when the first passions of the Conquest had died away, the story still divided men along national lines: for the Normans Waltheof was a traitor; for the English a hero and a martyr.

By the 1130s, attitudes toward Waldef were changing, a sign that the animosity and sense of division that followed the Conquest were beginning to die away. Waldef became a national hero, a martyr, and his cult no longer was limited to Englishmen. By the time the Cistercian biographer Jocelin of Furness shortly after 1200 wrote an account of Waldef's grandson, the fact of treason had been reversed. Now it was King William who had betrayed Waldef, whom Jocelin described as preparing himself for martyrdom as he "turned his whole being to God, with frequent confession of sins, continual shedding of tears, assiduous prayers and genuflections" (AS, August, vol. 1, p. 250).

As an Englishman of the North, Aelred must have grown up with stories about the heroic and tragic Count Waldef. As we shall see, Aelred spent time at the court of Scotland with the son of Count Waldef's daughter, Maud. Waldef's grandson, who was also called Waldef, became the stepson of King David of Scotland. Waldef junior's mother, Maud, married David in 1114, ten years before he became king. Maud's first husband — and Waldef junior's father — had been Simon earl of Huntingdon. From the mid-1120s, by which time Aelred would have been resident at the Scottish court, he would have heard stories about grandfather Waldef and the great betrayals of the 1060s and 1070s.

By the time of Aelred's youth, the old betrayals were at such a distance that their memory no longer reflected national divisions and discord. Now the events of the 1060s and 1070s could be looked upon as a warning against the type of dissension that again descended upon England in the so-called Anarchy of the 1130s and 1140s, after the death of King Henry I, the last of William the Conqueror's sons. Aelred in his twenties and thirties was to experience the consequences of dynastic rivalries. In his own writings, he would come to celebrate a final reconciliation between Anglo-Saxons and Normans with the coming of Henry II in 1154.

Aelred's life was thus deeply influenced by three royal families: English, Scottish, and Norman. The old English line descending from Edmund Ironside through his granddaughter Margaret had married

CONNECTIONS BETWEEN THE ROYAL HOUSES OF ENGLAND AND SCOTLAND

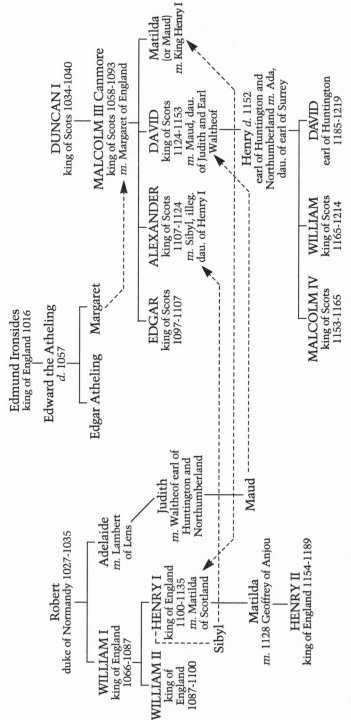

From W.L. Warren, Henry II, p. 176. Berkeley and Los Angeles: University of California Press. 1977. Used with permission.

into the Scottish line. Margaret of England and her husband, the Scottish king Malcolm Canmore (1058–93), brought three sons and two daughters into the world. Among them were Edgar (Scottish king 1097–1107), Alexander (king 1107–24), David (king 1124–53), and Matilda, or Maud, who married King Henry I of England (1100–1135). Henry I and Maud had no sons, but their daughter, also called Matilda, or Maud, first married the German emperor and after his death became the wife of Geoffrey, count of Anjou. Matilda tried unsuccessfully to rule over England in the years after Henry I's death, but it was only with the accession of her son, Henry II, in 1154 that civil war between Matilda and her rival, Stephen of Blois, ended.

For the reader, these dynastic conflicts and intermarriages may well be confusing, but as with most royal families in the history of Europe, one fact is clear. The different lines intermingled. Two of Aelred's close friends at the court of King David of Scotland were products of royal entanglements: Henry, earl of Huntingdon and Northumberland, was the son of King David and Maud the daughter of Judith and Earl Waldef; Waldef, the grandson of the first Waldef, became the stepson of King David. As explained above, Waldef junior was the son of David's wife, Maud, the daughter of Earl Waldef and Judith, niece of William the Conqueror. Everyone was related, and by the 1120s, when Aelred went to Scotland, his Anglo-Saxon past was not a liability. By this time the Norman Conquests had given way to a new aristocracy that intermingled old blood with new.

Aelred was not himself of royal or even of aristocratic blood, but he had access to the highest circles. At the death of King David in 1153, Aelred wrote a brief treatise to lament the man who had been so important for him in his early life. Although much of the work is made up of traditional rhetorical materials, Aelred still conveyed something of the political and religious role that David had played for the Scottish people. He pointed to the many religious houses founded by David (Eulog, p. 272) and to his justice and affability, making him accessible to his people (p. 273). Aelred described David's reaction to the death of his son Henry, Aelred's friend who died in 1152 and left the kingdom with an underage heir. Aelred addressed a desolate Scotland, "Who will console you? Who will take mercy on you.... Your light is extinguished. Your God has vanished" (pp. 278–79).

Even though this account might seem exaggerated, Aelred's evaluation of David as a great ruler remains to this day the judgment of most historians. He is seen as a reformer of the church, a lawgiver, and a superb administrator. Under him, Scotland, always divided between the "civilized" lowlands and the wild highlands, became one country. Aelred describes these changes as if David were a good abbot who turned his palace into a cloister. But behind the saintly and monastic facade,

Aelred reveals a dynamic personality whose legend lives on to this day in Scotland.

Aelred was concerned with the exercise of political power, but his main interest was the growth of personal piety. "Being made all things to all people," David is described in words taken from Saint Paul (1 Cor 9:22; Eulog, p. 270). This phrase was a favorite for medieval hagiographers in writing about their candidates for sainthood. We can perhaps better understand how David developed in this mode if we turn to the monastic historian Orderic Vitalis, who in his *Ecclesiastical History*, written in the 1130s and 1140s in Normandy, included a section on Scotland:

David, the youngest of the brothers, by taking good counsel escaped from the fierce attacks of the Scots and took refuge at the court of Henry [I], king of England. While the Scots were troubled with civil strife, and the fury of war raged relentlessly in the heart of their country, he was in constant attendance at the court of his brother-in-law, grew up among the boys of the royal household, and earned the close friendship of a wise and powerful king. He received the arms of knighthood from the king's hand, and after being loaded with gifts sat at his side among the greatest magnates. (Bk. 8, p. 275)

King Henry I's generosity toward David was probably an expression of a royal policy set on making a firm ally in Scotland, but Orderic would not have used the expression *familiarem amiciciam*, firm friendship, if there had been only a political dimension to the bond. Like Aelred himself, Orderic was fascinated with the friendships of the magnates, and he saw the importance of a personal bond that David later in life might have recalled in speaking of his youth.

Orderic also tells a story that most historians today reject but that perhaps sheds light on the unpredictability and cruelty of life, even in the protected world of the court. After David married Maud, they had a son who was murdered by a clerk. This man had originally come from Norway, where he had been blinded and had his hands and feet cut off after he had committed a horrible sacrilege:

He had attacked a certain priest who was celebrating Mass, and when the people had withdrawn after receiving the sacraments he had struck him in the stomach with a huge knife and murdered him, horribly scattering his bowels over the altar. Afterward Earl David took him into his care in England for the love of God and provided him and his small daughter with food and clothing. Using the iron fingers with which he was fitted, being maimed, he cruelly stabbed his benefactor's two-year-old son while pretending to caress him, and so at the prompting of the devil he suddenly tore out the bowels of the suckling in his nurse's arms. In this way David's first-born child was killed. The murderer was bound to the tails of four wild horses and torn to pieces by them, as a terrible warning to evil-doers. (p. 277)

I have quoted this gruesome tale in full because, whether true or false, it reflects the kind of talk that circulated in court and monastery in the early years of Aelred's life. David's son, Henry, who was to become Aelred's close friend, may not have been the first-born son at all. His older brother was rumored to have died in a hideous manner. Aelred's idealized portrait of the life of King David perhaps leaves out the rumor of a terrible event from the king's youth. There was no gutter press in the twelfth century, but even respectable historians like Orderic at times picked up the scent of something evil in the highest circles.

Whatever the truth of the tale, it is probable that David was able to survive to become king of Scotland because he had to spend his youth at the Anglo-Norman court of Henry I. Besides looking after his physical safety, his sister Maud, Henry's queen, may also have influenced his religious perceptions. Aelred tells in his *Genealogy of the English Kings* a story about Maud that David himself had told him. While David was staying at court, he one night was summoned to his sister Maud. He found her nursing lepers and kissing them "most devoutly." "What are you doing, my lady?" he asked her, "If the king knew this, you would never be allowed to kiss his lips, since you pollute yourself with the feet of lepers!" David told Aelred how Maud smiled and replied, "Who does not know that the feet of the eternal king are to be preferred to the lips of a king who will die?" (Gen Angl, PL 195:736) Aelred says that Maud had called in her brother so that by her example he would learn to perform similar acts of charity.

The story recalls later tales about Saint Francis of Assisi and his desire to kiss the sores of lepers. But here we are almost a century distant from what will become Franciscan piety. Aelred visualized a world in which queens gave up physical contact with kings because they preferred the bodies of lepers. Time and again in Aelred we are reminded of the existence of the body and its requirements, not as something to be denied, but to be embraced in the love of God and neighbor. However repulsive this legend of Maud and her lepers might seem, it conveys perfectly Aelred's belief in the importance of seeking out the embrace of other people.

Acts of cruelty and heroic manifestations of charity characterize the society from which Aelred emerged. In a world turned upside down, people were remembered for acting in extreme ways. This attention to extreme behavior was especially true in the north of England, in the areas called Cumbria and Northumbria, contiguous to Scotland and lacking any clear boundaries with the Scottish kingdom. South of the Humber, there was more control. At Canterbury the Anglo-Saxon monks had to put up with the regime of their new archbishop, Lanfranc (1069–1093). He disregarded their saints and even rejected them, while his successor Anselm (d. 1109) was much more generous in showing reverence for the English past. Anselm's biographer Eadmer was one of the many frustrated Anglo-Saxon monks who looked to the new archbishop for justice and piety after the traumatic years under Lanfranc. To a certain extent, Anselm did not let Eadmer down, for the new archbishop did his best to encourage the cults of the ancient Canterbury saints. In other respects, however, Anselm's years as archbishop from 1093 to 1109 were a disaster, with periods of exile abroad in protest against royal policies.

Anselm became reconciled with King Henry I and returned to Canterbury. After his death Eadmer continued in his writing of history to wage one battle that he considered essential for his church: its primacy in England over the see of York, the northern upstart whose claims were entwined with the reemergence of Scottish bishoprics. Eadmer, like many of his brethren, defended his own Anglo-Saxon identity in terms of saints and privileges in the new Norman world. He would not allow anyone to forget he had history on his side.

Aelred, who was born the year after Anselm's death in 1109 and while Eadmer still lived, would have well understood this defense of the past. In writing about the saints of his birthplace, Hexham, he included a story of a disrespectful clerk (probably a Norman) who challenged the validity of the cult of one of the Hexham saints. The clerk was promptly punished by being disabled and was able to be cured only by calling on the very saint whose powers he had doubted (Hexham, ch. 10, p. 189). Eadmer would have relished such a story, which belongs to a literary category of revenge motifs, popular before 1200, in which an angry saint defends his honor and reputation. Like the saints themselves, the Anglo-Saxon monks at Canterbury and elsewhere had to defend their honor from a new ruling class that looked upon the monks and their lay relatives as relics from the past. The only possible response was to show the power of the English saints.

Aelred did not have a vocabulary of cultural integration and identity. He did not, as we do, distinguish sharply between Anglo-Saxon and Norman, nor did he lament the facts of the recent past. Apparently he rarely thought of himself as belonging to an ethnic background that was on the losing side. But he was in fact a member of a race that had forfeited the rule of the land where it lived. Another source from the same period provides a sense of these humiliations, the biography of a holy woman, Christina of Markyate, dated to the first half of the twelfth century. Christina came from a prosperous Anglo-Saxon family from central England. Her family tried to get on by doing its best to accept the new regime. This effort meant being on good terms with a high royal official, Ranulf, or Ralph, Flambard, bishop of Durham and one of the least sympathetic creatures of the Norman administration. Christina's parents handed their daughter over to Flambard for her sexual debut. The girl, however, was not willing to oblige the bishop and managed to escape from him:

Whilst Ralph the bishop of Durham was justiciar of the whole of England, holding the second place after the king, but before he became a bishop, he had taken to himself Christina's maternal aunt, named Alveva, and had children by her. Afterward he gave her in marriage to one of the citizens of Huntingdon and for her sake held the rest of her kin in high esteem. On his way from Northumbria to London and on his return from there he always lodged with her. On one occasion when he was there Autti, his friend, had come as usual with his children to see him. The bishop gazed intently at his beautiful daughter, and immediately Satan put it into his heart to desire her.

This distasteful episode expresses in an extreme way what was in store for many old English families: they had to find ways of cooperating with their new masters. Even if it meant surrendering their daughters to the Normans. Until about 1100, there remained hope that a new Danish invasion would put an end to the Normans in England. Thereafter it was clear that the new monarchy and its henchmen were permanent fixtures in a population that, after all, was still largely English. The rulers, however, were not of English blood, at least until Henry II came to the throne and through his grandmother combined Scottish with Anglo-Saxon blood.

Ranulf Flambard chased Christina while he was bishop of Durham, a position that he held from 1099 to 1128. His stay in Northampton on trips between Durham and London points to the Norman effort to unite North England with the South through loyal royal servants who kept in regular contact with the king and court. Aelred grew up in a world where everyone who wanted to be anyone had to reconcile themselves with the Norman presence, whether they liked it or not. Eadmer might try to defend his Anglo-Saxon saints, but his archbishop, Anselm, had to accommodate Norman kings. Christina might try to protect her virginity and to find sympathetic Anglo-Saxon hermits who would shelter her, but in the end her choice to become a recluse was secured only by a Norman cleric, Geoffrey, the brash abbot of Saint Albans. Even in Scotland, the success of King David was due in large measure not to his vision of a unified country but to his acceptance of Norman institutions and personnel at his court.

It has become fashionable in recent years to look on the Anglo-Saxons as a harried, tragic people, tricked by the Normans and betrayed by some of their own leaders. This view has replaced an earlier one in which the Anglo-Saxon church and state were considered to be corrupt and weak. In our age of ethnic pride and new nationalism, the Norman Conquest is seen as the defeat of a beautiful aristocratic world, enjoying a vernacular language that united people, church, and court. Such an impression of the Anglo-Saxons perhaps reflects our own search for identity more than the facts of life for these people. But what happened after 1066 was indeed tragic for many. A whole aristocracy disappeared, and the population at large had to conform to the demands of a new regime. In the course of a few decades, a culture and language largely disappeared from written records. Anglo-Norman government, which in the twelfth century conveys itself to us in Latin, turned into a formidable structure in terms of government and church organization. But this new regime was consolidated only after the accession of Henry II. From the point of view of the 1130s and 1140s, when the English crown again was up for grabs, anything was possible.

How did this period of uncertainty affect the young Aelred from Hexham? Aelred was fortunate enough to be able to look northward. At the Scottish court, a Normanized David had brought stability. David was at a distance from the controversies about the English crown, even though he did involve himself. Aelred remembered his stay at the Scottish court with great fondness. As he wrote of David's son Henry:

With him I lived from the time he was in the cradle, and as a boy with a boy I grew up with him. In his adolescence I as a youth knew him. In my body but never in terms of mental attachment, I left him to serve Christ. He was in the full bloom of his prime, as also his father, now flourishing in the flower of old age. I have loved him above all mortals. (Gen Angl, PL 195:736–37)

Aelred did not have to choose between a Norman or an English identity. At an early age he left England and went to a part of Scotland where the Norman presence meant the memory of good King Henry I, who had knighted King David, and who in turn named his son Henry. David could look back on his days at the court of Henry I as the foundation of his rule in Scotland.

While the Norman Henry I still lived, until 1135, David could rule Scotland with assurances of generous friendship. Whatever problems there were behind the idyllic facade, a youth from Hexham, the son of a priest, could profit from this moment of harmony and find a relatively secure niche at court. Aelred's own vision of a reconciliation of royal houses, which he expresses in his later historical writings, originated in his Scottish-Norman experience.

2

the Bodies of saints

*t*O TRACE AELRED'S ORIGINS, we have to go behind the events of the eleventh and early twelfth centuries to the early Middle Ages. Aelred's homeland, Northumbria, was not really England nor was it Scotland. It was somewhere in between, with its own traditions and customs. Most of all, it had its own saints. The premier English historian, Bede the Venerable, in the eighth century told the story of church and society in England as if there had been one country from early times. But even Bede's art does not hide the fact that he drew on two traditions, that of Celtic monasticism with its fierce independence from outside influences and that of Roman religion with its claim to universalism and ancient authority. At the Synod of Whitby in 664, Rome appeared to win. The Celtic fathers gave way to Roman demands. But the saints of the North remained as special reminders of a non-Roman inheritance.

First among equals for the northern saints we meet Cuthbert (c. 634–87), who preferred life as monk and hermit but ended his life as bishop of Lindisfarne (685–87). After the synod of Whitby, Cuthbert became prior of a monastic community at Lindisfarne, but he spent as much time as possible as a hermit on a neighboring island. In 676 he made himself unavailable by moving his hermitage even further away from the monks. Such isolation, as often is the case, made the hermit more attractive than ever. In 685 he was made bishop of Hexham, a see he immediately exchanged for Lindisfarne.

Like so many other early medieval saints, Cuthbert became even more important in death than in life. His body was kept in a shrine at Lindisfarne. After the Danish destruction of the monastery in 875, its inhabitants began an odyssey with Cuthbert's incorrupt remains. Their wanderings lasted for 120 years. The monks brought him inland, to places such as Ripon and Chester-le-Street, but the final destination, in 995, was Durham. A church was built to house the shrine, and Cuthbert's relics were moved there in 999.

The young Aelred, whose father's family came from Durham, would certainly have known about Saint Cuthbert and his wanderings. Aelred's great-grandfather, Alured Westou, had been sacristan and

AELRED'S KNOWN ANCESTORS

Hunred, living in 875

Eardulf

Eadred

Collan, provost of Hexham c. A.D. 1000

Eadred, provost of Hexham

daughter *m. Alured*, son of Westou, surnamed
Larwa, sacrist of Durham, priest of Hexham c. 1020

Collan, provost of Hexham
between 1042-1056

Eilaf, surnamed Larwa, treasurer of
Durham and priest of Hexham in 1085

Hemming, priest
of Brancepeth

Ulkill, priest of
Sedgfield

Aldred, shrinekeeper at Hexham
and then a canon there

Eilaf, priest of Hexham
died a monk at Durham in 1138

Ethelwold

daughter, to whom her brother Aelred
addressed his *Rule of Life for a Recluse*

Samuel

Aelred, monk and
abbot of Rievaulx,

Taken from The Priory of Hexham: Its Chroniclers, Endowments, and Annals, *Vol. 1,
edited by James Raine, published for the Surtees Society by Andrews and Co., Durham, 1864.*

priest at the church at Durham. He was charged with looking after the sacred objects of the place, especially those of Cuthbert. Alured was given the honorary title of *larwa*, or teacher, and Aelred proudly collected stories about this man and his sons. Around the middle of the twelfth century, Aelred told a monk of Durham, Reginald, about his legendary ancestor Alured, who had gained "such great closeness" to Cuthbert that he used to cut the hair of the saint, dead, yet living in his grave. Sometimes great-grandfather Alured also did Cuthbert's nails:

Indeed [Alured] sometimes had intimate conversation with him [Cuthbert], who would carefully instruct him as to where he might find the relics of Saint Bede the Doctor and other saints, or how he should transport them or where he could deposit them. (Cuthbert, ch. 16, p. 29)

One day the canons of Durham were sitting and talking about the beauty of their church, known as Alba Ecclesia, the White Church, with its two towers of stone. Aelred's ancestor predicted that someday this church would be replaced by a much grander and more beautiful edifice "in honor of Saint Cuthbert."

This prophecy Reginald of Durham could see fulfilled in the magnificent Norman structure that was already completed by 1130. Durham cathedral and its neighboring bishop's castle became the symbol of Norman power in the North. It also bore witness to the continuing presence of Saint Cuthbert, buried inside. Set upon a huge rock formation overlooking the Wear, these buildings symbolized new and old forms of political and spiritual strength.

The Norman cathedral manifested the power of Saint Cuthbert. His body remained marvelously intact. Indeed, as Reginald pointed out in his *Life and Miracles of Cuthbert*, the saint's limbs showed no evidence of *rigor mortis*. They remained wonderfully pliant: "Only Saint Cuthbert has been enriched with the privilege of this gift by heaven," Reginald trumpeted (Cuthbert, p. 4).

In 1083, after the murder of his predecessor Walcher, the new bishop, William of Saint Carilef, installed a monastic community in the cathedral church. Until then the priests of Durham had been men who according to Reginald had lived "in the manner of canons, which are now called seculars ... and were carrying out monastic exercises in church offices" (Cuthbert, p. 29). Reginald does not add the essential point that these were married men, who filled the cathedral precinct with their families. Alured Westou had at least one son, Eilaf. He had to live with the fact that Bishop William at Durham chose to summon monks from the revived communities of Wearmouth and Jarrow, where the Venerable Bede centuries earlier had lived. The new bishop brought the Gregorian Reform and its requirement of clerical celibacy. The days of married canons at Durham were numbered. Eilaf the priest, son of Alured and grandfather of Aelred, had to find a living elsewhere.

King William I tried to ensure the new bishop's power by giving him his lands around Durham as a palatinate, making him and his successors at one and the same time ecclesiastical and secular rulers. Such a status well pleased William of Saint Carilef and his successor Ranulf Flambard. They went about consolidating their position by building a new church for Saint Cuthbert. This was the grand edifice that Aelred's great-grandfather had foreseen. To this day it remains a rare achievement of Romanesque architecture, one of the earliest cathedrals with a stone roof held up by great columns in a manner that heralds the coming of the Gothic style. In the words of one guidebook:

The exterior of Durham, with its three massive towers, its enormous bulk, and its superb position on a rocky promontory round which the river Wear sweeps in a grand wooded defile, makes perhaps the most impressive picture of any cathedral in Europe.

The piers and arches of the central tower, and a large part of the transepts, were completed before the death of Bishop William toward the end of the eleventh century. He survived an unsuccessful revolt against William's son Rufus in 1088 and continued at his post. The Durham nave is the achievement of the next bishop, the lecherous Ranulf Flambard. Both sections of the church remind the viewer that sublime church architecture and slimy political behavior can originate in the same mind.

In 1133, the year before Aelred entered Rievaulx, the transverse arches of the nave were finished at Durham. We do not know if Aelred spent any time there, but Durham would have been a good place to get a solid Latin education. We know from Reginald of Durham, however, that Aelred was proud of the stories about Saint Cuthbert and Durham that he had heard from his father. Reginald dedicated his work to Aelred and even spoke of him as a mother from whose breasts he had drunk "milk of refreshment and consolation" (Cuthbert, p. 1). The passage indicates that Reginald respected Aelred for his learning.

A common interest in Saint Cuthbert and his power provided the groundwork for a bond of sentiment. Yet there is nothing sentimental about some of the stories Aelred told. Cuthbert was remembered as punishing those who did not look after his bones, as in the case of a rich man who refused to house his body. His mansion was destroyed, except for the barn where the remains had lain:

All these things which we have described, as we have heard from our venerable father Ethelred [Aelred] abbot of Rievaulx, and so by his testimony, we have inserted onto our parchment. These things are testified, as he has asserted, accordingly as they were taught by his ancestors [*ab atavis suis pro-genitoribus praecepta sunt*]. Therefore these events, which they themselves saw, in truth took place. (Cuthbert, ch. 16, p. 32)

We notice here that Reginald, writing after 1147 when Aelred was made abbot, still called him by his Anglo-Saxon name, Ethelred. He not only dedicated his book to him; he returned to Aelred's name on several occasions in order to back up stories with the abbot's witness.

Aelred had only repeated what he had heard years before as a boy. Yet even as a Cistercian in a Yorkshire monastery far from Durham, he was able to add to his repertoire of Cuthbert stories. Toward the end of his life, he told Reginald how he had gone, in spite of illness, to the Cistercian General Chapter at Cîteaux in Burgundy. He put his faith in Saint Cuthbert to look after him, "because he kept his special memory more intimately than that of all other saints" (Cuthbert, ch. 83, p. 176). During the journey he was thinking of writing a hymn to honor Cuthbert, but the rigors of the trip and the business at the Chapter did not give him the necessary time. On the return to England, stormy weather for more than two weeks kept back the party of English and assumedly also Scottish Cistercian abbots. Then Aelred remembered his intention of writing something for Cuthbert. "I know," he told his fellow abbots, "and I trust in the mercy of Saint Cuthbert, that as soon as I will finish the work intended for him, I will be able to bring good news to you." Aelred blamed himself for the bad weather and, upon the completion of the hymn (now lost to us), credited Cuthbert with taking care of the weather for the monastic party. No other travelers, however, could make it across the Channel. Reginald tells how the sailors praised the power of Saint Cuthbert.

Reginald concludes: "These things the Lord of Rievaulx would tell us as often as he could" (p. 177) This is a story of a type found in the section on post-mortem miracles in innumerable medieval saints' lives. Even though Aelred was a member of a monastic order that dedicated all its churches to Mary and that had great devotion to the Mother of God, his first loyalty among the saints was to Cuthbert. He never lost touch with the world of marvels and saintly intervention with which he had grown up. Reginald lamented that "ancient times" provided more miracles because then "innocent simplicity flourished more than in modern times" (Cuthbert, ch. 16, p. 28). Nevertheless his contact with Aelred provided Reginald with an unbroken link between the earlier age of miracles and his own time.

Aelred was a traditionalist when it came to such miracles. Twelfth-century churchmen often showed critical sense, necessary at a time when evidence was required before they could submit briefs for canonization to Rome instead of deciding the matter on the spot. In such a context Aelred's faith in Cuthbert seems slightly old-fashioned. But in Northumbria, Aelred, just as Eadmer in Kent, felt a deep respect for the old saints and their cults. He was convinced that they continued to work miracles.

A few years before his death, Aelred went on a visitation to Rievaulx's daughterhouse Dundrennan in Scotland. There he stopped at a town that had taken the name of Cuthbert, Kircudbright. At the church he celebrated the feast of Saint Cuthbert, which falls on March 20. A penitent arrived dressed in a belt of iron. When he entered the church, the iron belt broke into pieces and fell at his feet. So Cuthbert again had shown his power, Aelred and Reginald concluded: "He is close to all who call upon him through confession of truth and justice" (Cuthbert, ch. 84, p. 178).

Another manifestation of Cuthbert's power that also can be dated to the 1160s concerns a stag that a knight named Robert in the Scottish province of Lothian tried to capture. It sought refuge in the cemetery of a church dedicated to Saint Cuthbert. The dogs chasing the animal were not able to get inside the graveyard, and the stag remained there in sanctuary. A young man defied the power of Cuthbert and got into the precinct to attack the animal. The stag turned around and charged at a group of people watching. With its antlers it gored the evil man's baby son, who subsequently died. "Thus Saint Cuthbert deservedly ordered that death be inflicted on the son of the man who chose to cheat his guest of his tranquillity" (Cuthbert, ch. 88, p. 185).

The dogs then killed the stag, but no one dared to touch its carcass or eat of its flesh, which was left to rot. Six months later, a craftsman defied the spot by trying to cut up the carcass. Even though it seemed to be dried out by then, blood shot forth and struck him in the forehead. Still, he dragged the animal to his home but was punished when blood began to ooze from the animal and to fill the house, to such an extent that neighbors could see a river of red emerging from the building. "What should he do, where should he go, he was at a loss, for everywhere he sensed the danger of evil hanging over him?" (Cuthbert, ch. 88, p. 186). The wrath of God was on him. Reginald concluded that Saint Cuthbert continued to renew ancient miracles. He compared Cuthbert's doings with deeds of earlier saints, such as Martin of Tours in the fourth century.

The Durham canon seems to have contradicted an earlier assertion that the age of miracles was over. Thanks partly to the stories Aelred had given to Reginald, Cuthbert's continuing virility, even for the sake of dumb creatures, was still being shown forth.

The legend of the stag, in its search for sanctuary and shedding of blood, mixes folk tale with Christian lore. Reginald recounted it with great relish and detail, but it was Aelred's story. As an old man, full of

learning and experience, he had not hesitated to repeat a tale that to
some of the churchmen of his day at best might have sounded naive.
But Aelred had no doubts. In such events he saw the same Cuthbert
with whom he had grown up, the Cuthbert whose church now domi-
nated Durham and the north of England, and whose body somehow
was still alive. This potent, vengeful saint remained Aelred's hero,
refuge, and hope.

While Cuthbert remained the most important saint for Aelred, the
saints of Hexham came a close second. Aelred himself wrote of these
saints and their powers in connection with the translation of their
relics in 1155. His treatise, *On the Saints of the Church of Hexham
and Their Miracles*, was probably commissioned by the very community of Augustinian canons that took over the church at Hexham
where Aelred's father and grandfather once resided. As in so much else
in Aelred's life, the writing of this work shows an uncanny talent for
reconciling past and present, family and monastic community, Anglo-
Saxon and Norman presence. From what Aelred says, there would
seem to be no conflict between the concerns for these saints shown
by his ancestors and by their Augustinian successors.

Aelred did not retell the lives of these saints of the distant past. He
assumed his audience knew the stories of men like Eata, who died in
686 as bishop at Hexham, and his successor Acca (d. 740). Eata's life,
as those of other Hexham bishops, was already contained in Bede's
account, so Aelred limited himself to the history of Hexham after the
Danish invasion of England at the end of the ninth century. For a long
time, he wrote, the church was without a priest (Hexham, ch. 11,
p. 190). The Danes in their destruction of Northumbria had obliter-
ated everything made of wood. An excellent library perished, and the
monuments of the saints were left in ruins. Revival came from Durham when Alured, son of Westou, teacher or *larwa*, came to Hexham
with the intention of removing the relics of Acca.

According to the family tradition, Alured came to realize that the
church of Hexham would be reestablished. He gave up his removal
project and instead left the relics at Hexham. During the reign of Edward the Confessor, the dispersion of the relics was stopped and the
rebuilding of the ruins began. During this time Aelred's family still
resided at Durham. His father Eilaf was one of the secular canons of
the cathedral. But William the Conqueror imposed a new regime, after Englishmen in 1080 murdered Walcher, bishop of Durham. His
successor, William of Saint Carilef, as we have seen, reformed the
cathedral by bringing in monks and throwing out the clerics:

Among them the son of Alured [Eilaf], who had been in charge of the others,
when he received nothing from the bishop, went to the venerable archbishop

Thomas, the first of the Normans to rule over the church of York, asking that he give him the church of Hexham so he could rebuild it. The bishop accepted and handed the church over to him. (Hexham, ch. 11, p. 191)

Aelred's account seems straightforward. In reality the role of the archbishop of York in taking an initiative for changes at Hexham was probably more central than Aelred indicates. Eilaf, Aelred's grandfather, was demoted from being treasurer of Durham to being stand-in for a York canon at Hexham. Even though Aelred exaggerated his grandfather's position at Hexham, the family record maintained a keen memory of what it was like to leave the glories of Durham for the ruins of Hexham: "Coming to the place, the man found everything desolate. He was horrified to see the walls of the church without a roof, grass growing, the forest growing up." "Nothing of the original beauty was left. And such was the poverty of that land that for almost two years he could sustain himself and his family only by hunting and fowling" (Hexham, ch. 11, p. 191).

Aelred's grandfather died in 1085, twenty-five years before his own birth, so Aelred would have had to hear this sad story from the lips of his father, also called Eilaf. Eilaf senior had begun the restoration of Hexham by placing an altar in the eastern part of the church. He did not get very far, but Eilaf junior, who considered himself to be the hereditary priest of Hexham, continued the work. We will return in the next chapter to Aelred's father's vocation and his son's evaluation of its importance and limitations. Here it is sufficient to point out that just as Cuthbert remained very much alive at Durham, so too the early bishops of Hexham continued to play a lively role in the history of that place.

A favorite story of Aelred's, which he must have gotten from his father, concerns the father of King David of Scotland, Malcolm Canmore. Malcolm made several raids into Northumberland, the last of which in 1093 brought on his death. On such occasions Malcolm is supposed to have spared the people of Hexham because of his reverence for their saints, but one time his messengers fell into the hands of robbers and blamed the Hexham population for what had happened to them. Malcolm became furious and decided to punish the town. He got his army ready, and it looked bad for Hexham. In Aelred's words, "There was no possibility of resistance, no protection in flight, no solace in the help of any man" (Hexham, ch. 2, p. 177). The youths of the town, together with women and small children, went to the church to pray for God's help and that of the saints. Meanwhile the priest in charge of the church, probably Eilaf, and some of the clergy crossed the Tyne River to the camp of Malcolm. They brought relics to purge themselves of the crime of which they were accused and to ask to be spared.

Malcolm was not appeased. He summoned warriors from Galloway, who were considered to be the fiercest of all, and promised that the next day they would be in the front line in attacking Hexham. They would not spare anyone, regardless of sex or age. Aelred described the scene of terror when the delegation returned to Hexham: women tore their hair, exposed their breasts and cried out, making a "horrid spectacle" (Hexham, ch. 2, p. 179). The men, he says, behaved "more moderately" in asking for the help of the saints of Hexham. "Some sighed and cried out for Wilfrid, others for Cuthbert, others Acca, others Alcmund."

Aelred's father then had a dream. He thought he had gone outside the church and there met two men who were wonderfully dressed. They asked him to watch over their horses until they finished praying in church. When they came outside again, they asked Eilaf why there was so much weeping, clamor, and fear in the church. The priest answered that this was hardly surprising because all had been condemned to death: "We are considered by the king of Scotland to be like sheep for the slaughter" (Hexham, ch. 2, p. 179). One of the men told the priest not to be afraid, "for I am with you, to rescue you." He promised to extend his net from the watershed of the Tyne to its mouth so that no one could cross it or do anything evil to the people of Hexham:

I am called Wilfrid, and behold Saint Cuthbert is here with me. Coming through Durham I brought him, so that we together could come to our brothers who rest in this church and preserve this place and people.

(Hexham, ch. 2, p. 179)

At dawn a thick fog made it impossible for the Scots to find their way. The Galwegian fighters ended up in the west, on the borders of Cumbria. Malcolm did not know what to do. Then a flood came that for three days blocked the king's passage of the river. Finally he concluded, "What are we doing? We had better get out of here, for these saints are at home."

The coming of the valley fog may well have been a result of heavy rains in the hills to the west, which eventually brought flooding. But Aelred did not need any natural explanations. He was convinced, as his father was, that the bodies of the saints at Hexham saved its clergy and people. Aelred ended this anecdote with a general lesson in which he pointed out the need to care not only for the body but also for the soul. He insisted that the saints' concern is guaranteed those who reverence them, wherever we may be. "Even though the body is absent, the spirit is present" (Hexham, p. 181). Aelred sought to avoid the trap of making contact with physical remains of saints as the only way to get access to their spiritual power. But his very story, centered on relics and their presence in the church at Hexham, indicates how much he counted on the bones that his father and grandfather had guarded at Hexham.

In this collection for the canons of Hexham, Aelred's own stories reveal the importance of the saints' bodies and their locations. In 1032, in the time of Aelred's great-grandfather Alured Westou at Durham, a cleric, who had in his possession the church of Hexham, had a vision of a man dressed in the clothes of a bishop (Hexham, ch. 12, pp. 195–96). He struck the cleric lightly, as if to wake him from sleep, and ordered him to tell Alured at Durham "to gather together the people of Hexham and take my body from its resting place and put it in a higher and more worthy place in the church." The visionary figure identified itself as Alcmund, bishop of Hexham (767–81), who was buried next to his predecessor Acca.

The man went to Alured and told him of his vision. Alured promptly went to the place pointed out and initiated an excavation. After three hours, nothing at all had been found. The diggers continued until noon, with no result, so some of the people watching began to laugh, thinking that the cleric had been suffering from a delusion. Others, Aelred records, were silently accusing the priest for putting his faith in dreams. But Alured continued. He took a shovel and encouraged the others, by now tired out, to keep on digging. "Here," he said, "Here without a doubt lies Alcmund." By about three in the afternoon, Alcmund's remains came to view. Amid general rejoicing the bones were covered in the finest garments and put into a fitting container.

It was too late in the day to celebrate mass, so the men set the remains in the eastern porch of the church, dedicated to Saint Peter, for the night. Alured, whose first loyalty after all was to his church at Durham, decided to take some of the relics back home with him. He removed a bone from the skeleton. The next morning, when mass was to be said, it was impossible for anyone to lift the container with Alcmund. Everything was stopped, and that night while the man who had had the earlier vision prayed for help, Alcmund appeared to him and gave him a hard look:

What is it that you wanted to do? Is it in such a way you brought me, cut apart in my members, to the church, so that I being mutilated might be present to the holy Apostle Andrew at his holy altar? I who for so many years served him with my whole body and mind. (Hexham, ch. 12, p. 197)

Alcmund showed off his hand, from which the middle part of one finger was missing. "Get up, he said, and insist to the people that he who took away my finger restore it, so that my members in their wholeness may rest again in a place of quiet, and so that they who in my honor have devoutly assembled here can get the reward of their labor."

In the morning, when the saint's message was publicized, Alured Westou revealed what he had done and put the bone fragment back in place. There was great rejoicing. At last it was possible to transfer Alcmund's remains to their rightful place. The date became the general feast day for all the saints of Hexham.

Aelred added to this narrative a story of how a cleric of Hexham together with a servant was once hurrying back to the church from a trip in order to be there in time for the feast. Their boat turned over, and the servant Uthred was thrown into the river. Aelred dramatizes the event, emphasizing human emotion by shifting from the past tense to the historical present: "Those who were present cried out; they rush down, weep, rush about here and there, protesting with sighs and cries their misfortune. But what are they to do?" (Hexham, ch. 12, p. 198). Not surprisingly, it was the prayers offered to Saint Alcmund that saved the man, who suddenly stood before the distracted people, holding his lance, and telling them how Saint Alcmund had kept him safe in the water.

One can imagine how the boy Aelred on long winter evenings, while the wind howled outside and the world was covered with blackness, hung on every word his father told about the power of the saints and their rescues. His dad was the guardian of the saints and their treasures. His dad's grandfather had tried to pick up a bone for Durham and had been warned. In the account he wrote as abbot of Rievaulx, Aelred did not criticize Alured Westou. His great-grandfather had found out for himself that the saints of Hexham belonged intact at Hexham.

Durham had Cuthbert, while Hexham had many bishops. This population of saints could be a real problem. In 1154 the canons of Hexham came across a container with relics to which no name was attached. Aelred remembered that when he had been a small boy, the people of Hexham had believed that here the bones of Acca, Alcmund, Frithebert (bishop 734–66), and Tilbert (781–89) all rested. These bones had to be sorted out in the great translation of 1155 at which Aelred assisted as abbot of Rievaulx. It is typical for Aelred that he added his own boyhood memories to the stories of miracles and earlier translations (Hexham, ch. 13, pp. 199–200).

In a real sense, Aelred continued in the position of his paternal ancestors as caretaker of the Hexham saints. Even though he probably left Hexham at an early age, his work on the saints of Hexham shows that he continued to cherish memories of miraculous power and family concerns. What his father, Eilaf, passed onto him was not just distant memories but also events that had happened in Aelred's own lifetime. In 1113, when Aelred was three, the archbishop of York, Thomas II, apparently disappointed that his episcopal seat lacked the shrine of a local saint, tried to get hold of Bishop Eata's relics for York (Hexham, ch. 15, p. 202). As Aelred put it: "They [the clergy of York] thought it was inglorious that the church of Hexham had five, while York did not even have one bishop" of saintly provenance.

Hexham had by now been given over to an Augustinian community. Its members were dependent on the powerful lord of York, and they did not dare to protest. In Aelred's words: "There was none who stood in the way, none who opened his mouth." Still, Aelred conceded, the brothers of Hexham did their best to resist through prayer. "They prostrated themselves before the place which served as that heavenly treasure; they wept, they begged that [Eata] not desert them, that he not prefer the riches of York to his own poverty." The text indicates that the brothers of Hexham were terrified that if Eata were removed, Hexham would lose its status as a place of pilgrimage, and so their own foundation would be impoverished.

The night before the translation was to take place, the archbishop had a dream in which a man in episcopal robes, with a hard look on his face, appeared to him: "Why do you think it fit to disturb my quiet?" the episcopal figure demanded, "From the place where I sleep and find rest with my brothers would you transfer me to other nations? This is not the will of the Lord, but is your presumption, for which you now will pay the penalty." The figure lifted up the pastoral staff he held in his hand and struck the archbishop's upper arm twice. Terrified from the blow, he woke up from his dream with a shout. This awoke his clerics, who found him shaking all over. In the morning the archbishop called the Augustinian canons to him and asked their forgiveness. He promised that in this matter he never again would try to impose his will on them and asked for their prayers. The canons were jubilant, while the York clerics "having been frustrated in their hope were in great confusion" (Hexham, ch. 15, p. 203). For three more days the archbishop's arm hurt, but on the fourth, the pain left him and he left town.

No other story shows quite so well how the canons of Hexham — and Aelred — understood their common inheritance. Hexham was their country, while York was another "nation." The bishops of Hexham deserved to rest undisturbed in home ground, not abroad. More than four decades after the event, Aelred retold the story with a sense of triumph and relief.

Aelred's tale put the Augustinians at the center and omitted his father. In Aelred's mind Eilaf had done his very best to look after the church of Hexham. But the exclusive responsibility he had taken on at the death of Eilaf senior ceased in 1113, when Archbishop Thomas handed over Hexham to the canons. Eilaf kept the care of the parish and enough income for his family. Aelred claimed that his father took the initiative for the coming of the canons so that the shrines would be better cared for. But behind Aelred's explanation, it is apparent that Eilaf had to cope with a new regime and had little choice but to succumb to it.

By the early twelfth century, Eilaf had become a relic of the past. He was a married priest at a time in the history of the Western church when it was becoming difficult to combine priesthood and marriage. The so-called Gregorian Reform, a long process that began in the mid-eleventh century and continued into the twelfth, required clerical celibacy. The man who touched sacred objects had to keep himself separate from the rest of God's people. He asserted his apartness by living alone, with no bedmate, and certainly with no children.

For centuries clerics had gotten along well enough by having wives and fathering children. Aelred's own family is a case in point: a dynasty of priests, with the father handing down to his son a training and education that combined family traditions and wealth with church functions. Even after 1083, when such a way of life no longer was possible at Durham, Hexham had become a refuge for the offspring of Alured Westou. But by the early years of the twelfth century, despite all the protection of the old saints, the new rules were being enforced.

Aelred does not seem to have felt ashamed of his father and what he represented. He looked at his father as a sinner, but one who made up for his illicit life by the degree of his devotion to his duties at Hexham: "Although he was a sinner in living otherwise than was right, he showed himself pious and solicitous in renovating, decorating, and preserving the churches of Christ" (Hexham, ch. 11, p. 191). Aelred wrote these lines in 1154 with great conviction, for he could recall how in 1138, a few years after he had entered Rievaulx, Eilaf at Durham had surrendered his family properties and claims to the prior of Hexham. Witnesses at the scene were his three sons, Samuel, Ethelwold, and Ethelred (our Aelred), who must have sensed that this ceremony meant the final passing of the world in which they had grown up.

We know nothing more about Samuel and Ethelwold. Aelred is also supposed to have had a sister, whose name has not survived. Her existence at least one historian considers to be purely a literary convention. But we do know that the dying Eilaf professed himself as a monk of Saint Cuthbert, thus closing the family circle that had started at Durham. By 1138 Aelred had set out in a new direction. As a monk within a reformed order, he stood outside the familiar pattern and himself initiated a different way of life. Just as the choice to have an active sexual life was Eilaf's undoing, so too the choice to abstain from sexual activity was Aelred's passport into a new life. Sexual abstinence would not be easy for Aelred, and yet he does not seem to have condemned his father for the lives his sexuality had helped create. Aelred believed that his father, Eilaf, had lived a good and useful life. He recorded how Eilaf at the east end of the Hexham church laid down a stone pavement and erected an altar. The saints' relics that lay there he dug up carefully and then prepared a shrine for them above the high altar. While the new structure was being prepared, he placed the relics in the south porch of the church, which is dedicated to Saint Michael. He entrusted their care for the time being to his younger brother Aldred, who is described as a young man (*adolescentem*).

Aldred was once tempted to remove some of the relics for his own use. As Aelred says, his uncle asked whether "this church alone ought not to glory in such a gift when so many bones could be sufficient for many churches" (Hexham, ch. 11, p. 192). Afraid of touching the sanctuary with his hand, Aldred first said the seven penitential psalms and then went to the porch. But there he met such a blast of heat emanating from the relics that he felt as if he were at the mouth of a furnace. Terrified he left, prostrating himself again, weeping, striking his breast, repeating his psalms, and then getting up for a new try. But the same heat drove him off, and so Aldred did not again dare. When his brother Eilaf heard of this episode, he wept and went "with great devotion" to the relics and put them in a container on top of a stone table, which he had made ready for them.

This narrative forms a point of departure for Aelred's explanation for his father's handing over the church of Hexham to the canons:

As the devotion of this priest afterwards grew towards the saints, he began to think within himself of his own lack of worth, of the holiness of the church, and of the reverence due to the saints. And he judged himself to be unworthy to have access to such great fathers. (Hexham, ch. 11, p. 192)

The question of *dignitas* is central for Aelred, not the dignity of human self-worth as we usually define it today, but the legal right to carry out a public function, such as the care of the saints' bones at Hexham.

Eilaf's motive for giving up his position may have had much more to do with political facts than religious devotion. Aelred nevertheless chose to remember his father as making his own decision to leave his hereditary office, instead of being forced by the new regime to give it up. Richard, canon of Hexham and new-style historian of the church there, wrote in his account from the mid-twelfth century that the canons could have taken away Eilaf's position and income. They chose, however, not to do so, "so that he not be able to complain about them, whether justly or unjustly, and injure their reputation in some way." Here Eilaf is seen as a potential troublemaker, and the hero of the piece is the archbishop of York, Thomas II, who on his election in 1108 came to Hexham. Recalling its former glory, the archbishop "grieved with great compassionate sorrow on the state of the place and thought about how to revive it." Richard of Hexham thus looked upon Eilaf's contribution as minimal or even negative.

This hint of hostility between the Hexham canons and the archbishop of York on the one hand and Aelred's family on the other is strengthened by an anecdote told by Aelred's biographer Walter Daniel. When Aelred was three, in 1113, he amazed everyone by providing the news that the archbishop of York was dead. His father is supposed to have made a joke of his baby son's assertion by saying, "He is dead who lives an evil life" (WD, p. 72). Aelred Squire, the most thorough biographer of Aelred in our time, thinks that the child Aelred would not have picked up the tensions that must have prevailed at home during this period. I would disagree. Perhaps the three-year-old Aelred did not understand precisely what his father meant, but he may well have sensed an atmosphere of insecurity.

In any case, the Aelred who wrote an account of Hexham's saints, in describing a painful transfer of property, rights, and traditions away from his family, conceded that his father had been a representative of a dying world. He chose to criticize his father's way of life as a married priest, but he loyally insisted that Eilaf had been a conscientious and energetic keeper of the relics. Here Richard of Hexham seems not to have agreed. For him Eilaf left matters in a mess, and only the canons and their champion, the archbishop, were able to straighten them out.

In Aelred we meet the memory of a once-sturdy hereditary structure of priestly dynasties that had preceded the reform. Aelred could have ignored his ancestry and concentrated in his writings on matters that did not touch his family. But on several occasions, and especially in 1155, he chose to return to the world of his paternal ancestors. To a certain extent, he gave it his blessing. In his mind its members had done a decent job and had preserved a vital heritage. For Aelred this inheritance was an essential part of his own life and spirituality. We cannot understand the bard of spiritual friendship without also seeing him as the defender of saints' bones and of family traditions. For Aelred loyalty to God, to family, and to history mattered even more than the adoption of the new celibate requirements for priests.

Like his father, his grandfather, and his great-grandfather, Aelred found it important to take care of the saints. At the very end of his final work, *On the Soul*, Aelred returned to a theme that seems to have been one of the major concerns in his life:

Therefore we should honor, praise and glorify the saints with all possible devotion. We should contemplate their bliss, as far as lies within our power, imitate their behaviour and desire their company. For surely they have a care for us and they pray for us all the more devoutly in proportion as they realize that their own supreme happiness is unattainable without us.

(Anima, p. 149)

Unlike his uncle Aldred, Aelred apparently never tried to take for himself any saints' bones. When he became a Cistercian monk, he, at least in theory, left behind all the relics of his family life and past. In truth, however, he cherished and guarded the memories of his past.

As a born lover of history and its tales, Aelred found in the saints of Durham and Hexham the point of departure for his own sense of community spirituality. The power of the saints was his own power to move and change the men around him. He had confidence in the saints and believed that they needed him almost as much as he them. Aelred's trust in God's friends made it easier for him to move from the fragile but vital world of the biological family into a new world of Christian community. In between Hexham and Rievaulx was the world of the court of King David, but this environment did not give Aelred the sense of belonging that he sought. Instead of denying or trying to escape his background by becoming a monk, Aelred made his life richer. There were hardly any dead saints at Rievaulx, but many living ones. These he could touch without being, like his ancestor, driven away by the hot breath of guilt.

3

an absent mother

hOWEVER MUCH he was in contact with his father's heritage, Aelred was reticent about his mother. In Walter Daniel's account of the infant Aelred, whose face shone "with a radiance of solar light," Aelred's mother is barely mentioned (WD, p. 71). When Aelred was "old enough to understand it," Daniel says, his father, his mother, and his brothers told him about the incident. This passage at least indicates that Aelred's mother was still alive when he was five or six years old.

In his own writings Aelred only once refers to his mother. His reference, oblique in manner, is in terms of sin. Writing to his sister in the *Rule of Life for a Recluse*, probably in the early 1160s, Aelred mentioned the blessings God had given both of them:

I consider it to be no small benefit that he brought good out of the evil committed by our parents and created us from their flesh, animating us with the breath of life and setting us apart from those who were either ejected from the womb prematurely or stifled within the womb, conceived, it would seem, for punishment rather than for life. (Inst Inc 32, pp. 92–93)

Aelred here expresses gratitude that he and his sister survived their mother's pregnancy. He follows the teaching of Augustine that the souls of the unbaptized are damned. Every miscarriage thereby means a lost soul. But even though he and his sister were fortunate to be born and baptized, Aelred thinks they were created in "evil." This is not the evil of original sin in the Augustinian sense but a much more particular evil because they were conceived in the forbidden union of a priest and a woman who could never be his lawful wife.

The above passage suggests that Aelred saw himself as the result of an act that in God's ordering of things should not have taken place. His purpose in writing his sister was to praise the gifts of life, health, and the sacraments of the church, but he did not hide his distress with his clouded beginnings. Aelred may have been influenced by the sense of sin in the infant expressed in a work he loved, Saint Augustine's *Confessions*. But Augustine found the origins of sin deep in his own being and in the human race as a whole, while Aelred traced sin particularly to his own parents. For Augustine, his mother, Monica, was

a saint who suffered for years in her attempts to bring her son to see
the light. For Aelred, his mother, once she had brought him into the
world, practically ceased to exist.

Aelred's silence about his mother proves nothing, for silence in a
source can mean almost anything. But the silence still matters, for
Aelred's life covers a period when sensitive, intelligent men who entered the church and left behind records of themselves often wrote
or talked about their mothers. Anselm, abbot of Bec and then archbishop of Canterbury, spoke lovingly of his mother to his monk and
biographer, Eadmer. Guibert, abbot of Nogent in France and Aelred's
contemporary, dedicated a large part of his landmark autobiography to
describing his mother. However much Guibert may have been a split
personality, with deep hostility to his mother, he at the same time
worshipped his mother and made her into a Mary figure.

Such considerations were central for the American medievalist
John Benton, whose study of Guibert from 1970 has influenced a generation of historians. Benton was acutely aware of the importance of
mothers. He concluded an essay entitled "Consciousness of Self and
Perceptions of Individuality:" "as we seek to know more about the
growth of self-awareness in the renaissance of the twelfth century
we should look most closely at the influence of Mother Church and
biological mothers."

Benton's suggestion can be helpful if we consider the life of the
most eminent Cistercian monk of the period, Bernard of Clairvaux
(1090–1153). We know, for example, that Bernard's mother, Aleth,
insisted on bringing up her children on milk from her own breasts, instead of handing them over to a wet nurse. While Bernard's biographer
William of Saint Thierry provides such central remarks about Aleth's
role in Bernard's life, Aelred's biographer, Walter Daniel, does not even
reveal Aelred's mother's name. Her family background is uncertain.
Sir Maurice Powicke, who perhaps more than any other historian of
our century has looked into Aelred's origins, provides no help at all. It
was sufficient for him to concentrate on Aelred's father.

Why this silence? There are two answers: an easy one and a more
speculative one. The easy answer is that Aelred, as he indicated to his
sister, was embarrassed that he was the son of a married priest. He
could partially excuse his father because of Eilaf's conscientious service to the church of Hexham, but any mention of his mother would
have underlined the sinful relationship that his father had maintained
in spite of the reform movement in the church. By speaking only of
his father, Aelred, as it were, minimized the damage. Aelred did not
hide the truth of his own origins, but he protected the memory of
both mother and father.

However attractive, this explanation for Aelred's silence is almost too neat. How could Aelred so consistently have avoided all mention of his mother? After all, he wrote dozens of sermons and treatises where he frequently spoke of himself. Walter Daniel hung on his every word, and even though he in his biography avoided describing Aelred's family background, Walter wrote a supplement to the biography, a "Letter to Maurice," to defend Aelred's reputation. Here, as we saw above, he mentioned Aelred's family.

Walter's reticence about Aelred's parents is probably due to the fact that Aelred himself did not speak to his monks of his earliest years. Here I would like to present a more speculative explanation for Aelred's silence. I think there are two factors to consider: first, the likelihood that Aelred already at an early age, probably six or seven, was sent to the Scottish court; second, Aelred's own psychological makeup.

Most historians have assumed that Aelred went to Scotland in his early teens, in about 1124, when David became king. This interpretation is hard to reconcile with Aelred's speaking of his having lived together with David's son Henry "from the cradle." Since Henry was several years younger than Aelred, the phrase may indicate that Aelred as a six- or seven-year-old encountered the one- or two-year-old Henry.

Until 1107 David had been at the court of King Henry I of England, and in 1114 Henry arranged his marriage to the daughter of Earl Waldef, Maud. After this time David probably divided his time between England and Scotland. Whether Henry was his first or second son, the child could have been born in 1115 or 1116. At about this time Aelred may have been sent to the Scottish court. By then his father, Eilaf, would have been aware that his sons had no future at Hexham. After the establishment of the Augustinian canons in 1113, the new archbishop of York, Thurstan, introduced a new prior, Aschatil, who came from Huntingdon. As an expert on Aelred, Marsha Dutton, writes:

The dismissal of Eilaf from the church in Hexham and his replacement by canons put a certain end to his sons' expectations there. The arrival of Aschatil had at last accomplished what the threats and rulings of popes and archbishops could not. Aelred and his brothers would have to choose between marriage and priesthood and could enjoy the latter only within the cloister; under no terms could they live as had their ancestors.

As Dutton has pointed out, canon law now forbade that the sons of priests could become priests. They had to look elsewhere for a career and a future. What better place than the court of Scotland, with its mixture of English and Norman traditions and its firm links with the old families of Northumbria? Eilaf invested the same care in looking after his sons as he had done in providing for the saints of Hexham. By 1115, he knew that his son's future was away from Hexham. So he sent him to Scotland. My early dating of this event remains only a hypothesis that I am unable to prove, but it fits the facts as we have them.

Aelred's separation from his mother at the age of five or six would help explain why he says so little about her. I am aware that children who lose their parents so early can easily end up romanticizing or fantasizing about them. But in Aelred's case, the separation expressed itself in his adult life, after he had chosen the Cistercian way, in terms of silence.

Another indication of Aelred's relationship to his mother may be evident in what he indicates in his writings about his attitude toward women. Here Aelred conveys himself as a man who had little room for women in his emotional and spiritual life. Such an evaluation might seem to be in conflict with Aelred's *Rule of Life for a Recluse*, written for his sister. But a close look at the text indicates how in many places Aelred says much more about himself than he does about his sister and her needs. He fantasized about how she would lie awake on her bed at night and be tempted to masturbate (Inst Inc 16). He worried about homosexual behavior as well:

...that abominable sin which inflames a man with passion for a man or a woman for a woman meets with more relentless condemnation than any other crime. But virginity is often lost and chastity outraged without any commerce with another if the flesh is set on fire by a strong heat which subdues the will and takes the members by surprise. (Inst Incl, ch. 15, p. 64)

For centuries Aelred has been admired for the meditative materials he provided in this treatise on the life and sufferings of Jesus. His method would find imitation in late medieval tracts of spirituality, and he can be looked on as a point of departure for a new concentration on the humanity of Jesus. But much of this treatise deals with Aelred's shame and guilt about his past life. At moments he even seems slightly jealous of his sister, who kept her virginity, while he lost his: "With my wretchedness then in the loss of my chastity compare your own happiness in the protection accorded to your virginity by God's grace" (Inst Incl, ch. 32, pp. 93–94).

Every author writes directly or indirectly about himself or herself, and so there is no reason to judge Aelred for failing to concentrate on his sister and her needs. My point, however, is that Aelred lacks much feeling at all for religious women and their concerns. His prescriptions for his sister and for other recluses indicate either contempt for them in what he imagines to be a gossipy world, or else belief that they will be subject to violent sexual temptations. Anyone who reads this treatise carefully must come away with a sense that Aelred was not especially concerned with the world of the female recluse. He was curious about it, projected his self upon it, and had strong opinions, but he was an outsider to its inhabitants and their inner lives.

This conclusion may seem like a harsh judgment and perhaps one that will call down the wrath of those who honor and love Aelred in a one-dimensional manner. But it is impossible to ignore the cracks in the saintly facade. Like all saints, Aelred was a human being, and one who asked his audience to take into account the person he was. In turning to his sister, Aelred dealt with his own identity in order to take hers into account. For Aelred women hardly existed. His imaginations about women reflected his own male concerns.

Aelred was not a misogynist, for he did not actively hate women. Like many of the early Cistercians, he lived in a world so centered on good and attractive men that women remained on the periphery. But unlike some of his contemporaries, Aelred apparently did not have an elevated view of his mother. Nor did he transfer such a vision to the Virgin Mary. If we look at his sermons dedicated to Mary on her feast days, we find a competent wordsmith who used the few Gospel passages about Mary in order to consider his own problems and those of his monks. He saw Mary as a lady, who was to be served in a loyal fashion: "We owe her honor, because she is the mother of our Lord. For he who does not honor the mother doubtlessly dishonors the son" (Serm 23.6, In Nativitate Sanctae Mariae, p. 185).

Aelred did not express emotions of the type to be found, for example, in Anselm of Canterbury's prayers to Mary, especially his final one: "Let the cry of my need, as long as it persists, be with you, and the care of your goodness, as long as I need it, be with me." Anselm turned to Mary as a comforter and a source of endless mercy, while Aelred warned his monks against thinking that if they sinned against Jesus, they could always flee to his mother for consolation and forgiveness:

Let no one say: "Even though I should do this or that against the Lord, I don't care that much; for I shall serve holy Mary and be secure." It is not so! Immediately when a man offends the son, without doubt he also offends the mother. (Serm 23.12, p. 187)

Aelred rejected the very idea of tales about Mary in which she, so long as the sinner is devoted to her, is all-forgiving in spite of offenses against her Son. A contemporary of Aelred, Anselm of Canterbury's nephew, who died in England as abbot of Bury Saint Edmunds in 1148, spent his life in spreading these tales about the Virgin's miracles and mercy. For Aelred such promises of last-minute salvation because of a "Hail Mary" contradicted his sense of fairness and justice. Mary always had secondary importance in comparison to the overwhelming fact of Jesus.

It is not by accident that Aelred chose to shift attention from Mary as mother to Mary as our sister. "See how much we can count on her because she is our sister," he insisted (Serm 23.13, p. 187). As a mother and a lady, Mary for Aelred required service more than love. As a sister, she became more approachable. Aelred knew how to respect and deal with a sister, while he apparently had only a limited sense of a mother's love.

In writing about a nun at Watton, a house not far from Rievaulx, who broke her vow of chastity and became pregnant, Aelred celebrated a miracle that had come about when the child disappeared from sight. This little treatise, *The Nun of Watton*, has drawn considerable attention in recent years, a beneficiary of increased interest in women in the Middle Ages and women's studies. Aelred does not emerge well from his exposition of how the community at Watton dealt with the nun and her lover. The sisters themselves castrated the man, while the nun was put into prison. In making use of this work in order to understand Aelred's life and attitudes, it is important to realize that here as elsewhere Aelred blames the man more than the woman for sexual lust. As he wrote of the culprit: "He was contemplating the thought of sexual defilement [*stuprum*], while she afterwards said that she was thinking of love alone" (PL 195:791–92).

In Aelred's view, the girl could be excused to some extent because she was put into the monastery at the age of four without any opportunity to choose for herself. She was tempted by the presence of male workers in her own precinct. Aelred indicates that the priest in charge of the house, his friend Gilbert of Sempringham, did not take proper precautions.

In Aelred we do not find a common medieval clerical cliché about how women's insatiable desires lead men astray. Aelred saw a case of mutual consent. As for the religious life itself at Watton, he described it in general as a place of great fervor, with friendship among the nuns and visions reflecting this intensity. It would be wrong to interpret the anger of the nuns that led to the mutilation of the young man solely as an expression of the nuns' sexual frustrations. Their reaction must be placed in the context of fear and uncertainty experienced in a house for both men and women in an age when such communities were under suspicion. The nuns had every reason to believe that this single incident, if it ever came to public knowledge, not only would undermine their reputation but also lead to their dissolution. They prayed that God "spare the place" (Watt, PL 195:794).

Aelred's main point in telling the story was to show God's mercy on a sinner. The chains in which the sisters had put the nun fell off miraculously, an indication that she was forgiven. Best of all, the baby disappeared from the scene. However much we may wonder what exactly happened, Aelred was satisfied with the explanation that the woman had had a vision of the dead archbishop of York, Henry Murdac, who appeared to her just before she was to give birth. Henry, a Cistercian of course, acted as the perfect problem-solver. He removed the baby. The next morning the nuns of Watton were as deeply suspicious as modern people might be and accused the girl of giving birth in secret and killing the baby. They felt her body and even squeezed her breasts, but there were no signs of the pregnancy.

So far as Aelred was concerned, God had shown his mercy on the girl and had forgiven her: "All things are pure, all are clean, everything is beautiful." Aelred got involved when Gilbert called him to Watton, probably in order to use Aelred's authority to guard his monastery against vicious gossip. Aelred questioned the various witnesses but could only find confirmation of the story. He was even shown the chain that had fallen off the girl. The sisters, still deeply upset, asked him if they should not replace it! "I forbade it, saying this was not right and would be an indication of lack of belief" (Watt, PL 195:796). Aelred returned to Rievaulx "praising and glorifying the Lord in everything we had heard and seen and which the holy virgins had told us."

A few days later a letter was brought from Gilbert with the news that the other chain had fallen off. Gilbert, again looking for authority to back his own, asked what should be done. Aelred replied that what God "has loosened, you are not to bind." The girl would no longer be imprisoned.

Aelred is virtually the only source we have for the events at Watton. His account perhaps shows the gulf between modern secular attitudes toward sexuality and the medieval monastic view. Aelred felt no need to apologize and defend his own attitude. Something awful had happened in the sexual violation of the cloister, but then God showed his forgiveness. In dealing with the facts of physical attraction and union between a man and a woman, Aelred showed no sympathy, except perhaps in blaming the man slightly more than the woman. Aelred described events at Watton as an outside expert called in to interpret the situation in order to understand God's will and to protect the reputation of the place. For him it was all very strange.

Even if women for Aelred were secondary, he could feel drawn to them because of their religious experiences, as he shows in a Sermon on Isaiah, where he allowed himself to describe how women in a religious community supported each other's spiritual growth through their visions (Oner 3, PL 195:370–72). But Aelred was not really concerned with women as individual human beings. Like Mary herself, they bore witness to God's workings in the world. But in doing so, they required male guidance and supervision.

Even when women were closely watched, as at Watton, terrible things could still happen. Yet Aelred did not condemn Gilbert's religious experiment. This was his business, and Aelred was willing to help out a friend by making an inquiry at Watton. In the end his involvement resulted from his friendship with a man and not from concern for the welfare of women.

Where is Aelred's mother in such a story? Aelred's work on the nun of Watton reflects perfectly his attitudes toward mothers and women in general. He was not keen on motherhood. Aelred's response to the events at Watton indicates that women were of concern to him only insofar as they were brought to his attention. It may merely be a literary commonplace that he began his *Rule of Life* for his sister by saying that she "for many years" had been asking him for such a treatment. But Aelred may well have long put off such a task because for him the world of men was far more important than that of women. Here he reflected the official Cistercian attitude in the early years of the Order, according to which the new monasticism was for men only.

In telling of his childhood, Aelred did not mention women. In his pastoral and political functions as abbot of Rievaulx, Aelred continued to keep women at a distance. Only in describing Mary's concern for her son Jesus at the age of twelve, when he was lost to her for three days, does Aelred imagine a mother's love for a son:

Tell me, my dearest Lady, Mother of my Lord, what were your feelings, your surprise, your joy, when you found your dearest son, the boy Jesus, not among boys but among teachers, and beheld the gaze of all eyes bent on him...? "I found," she says, "him whom my soul loves. I held him fast and would not let him go" (Song 3:4). Hold him fast, dearest Lady, hold him fast whom you love, cast yourself upon his neck, embrace him, kiss him and make up for his absence during three days with increased delight. (Iesu, ch. 8, pp. 11–12)

Aelred here used one of his favorite passages from the Song of Songs to describe Mary's delight in finding her son. He visualized the reunion as a physical one, with embraces and kisses. But it is noteworthy that Aelred wrote nothing about how Jesus in return must have felt love for Mary.

In Aelred love goes only one way: the mother needs the son much more than the son the mother. Aelred was convinced that Mary was distressed not because she worried about her son's well-being (for Aelred thought she knew he was God and could take care of himself): "it was only that you could not bear to be deprived even for a while of the ineffable delights you found in his presence" (Iesu, ch. 8, p. 12). Aelred used Mary's need for contact with Jesus as an image of our common yearning for him:

For the Lord Jesus is so dear to those who have some experience of him, so beautiful to those who look upon him, so sweet to those who embrace him, that a short absence on his part gives rise to the greatest pain. (Iesu, p. 12)

We need Jesus. Sometimes he will go away and leave us devastated. Aelred makes this point in the first section of his meditation *Jesus at the Age of Twelve.* The love of Mary for her son is very much a secondary theme. Aelred even hints at criticism of Mary for not taking good enough care of her son and allowing him to get separated from her: "Indeed, my Lady, if you will allow me to say so, why did you lose your dearest Son so easily, why did you watch over him with such little care, why were you so late in noticing that he was missing?" (Iesu, ch. 2, p. 5). If Aelred really meant what he said here, he was indirectly challenging the new devotion to Mary that saw her as almost all-powerful. He saw Mary at this moment as a weak human being, perhaps going off to gossip with the other women, and taking her time to find out where her son might be.

Why did Aelred write about Mary in such a way? I want to suggest that he distanced himself from her because he had had a mother to whom he could not or would not show his feelings. For Aelred the joy of life was the company of other men, first his brothers in the flesh, and then his brothers in the spirit. It is they who found at their center the young Jesus for whose presence they longed, as the boys Aelred saw outside the Temple at Jerusalem (Iesu, ch. 5, p. 9). These boys could say to Jesus — or to Aelred, "Who will grant me to have you as my brother, sucking my mother's breasts, to find you outside and kiss you?" (Song 8:1) Mothers are necessary for the milk they give, but Aelred wanted to share his mother's milk with the boys whom he loved. Ultimately he was more concerned with them than with his mother. Aelred concentrated on the male body, its functions and needs, much more than on the female body. He thought of Jesus, not of Mary:

Where were you, good Jesus, during those three days? Who provided you with food and drink? Who made up a bed for you? Who took off your shoes? Who tended your boyish limbs with oil and baths? (Iesu, ch. 6, p. 10)

Aelred's fantasy about a massage for Jesus was perfectly legitimate in view of the fact that his flesh was pure and holy. Whatever Aelred felt about his own body and those of other men, the body of Jesus was available to him in his thoughts, in the sacrament of the altar, in the glory of the Resurrection, and in the hope of Judgment Day. He brought into his narrative the episode (Lk 7:36) in which Mary Magdalene anointed Jesus' body. This incident did not fit into Aelred's description of Jesus in the Temple, but it provided another instance of contact with Jesus in terms of his beautiful and delightful flesh:

Kiss, kiss, kiss, blessed sinner, kiss those dearest, sweetest, most beautiful of feet, by which the serpent's head is crushed (Gen 3:15)....Kiss, I say, those feet, press your fortunate lips to them, so that after you no sinner may be afraid of them, no one, whatever crimes he has committed, may flee from them....Kiss them, embrace them, hold them fast, those feet venerated by angels and men alike. (Iesu, ch. 27, pp. 34–35)

Jesus is here, as at the Temple in Jerusalem, the *object of love*, the one being onto whom Aelred could pour his passions and desires. There needed be no restraint, guilt, or hesitation. As Mary Magdalene, Aelred turned to Jesus as the one to whom he could entrust himself completely:

There certainly is the place for you safely to shed your tears, to atone for your impure kisses with holy kisses, to pour out all the ointment of your devotion free from fear, without any touch or movement of vice to tempt you.

(Iesu, ch. 27, p. 34)

Here it did not matter whether the sinner of the Gospel account was a woman or a man. Aelred identified himself completely with her as a sinner:

I will cling to your feet, my Jesus, I will hold them fast with my hands, press my lips to them, and I will not stop weeping and kiss them until I am told, "Many sins have been forgiven her, because she has loved much."

(Iesu, ch. 27, pp. 34–35)

Modern writers have for the most part given Aelred's meditation *Jesus at the Age of Twelve* a wide berth. Or they have interpreted it solely as a guide to the contemplative life in which his powerful physical language is seen purely in spiritual terms. The effusiveness of the language, taken literally, can be almost embarrassing. This is, indeed, a treatise on the contemplative life, but at another level it is also a part of Aelred's autobiography. Here he could desire the body of Christ as a human body. Jesus was his brother whom he wanted to "find outside and kiss." In turn, Jesus would give Aelred "a certain heavenly and divine kiss" (Iesu, ch. 24, p. 32).

The Aelred who reflected on the Gospel passages concerning the young Jesus and his performance in the Temple thus gave his interpretation a deeply personal dimension. He needed Jesus and often felt that he could not reach him. He wrote about "delays" in his comings, which led to "tears...groans...sighs....At one moment the words express your feelings, at the next moment your feelings stifle the words" (Iesu, ch. 21, pp. 28–29).

Aelred's eloquence in describing the spiritual and emotional aspects of his search for Jesus provides a sense of the richness of his inner life. In providing a new language and imagery of meditation for the individual's quest for Jesus, Aelred conveyed his own pain and desire:

The soul is inflamed with the fire of an unutterable longing and enters upon a certain spiritual contest with God, until the whisper of a gentle breeze makes itself felt in its inmost depths. It gently captivates the affections, imposing silence on all movements, all anxieties, all words, all thoughts; it raises the soul in contemplation up to the very gates of the heavenly Jerusalem. Then he who has been sought so long, so often implored, so ardently desired, comely of aspect beyond the sons of men (Ps 44:3), looking out as it were through the lattice-work, invites to kisses: "Rise up, hasten, my friend and come." (Song 2:9, Iesu, ch. 22, pp. 29–30)

Here as elsewhere in Aelred, only the intense language of the Song of Songs is sufficient to express his yearning for Jesus. However much he means kisses in a purely spiritual sense of contact between the soul and Jesus, he sees his lover as a beautiful man. The soul, *anima*, is feminine and so looks out discreetly from its secret place. But Aelred is a man seeking another man, the one whom he can hold fast and not let go (Song 3:4).

To read the spiritual language of Aelred in such a manner may seem to those who study and make use of him in their own religious lives as something almost blasphemous. But I am not saying that Aelred had a "crush" on Jesus. He was embracing Jesus with the totality of his being. Aelred in this treatise encompasses the full spectrum of human experience. He did not feel obliged to divorce spirituality from sexuality. He sought Jesus with his whole being, body, mind, soul. This is the point of his treatise: an intimate meeting of the human person with the person of Jesus. Aelred insisted on his right to reach out and grasp the flesh of the Lord, just as the youths of the Jerusalem once had been able to do.

In such works, Aelred reveals that he did not suffer from an absent or silent mother. For him the primary bonds of his life were with men: his father, his male friends, and his brothers. The missing mother in Aelred does not provide some psychic key to a wounded or incomplete person. The lack of concern for women does not open the door to a man afraid of women. Aelred must have imbibed the milk of love from his mother, but he soon left her to go out into a world where women were not of primary importance. He could turn to King David of the Old Testament, to Christ the King, or to King David of Scotland:

...if you are afraid, if you tremble with fear, if at moments you fear being overcome, if then you run to your Jesus in your anxiety, weeping, telling him of the dangers, imploring his help, he whom you love will come to your side as a most powerful king. As David prayed, "He will take up arms and shield and arise to help you" (Ps 34:2)....But if you wish to have...the solution of some problem revealed to you..., then you are seeking a retreat where you may be alone with Jesus and talk to him. (Iesu, ch. 24, p. 31)

Aelred found the men he needed in the memories of Cuthbert and the bishops of Hexham, in the members of his father's family, and in the friends he made at the court of King David. If motherhood was important for him, it was the motherhood that Aelred came to discover in Jesus.

4

school friends and court intimacies

I N TELLING MONKS AND FRIENDS about himself, Aelred claimed that he was not very well educated. In medieval literature, we constantly run into authors who assert their lack of qualifications for the task of writing what they claimed they had been asked to write. Such was the case with Aelred, when Bernard of Clairvaux asked him to describe how love and asceticism harmonize in the context of monastic life. Aelred excused himself on the basis that he knew more about kitchens than libraries. In Bernard's words, used as an introduction to the *Mirror of Charity:*

You pointed out the reasons for your inability, saying that you are little skilled in letters — almost illiterate, in fact — and that you have come to the desert [of the cloisters] not from the schools but from the kitchens, where subsisting peasant-like and rustic amid cliffs and mountains you sweat with axe and maul for your daily bread. (Spec Car, p. 70)

The meaning of this passage, which has been much discussed, seems quite clear to me. Aelred had in all innocence told Bernard that he knew a lot more about running a kitchen than about writing a theological work.

He had met Bernard on a mission for his abbot at Rievaulx, William, in 1141. Aelred had made a strong impression on Bernard, as we can see from one of the letters that Bernard wrote to Pope Innocent in order to help Aelred and those with him in their mission to the papal court concerning the election of the archbishop of York:

These men whom you see before you are true, honest, and God-fearing. They have been led by the spirit of God into your august presence with the sole intention of seeing and obtaining justice. Let your eyes rest upon these weary and poor men, for not without reason have they come to you from afar, undismayed by the great distance, the dangers of the sea, the snows of the Alps and, being poor men, the great expense of such a journey.... Their only motive is the love of God and I do not think that even their worst enemy could suspect them of being inspired in this business by either private interest or personal rancor.

At Clairvaux, or wherever they met on the way to Italy, Aelred had apparently convinced Bernard of his sincerity and solidity. Otherwise Bernard would not have backed him up so enthusiastically. He wrote similar letters to officials at the papal court and used all his influence to further the Cistercian cause at York. Bernard's involvement might have come about regardless of Aelred's presence, but the abbot of Clairvaux, by now one of the most powerful moral figures in Western Europe, was apparently fascinated by the monk from Rievaulx in his early thirties, who soon would become master of novices. Bernard thought it appropriate that a man who once had supervised a kitchen now would be providing spiritual nourishment:

How pleasing it is that by some presage of the future you have been transferred from the kitchen to the desert. Perhaps in the royal household serving bodily fare was entrusted to you for a time so that one day in the house of your King you might provide spiritual nourishment for spiritual persons, and refresh the hungry with the nourishment of God's Word. (Spec Car, p. 70)

In his conversations with Bernard, Aelred had apparently informed him that he had acted as steward at the court of King David, in charge of the procurement and serving of food. Similar information is found in Walter Daniel, who, with a tendency to rhetorical exaggeration, makes the position sound grander than it probably was (WD, p. 4).

Aelred had indeed occupied a significant position at the Scottish court, but it had not satisfied him. Outwardly, as he tells us, he was a great success. Inwardly, however, he was in turmoil:

Observing certain things about me, but ignorant of what was going on inside me, people kept saying: "O how well things are going for him! Yes, how well!" They had no idea that things were going badly for me there, where alone they could go well. Very deep within me was my wound, crucifying, terrifying and corrupting everything within me with an intolerable stench. Had you not quickly stretched out your hand to me, O Lord, unable to endure myself I might perhaps have resorted to the worst remedy of despair.

(Spec Car, 1.28.79, pp. 134–35)

In this much-quoted passage, as elsewhere in his writings, Aelred drew on the sense of self so rich in Augustine's *Confessions*, the book that, next to the Bible, probably influenced him most deeply.

Aelred's description of his mental state as an adolescent at the court of Scotland is also reflected in Bernard's letter to Aelred, where the abbot of Clairvaux described him as being "snatched . . . from the swamp of misery and the miry bog (Ps 39:3), from the ill-famed house of death and the mud of depravity." Bernard's images of filth and sexuality were not accidental: they hint at a fear and guilt that Aelred apparently had shared with him. As far as Bernard was concerned, Aelred was obliged to use the experience and understanding he had gained from these trials "to encourage sinners more fully to hope" as proof that the Lord had given "sight to a blind man (Ps 145:8), instructed an ignorant man (Pr 14:33) and taught an unskilled man" (Spec Car, p. 71).

Aelred received Bernard's blessing — and order — to use the content of his own life as an example, a moral *exemplum*, for the sake of others, especially the novices whom he came to teach. He was to write it all down, not as a new *Confessions*, but as a theological work dealing with the challenge of monastic life. The *Mirror of Charity* became the most complete and profound work of Aelred's authorship. I will return to it later in considering his period as master of novices. Here it is sufficient to point out that Aelred, when he composed the *Mirror* in his early thirties, looked back on his time at the court of Scotland as one of confusion and guilt.

One figure whose presence at King David's court might have had importance for Aelred was the king's brother, Ethelred, abbot of Dunkeld and earl of Fife. Ethelred was, of course, Aelred's Anglo-Saxon name. Aelred may, in fact, have been given his name in honor of the earl. David's and Ethelred's mother, Queen Margaret, as we have seen, was an Anglo-Saxon queen, the granddaughter of Edmund Ironside. In Aelred's name was established a link between his family and Scotland's royal house, with common English roots.

Writing about Aelred in the first years of the thirteenth century, Jocelin of Furness, a monk of the Cistercian house in Cumbria in northwest England, mentioned his education, or lack of it. In Powicke's translation:

He [Aelred] was a man of fine old English stock. He left school early and was brought up from boyhood in the court of King David with Henry the king's son and Waldef. In course of time he became first a monk, afterwards abbot of Rievaulx. His school learning was slight, but as a result of careful self-discipline in the exercise of his acute natural powers, he was cultured above many who have been thoroughly trained in secular learning. (WD, p. xxxiii)

Jocelin picked up on a tradition that had started with Aelred himself, in his protestations over his lack of formal learning. His term *juventus*, here translated as "boyhood," would indicate that he was in his late teens before he arrived at the court of David. Jocelin, however, never knew Aelred. His information is secondary. As I pointed out above, there is reason to believe that Aelred arrived in Scotland at an earlier age. He did not have to go straight into court service: he could have been trained in the liberal arts by a cleric at court or at a neighboring monastery. But he did not remain long at school.

Jocelin's most important point is one that Aelred himself made in his response to Bernard's order: he was self-taught. He made his own way in Latin letters, which fascinated him. Aelred's interest in learning was not that of the new medieval academic type emerging in the early decades of the twelfth century, the Abelard who delighted in performing feats of commentary on philosophical or biblical texts. Aelred learned not through logic or dialectic but by applying texts to his own life and situation. In him human experience was a point of departure for an interest in scholarly treatments of a subject. As he wrote in the justly famed opening lines of his *Spiritual Friendship:*

When I was still just a boy at school, and the attractiveness of my companions pleased me very much, I gave my whole soul to affection and devoted myself to love amid the ways and vices with which that age is often threatened. Nothing seemed to me more delightful, nothing more agreeable, nothing more useful, than to love. And so, torn between conflicting loves and friendships, I was drawn now here now there, and not knowing the law of true friendship, I was often deceived by its appearance. At length I got hold of the treatise which Tullius wrote on friendship, and it immediately appealed to me as useful because of the depth of his ideas and delightful because of the charm of his eloquence. (Am Sp, Prologue, p. 45)

As so often in Aelred, we find a description of the self that is heavily indebted to Augustine's *Confessions*. The need to love and be loved reflects Augustine's language and quest. Aelred was concerned that his loves lacked order, and he felt his emotions often out of control in the attractions he experienced toward other boys at school. In this volatile state, which we today would find quite characteristic for many adolescents, Aelred discovered Cicero's *De Amicitia*. This treatise provided him, he found, with "a formula for friendship," by which he could keep under control the "vacillations" of his "loves and attachments" (Am Sp, Prologue, p. 46).

Aelred indicated in this opening passage of *Spiritual Friendship* that after he joined the monastery, he lost for a period his former interest in Cicero, for only the language of the Bible fulfilled his needs. But Cicero remained with him all his life, not just as intellectual baggage, but as a point of departure for understanding himself. In school, at the court of King David, and finally in the monastery, Aelred found it possible to combine good Latin style with Christian thought and spirituality. Scholars argue to this day over to what extent the *Spiritual Friendship* is an original work or just a rehash of Cicero, but for Aelred it was not important to express himself in an original way. What he wanted was to combine personal experience with intellectual and moral standards.

It has long been known that Aelred was responsible for redoing a "semi-barbaric" life of a Celtic saint, that of the fifth-century missionary Ninian, bishop of Whithorn in Galloway in the southwest of Scotland. For more than a century it has been thought that Aelred prepared this biography for the second bishop of the reconstituted see of Whithorn, Christian (1154–86). But according to Powicke (WD, p. xcviii) Whithorn "was restored in or shortly before 1128," and so Aelred could have written his biography while he was in Scotland.

Thanks to the work of Aelred Squire, we know that already at the royal court Aelred acquired a literary reputation. A monk of Durham, Laurence, wrote to Aelred, addressing him as "steward of the royal house." Laurence informed Aelred that he had redone an earlier Latin *Life of Saint Brigid* of Ireland, which Aelred's father, who was Laurence's friend, had brought to him. Eilaf, as many other churchmen of his time, was apparently dissatisfied with the "semi-barbarous" style in which it was written. Now his friend Laurence had refashioned it according to the new literary standards of the twelfth century.

Laurence concluded the letter by calling Aelred his "dearest friend, for whom also in the king's court the pursuit of letters is a familiar occupation." It is significant that Laurence chose to dedicate his work not to Eilaf but to his son Aelred. Laurence may, of course, have wanted to draw attention to the Celtic saint in a milieu where there were people of influence who would appreciate such a literary work. But his decision to emphasize Aelred's position and learning indicate that even before he arrived at Rievaulx, Aelred had a reputation as a writer.

I think the *Life of Saint Ninian* is one of the first products of Aelred's pen, an expression of his school Latin experimenting with the genre of saints' lives, also known as hagiography. There is nothing in the account that indicates any special interest in monasticism. Aelred praised Ninian as a church reformer who organized dioceses, saw to the education of priests, and made sure they brought the word of God to the people. In other words, Aelred described Ninian as if he were an episcopal figure from the period of the Gregorian Reform, which, with the accession of King David in 1124, was finally being implemented in Scotland. Aelred's Ninian is a Gregorian figure without a monastic dimension.

Since little was known about Ninian at that time, Aelred needed to use his imagination and powers of expression to give life to the saint. In his Prologue he made it clear that his main purpose was simply to brush up the original source in order to make its Latin more appealing. This *Vita* was indeed a school exercise in which Aelred could display literary talent and idealism. For the pre-Cistercian Aelred, Ninian represented a type of heroic churchman who worked consistently for what he believed.

One link between this early work and his later writings is Aelred's use of the Song of Songs. Thus he described Ninian's quest for the Lord when Ninian considered his call: "What, shall I do? In my land I have sought him whom my soul loves and have not found him (Song

3:1). I shall get up and cross the sea and the land, seeking the truth which my soul loves."

Ninian had first gone to Rome, then to Scotland. Aelred could identify with Ninian's search for a purpose in life, his dynamism, and his decisiveness. When a girl accused a priest of making her pregnant, Ninian received a revelation informing him of the real father and so saved the honor of the church. He addressed the girl's tiny infant, who amazed everyone by speaking out the true father's name (V Nin, ch. 5, p. 146). Aelred described the miracles of Ninian in a vivid way, but his dependence on biblical quotations and references indicates that he had only limited materials available and could do little more than polish the Latin style and add a few appropriate biblical references. Only in complaining about the evils of his time did Aelred leave the strict narrative of events and allow himself room for comment:

It shames me, when I think about the most holy life of this most holy man, to consider our weakness of character and the cowardice of this wretched generation. Which of us, I ask, even among servants, when engaged in conversation, does not more frequently make jokes rather than be serious, perform idle acts rather than useful ones, and engage in carnal rather than in spiritual matters? Mouths which are meant to praise God, to celebrate sacred mysteries, and which divine grace has made holy, are daily polluted by slander and worldly conversation. These people are repelled by God's psalms, the prophets and the Gospel. In vain and base human activities they run around all the day long.... They are engaged in discussing rumors about the activities of base men. The seriousness of religion disappears in laughter and the telling of tales. The affairs of kings, the offices of bishops, the ministries of clerics, the disputes of princes, and above all, the lives and morals of everyone are discussed. We judge all things, except for ourselves. Even worse, we take bites at and eat each other so that we are devoured by each other. It was not so for the blessed Ninian, not so. (V Nin, ch. 9, p. 150)

If anyone at David's court read the young steward's polemical remarks, they must have caused a shock of recognition. As the son of a priest, Aelred could not himself become a priest, and yet here he was, tearing apart the morals of priests and courtiers alike. The passage conveys youthful impatience, dissatisfaction with the status quo, and desire to conform to higher standards. These accusations fit any human community in which there exists a gap between its purpose and its everyday existence. Aelred in his later sermons to his monks would make similar criticisms of life in the monastery. But the language here is geared not to a monastic community but to one where court and church meet. Privileged clerics, instead of carrying out their duties, preferred to gossip about their superiors and to slander each other.

Whenever Aelred wrote, he left the imprint of his person and his passions. He was dissatisfied and even outraged by the smugness and false intimacy of court. But he also hinted at his own problem of controlling his sexuality when he recalled how Saint Ninian one day, when reading the Psalter in the rain, was touched by an impure thought. Ninian realized what was happening to himself when the rain began to wet the parchment, previously unaffected by the downpour:

Then the brother, who was sitting by him, knowing what had taken place, with gentle reproof reminded him of his order and age, and showed him how unbecoming such things were in such as he. Immediately the man of God, coming to himself, blushed that he had been overtaken by an illicit thought, and in the same moment of time drove away the thought and stayed the shower. (V Nin, ch. 9, p. 18)

Aelred probably got this anecdote from his literary source. But by making use of the story in the same chapter in which he decried the morals of privileged clerics and courtiers, he highlighted one of his special concerns: sexual control.

In summing up his evaluation of Ninian, Aelred described him as a friend of Christ. Here again Aelred made use of the language of the Song of Songs to describe Ninian's attachment:

Christ, thus consoling the hesitating soul, said, "Arise, hasten, my friend, my dove, and come. Arise," he says, "arise, my dove, arise through the mind, hasten by desire, come by love." (V Nin, ch. 11; p. 21; cf. Song 2:13)

I wonder how Aelred's audience reacted to such language. A half-forgotten British saint came alive in his version of *Ninian* and took on flesh and meaning for a new age. Ninian became a friend and ally of all who were dissatisfied with the status quo and who wanted to carry out the reform of the church. In the context of Aelred's revived biography of Ninian, it is possible better to understand Laurence of Durham's decision to rewrite the life of Brigid of Ireland and to dedicate the work to Aelred. Aelred's *Life of Ninian* impressed Laurence and inspired him to modernize an ancient saint's life.

By placing the *Life of Ninian* at the beginning of Aelred's literary career, it becomes possible to understand Walter Daniel's failure to mention this work. Walter in his list of Aelred's writings claims to mention only what his master wrote at Rievaulx. Walter also leaves out Aelred's account of the Battle of the Standard in 1138, but this is a work of history from Aelred's early years at Rievaulx and one that Cistercian monks normally would not have been allowed to write. The *Life of Ninian*, on the other hand, would have been acceptable as a contribution to a growing Cistercian practice of writing hagiography.

Bernard of Clairvaux led the way in his *Life of Malachy*, the archbishop of Armagh. The exclusion of Ninian's biography from Walter's
list indicates that this work existed before Aelred entered Rievaulx.

If we want to consider further Aelred's way of life at the court of
King David, it would be wise to look at the requirements of kingship. In the twelfth century, kings moved around in order to exercise
their authority and make themselves visible to their subjects. Thus
we should not think of "the court of King David" as some stable lo-
cation at the town of Roxburgh, but as a kind of movable feast. As
Aelred indicated in his *Life of Ninian*, he found at times that the level
of discussion at court to be low and limiting. But Aelred still seems to
have been pleased to take on responsibility in looking after the material needs of the court. At the same time he had time for his studies
and literary activities.

For Aelred friendships were more important than anything else. As
he indicated in the Prologue to the *Spiritual Friendship*, he could not
help getting emotionally involved with his peers. He found such attachments both exciting and upsetting. His feelings for members of
his own sex were not necessarily a question of physical attraction. He
invested in other men the whole range of his emotions.

Any male who has experienced a culture in which women are
kept in the background and in which men are limited to each other's
company knows well how such a milieu functions. As late as the
early 1960s, seminaries for priests in the Roman Catholic Church,
especially those with high intellectual standards, created a hot-house
environment similar to the one in which Aelred thrived and suffered.
Some of the historians who have best understood Aelred emerged
from a similar background of schools with exclusively male popula-
tions: David Knowles, Sir Maurice Powicke, and Aelred Squire were all
products of the English public school system.

Aelred tells us little about the identities of his friends during this
period, but there were certainly two: Henry, the son of King David,
and Waldef, the grandson of the martyred Anglo-Saxon Waldef, and
now the stepson of David through the marriage of his mother Maud.
In 1153, at the death of King David, Aelred as abbot at Rievaulx wrote
a lament for David in which he also mentioned Henry, who had died
tragically the year before:

He was surely a most beautiful young man, lovable to all. I would briefly
recall all his virtues, but in everything he was like his father, except for being
a little gentler [*paulo suavior*]. (Eulog, ch. 8)

Aelred reviewed at great length David's habits and especially his last
year, even describing how all forms of "carnal contagion," even wet
dreams, ceased for him after the death of his wife (Eulog, ch. 6). But

Aelred did not include any detailed information about Henry. In his *Genealogy of the English Kings*, Aelred briefly described him as "a good and kind man, a man of gentle spirit and milk-like heart, and worthy in all things of his birth from such a great father" (Gen Angl, PL 195:736).

Aelred may have held back in describing Henry in order to put greater emphasis on his father, whom he greatly admired. Writing at Rievaulx in the 1150s, Aelred resorted to monastic categories in order to describe David. In terms of chastity, reverence toward God, religious devotion, and everyday life, David became for Aelred a monk-king. He gives only a limited sense of the dynamism David must have shown in being the first ruler to unite the northern and southern regions of Scotland. Only in Aelred's earlier *Battle of the Standard* does David emerge as an energetic ruler.

The other friend was Waldef, David's stepson, who becomes visible to us through the much later biography by Jocelin of Furness. As the historian Derek Baker has shown, there is perhaps more legend than reality in Jocelin's account. The work is characterized by a Cistercian effort, after about 1200, to salvage the memories of the early days of the Order and to offer examples of sanctity and sacrifice. Jocelin was more concerned with criticizing the abbots of his own day than with describing how Waldef ran his own monastery at Melrose in Scotland. But he indicates that Aelred had a deep effect on Waldef, for the royal stepson first became an Augustinian canon and then left his community at Kirkham to join Aelred's community at Rievaulx. Waldef's fear, according to Jocelin, was that he would not be tough enough to handle Cistercian ascetic requirements (AS, August, vol. 1, pp. 256–57). But Waldef sought advice from Aelred, who encouraged him to persist in his intention.

Jocelin wrote nothing about the life Aelred and Waldef shared at court, but he did tell how Waldef even then showed religious predilections. When out on hunting expeditions, Waldef preferred to hide himself in a tree and read a book or lapse into prayer. One time King David is supposed to have reproached his wife, Maud: "Your son is not of our sort. There is nothing in common between him and this world" (AS, August, vol. 1, p. 251). David predicted that Waldef would either die young or become a monk.

As a boy, Waldef had already foretold his future life. While his older brother Simon made castles out of sticks, Waldef played making churches. Jocelin had great respect for Count Simon and his work: "Having become a courageous knight, in the time of King Stephen he built new castles and conquered some that others had built. He joined to his county both cities and counties. Though he belonged to the

knighthood of the world, he still ended his life in a Christian manner"
(AS, August, vol. 1, p. 250).

Jocelin could not help admiring a good knight. The Cistercians
were sons and brothers of knights and could not get enough of them.
As novicemaster at Rievaulx, Aelred realized how easy it was for
people of his class to get excited by stories of King Arthur and his men
(Spec Car, 2.17.51, p. 199). The world of the aristocracy in the twelfth
century was one in which feats of bravery and acts of war won respect,
even from monastic writers.

Our sources provide mere glimpses of court life as it must have
been for Aelred during the 1120s and early 1130s. Here, however,
his biographer Walter Daniel provides some help. Telling of Aelred's
popularity as the king's trusted steward, he also indicated that Aelred's position created jealousies and accusations. As Walter writes, one
knight was particularly critical:

He had a mad hostility to the young man, because he enjoyed the King's
special affection and was so popular with everybody in the palace. In his
rage and envy he could not endure the sight of our Joseph and the gracious
qualities which made him cherished as a father by the other knights, and
honoured and given the first place by acclamation both in general and private
esteem. So he began to pursue him and in his hatred to molest him.

(WD, p. 5)

In the passage directly before this one, Walter Daniel described Aelred's attractiveness to other men in terms of his affability and good
will. The episode of the envious knight was obviously intended to
show how Aelred repaid evil with good. Later, in describing the atmosphere at Rievaulx, Walter again presented this jealous and wounded
person who challenged Aelred. The content of the knight's accusations
remains unclear:

He tried secretly to excite feelings of indignation against him among his
fellow-warriors by angry envious words and idle tales of detraction; at other
times he would burst out openly in his presence and spit his venom upon
him. (WD, pp. 5–6)

The man's anger reached a climax when he accused Aelred before King
David. Walter chose not to repeat the knight's words, "too foul for me
to speak or for others to hear." Walter only stated that the knight used
"filthy...language."

In this passage Powicke failed to translate the full meaning of the
words. The knight's language, Walter wrote, was that of "a prostitute
and not a knight" and "stank of wantonness" (luxuriam redoleret).
There was some kind of sexual slur involved. Because of these charges,
Aelred "was unworthy to have the disposal of the King's treasure and

to be in his personal service and enjoy such praise and distinction" (WD, p. 6).

Walter Daniel included this episode to show his fellow brothers that Aelred already at the court of King David showed patience and charity worthy of a monk. After twenty or forty years in the monastery, Walter pointed out, few men ever learn such meekness. Aelred's answer to the knight sums up the new courtesy and gentleness that would have such impact in coming decades both for lay aristocrats and for clerics:

"You say well, excellent knight," he [Aelred] replied, "you say well and everything you say is true; for I am sure you hate lying and love me. Who indeed is worthy to fight for King David or to serve him as he should be served?"

(WD, p. 7)

Walter's manipulation of the story in order to exhort his monastic audience minimizes the importance of the precise accusations made by the knight. But the language of this passage indicates strongly that the knight made sexual insinuations. It may well be that the knight clothed in obscene language what Aelred himself later hinted at in his *Mirror of Charity:*

The charming bond of friendship gratified me, though I always feared being hurt and inevitable separation some day in the future. I pondered the joy at their beginning, I observed their progress, and I foresaw their end. Now I saw that their beginnings could not escape blame, nor their midpoint an offense, nor their end condemnation. The specter of death was terrifying, because after death inevitable punishment awaited such a soul.

(Spec Car, 1.28.79, p. 134)

This passage breaks into two parts. The first two sentences sound like an echo of the *Confessions* of Augustine, who expressed anguish over the temporary quality of friendships in this world. But the last two sentences bring in a theme not specifically Augustinian: the sinfulness of such bonds. Aelred says outright that he knew that he would go to hell for having such attachments.

Aelred indicated here that at least one friendship "dearer... than all the delights of my life" was leading him to hell. Aelred's self-description and the knight's scurrilous accusations point to a relationship of sexual love with someone else at court. In the *Life of Waldef,* there is a colorful story about how a woman tried to tempt the budding Cistercian saint into bed, and how he resisted her (AS, August, vol. 1, pp. 251–52). In the *Life of Aelred,* we find no such temptresses. The absence of women, Aelred's confession of his own passion, and the knight's obscenities all indicate that Aelred at the court of King David lost his head, his heart, and perhaps his body to another young man.

For Walter Daniel this specter from Aelred's past posed a problem. He did not want to admit that Aelred had ever been sexually active. At first he claimed that his hero had lived like a monk at the court of David (WD, p. 4). This assertion was a literary commonplace and might have gone unchallenged in the 1170s if Aelred's youth by then had been forgotten. But Aelred apparently had a reputation, for there were complaints about a lack of veracity in Walter's account. He answered these charges in his apologetic *Letter to Maurice*, which in the manuscripts appears before the biography in order to strengthen Walter's claims. He had to admit "at this time Aelred sometimes deflowered his virginity" (WD, p. 76). Walter's expression is involuntarily humorous. In fact one can lose virginity only once, while Walter had Aelred deflowering his virginity "several times" (*aliquotiens*).

This remarkable passage indicates that Aelred was known for the way he had lived in the 1120s and 1130s. Walter could not get away with his idealizations of Aelred's behavior. Today it is sometimes claimed that Walter's language, as well as Aelred's in the *Mirror of Charity*, can be understood in terms of heterosexual behavior. But if we take the two most direct descriptions of his youthful attachments, it is hard to imagine Aelred as being attracted to members of the opposite sex:

Torn between conflicting loves and friendships, I was drawn now here, now there, and not knowing the law of true friendship, I was often deceived by its mere semblance. (Am Sp, Prologue, p. 45)

Recall now, as I said, my corruption at the time when a cloud of passion exhaled from the murky depths of my fleshly desires and youthful folly, without anyone being at hand to rescue me. The enticements of wicked men prevailed over me. They gave me the poison of self-indulgence to drink in the sweet cup of love. The combination of innocent affection and impure desire beguiled my inexperience. I slid down the precipice of vice and was engulfed in the whirlpool of debauchery. (Inst Incl, ch. 32, p. 94)

Earlier in the *Rule of Life for a Recluse*, Aelred wrote about how when he entered the monastery, he had had to deal "with the spirit of fornication." When this temptation calmed down, he found his heart "beset with forbidden affections" (Inst Incl, ch. 18, p. 67). Even though his language is vague, Aelred here indicated attraction to young and beautiful monks. Once his own inner struggle with his flesh had cooled, Aelred was horrified to discover that his desire to embrace the flesh of other men was as strong as ever.

Everything that Aelred or his biographer Walter Daniel wrote on this subject must be considered no more than circumstantial evidence for the case that Aelred was a man more drawn to other men than to women. For Walter what was important was not the nature of the accusations leveled against Aelred but the fact that Aelred responded in the manner of what we would call a gentleman. The young steward's position at the court, because of his dependability and likability to the king, was so solid that the knight could not undermine him. For Walter Daniel it was wonderful how Aelred eventually came to make the knight into his friend:

In a private interview he promised to be Aelred's firm friend in the future, and that he would ever abhor, in humility, every presumption of ill-will, and would most diligently show him peculiar veneration. (WD, p. 8)

In this affirmation of loyalty after attempted betrayal, we meet a new courtly ethos. Aelred's response in terms of love is a stock lesson in Christian love of neighbor, but also in the devotion of a man to his friend in the intense bonds that had grown up with the new Norman feudalism at David's court: "I love you and always shall love you much the more because by your hatred I grew in the love of my lord."

Obviously Walter could not have known Aelred's exact words, but he was no doubt retelling a story that Aelred probably had often repeated to the monks at Rievaulx. Walter was especially impressed because Aelred's response to the knight's challenge only strengthened his standing with King David.

Much of Walter Daniel's writing is rhetorical and hyperbolic, borne up on a structure of biblical quotations and reminiscences and intended as moral encouragement for monks. In these pages, however, I find a basis of truth: the rumors that existed at court about Aelred's sexual attachments and his ability to face accusations and to turn them to his own benefit. Here as elsewhere, Aelred showed a need to express himself to others, to tell them about his pain and sense of incompleteness, and to win their sympathy. Walter's characterization of Aelred as a peacemaker, who responded to hostility with love, explains his success both at court and in the monastery. Ultimately the two worlds were not so far apart, for in both of them men lived in close contact and needed to depend on each other in terms of loyalty and practical ability. Aelred manifested these two qualities and added a tender and trusting love that made him irresistible.

These were good years for Aelred. At the court there were many who appreciated his talents of diplomacy, organization, and affability. King David trusted him and made good use of him. At the same time Aelred pursued intellectual interests. He was preparing himself for some kind of church career and making a reputation for himself, so that even the monks of Durham took him into account. Walter's claim that David would have "honoured him with the first bishopric of the land" clashes with Marsha Dutton's claim that Aelred as the son of a priest could not have become a priest (WD, p. 3). Kings could

still do wonders with church decrees, especially with the help of tact-
ful advisors such as Aelred. The sky was the limit for this brilliant,
attractive young man.

For Aelred, however, there was a gap between outer success and
inner disposition. He could not come to terms with his inner life. He
felt that his friendships could too easily get out of control. Toward
one friend he wanted to surrender his whole being, and perhaps he
did. Whatever the case may have been, Aelred was worried and unhappy. Being at a center of the aristocratic life of his times, he felt
marginalized. As men with a split identity before and since, he used
his sensitivity to be a diplomat, a leader, and also a teacher.

In the midst of this success, Aelred felt that something was missing: a commitment, a quest, an all-embracing love that could integrate
abilities and intuitions into a life where the difference between inner
and outer worlds would disappear. In the language of his own time,
he was a sinner, with a terrible secret that had become public, but
which he could not share with anyone who could help. Later, to his
sister, he hinted that his pain had been so overwhelming that he had
desired self-destruction. His way of life called upon him the same
kind of punishment as Sodom and Gomorrah had received. But God
spared him:

Otherwise earth would have gaped open to swallow me, heaven's thunder-
bolts would have struck me down, rivers would have drowned me. For how
should creation endure such great wrong done to its Creator if its wrath were
not held in check by that same Creator, who does not desire the death of the
sinner but rather that he be converted and live? (Inst Incl, ch. 32, pp. 94–95)

Behind such statements in Aelred or in any other skilled medieval
writer, there are literary models, biblical language, and a desire to encourage imitation of a good example. Ultimately, however, medieval
authors still tell their audiences about themselves. Aelred took the experience of his own life to guide others. In writing of his own quest for
love, he used himself in order to offer hope.

5

valley of Bliss

ELRED JOINED THE MONKS at Rievaulx in 1134. The community was founded from Clairvaux in Champagne in 1132 with their abbot, William, who had been Bernard of Clairvaux's secretary. At this time the Cistercians were beginning to be noticed as a new monastic order. In claiming to return to the Rule of Saint Benedict as the inspiration of their lives, they in several ways challenged the monastic institutions that used the Rule.

Since the ninth century, Benedict's Rule had been a standard text for monastic communities in Western Europe. But individual monasteries were virtually on their own. There was no clarified structure of relationships among monasteries to make sure that the Rule was kept. Until the Cistercians, there were only hesitant attempts at organization. From the tenth century, the abbots of Cluny in Burgundy had managed to weave a complex web of dependent priories and affiliated monasteries. Elsewhere, especially in the Rhineland and the low-lying areas now occupied by Belgium and the Netherlands, various reform congregations appeared, eager to follow the letter of the Rule and to ally themselves with sympathetic monasteries.

The Cistercians emerged in the opening years of the twelfth century as one of many movements of reformed monasticism, but they soon outdistanced the others in terms of the number of their houses and the genius of their organization. The reasons for this success are much debated today, but there is no doubt that two personalities helped make a difference. The first was Stephen Harding, who came from a traditional English monastery and became one of the early abbots at the mother house of Citeaux. He was endowed with organizational genius and made sure that the monastic experiment quickly got written statutes and papal recognition.

The second major figure was Bernard, an offspring of the lower nobility in Burgundy, who entered Citeaux under Stephen Harding in 1113, just after Stephen had founded the first daughterhouse. Already in 1115, Stephen sent Bernard off to Champagne to found another house, Clairvaux. The new abbot showed immense talent in attracting young men to his monastery and then sending them away to found new daughterhouses. The Clairvaux granddaughter houses of Citeaux, as they were looked upon in the Cistercian conception, numbered about 150 by the time of Bernard's death in 1153.

The Cistercians can be looked on as the first international monastic order. They clarified the bonds between houses and insisted on a hierarchy of relationships between mother- and daughterhouses. At the same time, however, all abbots had equal voices in the yearly general assembly of the Order. In mid-September, all the abbots had to meet at the General Chapter at Citeaux in order to discuss matters of discipline and adopt new statutes. Abbots were also supposed to make yearly visitations of daughterhouses, and the abbots of daughterhouses were to investigate the affairs of mother houses. Cistercian abbots were ever moving across the face of Europe and boldly defying distances and dangers in order to bring conformity and regularity into monastic practices.

In the Rule of Saint Benedict the abbot is the absolute authority for all matters in his monastery. Claiming to return to the letter of the Rule, the Cistercians in fact changed it forever by imposing an outside authority on the monastery and subordinating the abbot to a monastic order. From now on, an international body, the General Chapter, could depose abbots that treated their monks badly or wasted the resources of their monasteries. There was, of course, a gap between theoretical powers and practical effects, but the very attempt to organize religious life on a large scale was in itself a watershed in the history of monasticism.

Aelred may have been indifferent toward the organizational genius and international structure of the new Cistercian Order. What attracted him to Rievaulx was the fervor of the monks. He was not drawn to fanaticism in terms of ascetic feats but instead sought warmth of community united to a desire for the experience of God. As Walter wrote, these men lived out literally the words in the Acts of the Apostles (4:32) that they were "of one heart and one soul" (WD, p. 12).

Aelred was sent in 1134 on a mission to England for King David and stopped at Helmsley, the castle of an important north-country Norman lord. The ruin of this imposing edifice can be visited today in the attractive Yorkshire market town, and its solid rock surface might seem almost out of place in the bourgeois surroundings. The lord of the castle, Walter Espec, combined in his person secular leadership and religious devotion. Walter Daniel called Espec a "leading baron of King Henry I" (p. 12). Two years earlier Espec had founded a house for Augustinian canons at nearby Kirkham. Here Aelred's friend Waldef had become prior.

The precise circumstances that brought Aelred to Helmsley remain a mystery. Powicke suggested that Aelred might have heard of the place from Waldef (WD, p. 10, note). Marsha Dutton insists that Walter's story, "however emotionally compelling," is "rationally unpersuasive":

Whatever one believes about Aelred's upbringing and vocation, the story of the conversion as Daniel tells it is not credible, and the young man who occupies its heart has nothing in common with the forceful, ambitious, assertive man who appears in history and in his own works of history and theology.

This modern critic has rightly accused Walter of the rhetorical exaggeration that makes it difficult to like or trust him. But beneath the effusiveness of his language, Walter does indeed indicate that Aelred grew up as a forceful, ambitious, and assertive man who knew how to make his way at court and now insisted on finding out about these remarkable monks. Aelred can be understood only if we combine religious sentiment with political ability. Both qualities were in Aelred, and both of them were necessary to get him into Rievaulx. Walter Daniel may be accurate in describing his tears at meeting the brothers. Here, after all, he had found a community of men who really loved each other. In Walter's words:

Personal standing is merged in the equality of each and all, there is no inequitable mark of exception, except the greater sanctity which is able to put one man above others. The only test of worth is the recognition of the best. The humbler a man is the greater he is among them. (WD, p. 12)

For a youth who had come from a doomed priestly dynasty and who had lived amid the arrogance of a new aristocracy, Rievaulx must have seemed like a wonderful alternative. It brought together sons of the Norman and French aristocracies who had given up position and pretension in order to enjoy each other's company in the Lord. Whatever Aelred might have attained in Scotland by living out his idealism and being close to other men in mind and body, he could realize his goals much more fully at Rievaulx. Here were men who genuinely cared for each other and who liked being together in a new form of fervor. In a world wild about hierarchy and rights, Rievaulx was a different kind of human society in which pride and propriety gave way to love and equality.

In this appealing form of human society and fellowship, Aelred sensed a new, egalitarian division of labor. Cistercian monks, at least in their first decades, cultivated the land themselves and tried to avoid using peasant labor. The lay brothers did the bulk of the work, but the monks were there too. Putting themselves apart from the normal structure of agrarian society, the monks avoided entangling involvements with questions of rights and obligations. Everyone in the monastery contributed, and no one was exempt:

Nowhere are there quarrels, nowhere conflicts, nowhere the wailing complaint of peasants about dreadful oppression, nowhere the pitiful outcry of poor people wronged; no legal trials, no secular courts. Everywhere is peace, everywhere tranquillity, and wonderful freedom from the hustle and bustle of worldly affairs. There is among the brothers such great unity, such great harmony, that what each has is considered belonging to everyone, and what everyone has to each one. (Spec Car, 2.17.43, p. 194)

Aelred probably wrote these lines when he was novicemaster at Rievaulx, not yet a full decade away from his previous life at the court in Scotland. He seems to have remembered acutely how difficult it was to be fair in the tensions of court life between the privileged and the less privileged. As steward, it was his job to make sure that there was the income necessary to feed the court. He may himself have had to collect from unwilling and complaining peasants. At Rievaulx this self-righteous world was replaced by one of spontaneous sharing.

Aelred did not seek democracy. He praised the fact that "for three hundred men . . . the will of one man alone is law" (Spec Car, 2.17.43, p. 195). His vision was one of unity, not of equality. Even so, there was an element of equality in the sharing of all tasks and the lack of favoritism. Aelred probably only barely sensed these special qualities when he first visited Rievaulx and talked with the prior, the guestmaster, and the gatekeeper. Their description of the monastery, however, clearly made a strong impression on him.

After visiting Rievaulx, Aelred returned to the castle at Helmsley. Then in the very early morning before dawn, he rode north on the main road to Scotland. It passes just above Rievaulx. Today there is a highway, the B1257, which a few kilometers further north turns into an expanse of brown and purple moors. But there is a turnoff to Rievaulx that leads down a very steep hill until the monastery buildings suddenly come into view.

According to Walter, Aelred did not want to make the decision on his own to return to Rievaulx. So he asked a servant accompanying him, "whom he called his friend," if the man would like to return to the monastery. The servant's consent may well merely have reflected sensitivity to the desire of his master. It is hard for anyone aware of medieval class society to share Walter's sentiments that God showed his goodness in the answer of the servant. But Walter merely repeated what Aelred himself used to say:

For as our father would tell us, if the friend he had asked if he wished to go down to the monastery or not had said, "I have no mind to go," he himself in that hour would not have gone down with him as he actually did. Take note here of the outshining humility of this gentlest of men, whose own will depended on the will of his servant. (WD, p. 15)

In rejecting Walter Daniel and offering her own *Life of Aelred* as a "reconstruction, built on a foundation of historical fact and rational hypothesis," Marsha Dutton concluded that "Aelred's life was all of one piece." I agree that it is of one piece, but the wholeness is already present in Walter, if we subtract the extremes of his rhetorical exuberance.

Dutton is probably right, however, that Walter telescoped Aelred's preparations to become a monk and made the conversion seem more sudden than it actually was. Aelred may well have arranged his trip south precisely because he had heard of this new breed of monks and wanted to have a look for himself. He was not satisfied with his life in Scotland and sought an alternative to which he could completely give himself.

There is no evidence in his own writings that Aelred entered Rievaulx because its monastic life provided the one way for him as the son of a priest to become a priest. In choosing Rievaulx, he embraced not sacerdotal power but community life in the praise of God. There, in Walter's words, "They all rejoice and are glad together." His servant-friend stuck with him, his one "relic" of the old life transformed and renewed (WD, pp. 15–16).

What is it that made a whole generation of bright and attractive young men from good families choose the monastery instead of the court? Aelred is only one of many youths in the first decades of the twelfth century on whom the Cistercians exercised an irresistible attraction. In our own century the Cistercians in their Trappist descendants in America had a similar period of popularity for young, partly educated men. In the 1940s and 1950s college boys and army men flocked to Trappist houses. At times when a society is bursting at its seams in terms of material exuberance and spiritual renewal, the contemplative life emerges from hidden sources and becomes a necessity for many people.

By the time Walter Daniel wrote about Aelred and tried to record this period of enthusiasm, the boom was already largely over. Literary works from the late twelfth century that praise the first decades of Cistercian expansion characterize the second period, when the monks were more concerned with consolidating material and legal gains than in living the life itself.

There is no formula to explain why people give up everything and choose an exacting way of life. I do not think Aelred was running away from himself and his identity by going to the monastery. He chose an existence that made it possible for him to be all that he wanted to be: brother and lover, intimate friend, inspired leader, writer and preacher, and man of prayer and of silence. In his multifaceted needs and desires, he was very much a human being determined to use his talents.

Aelred was worried about his own sexuality and probably afraid of becoming a successful court figure in Scotland. His learning would have given him a reputation as an outstanding cleric, while he saw his life as that of a hypocrite. He had perhaps had enough of the gossip and intrigues of court life, the search for signs of disfavor in the royal brow, and the realization that in politics, today's heroes are tomorrow's scoundrels.

Years later, when he was abbot, Aelred wrote a prayer that summarized his concerns. Before he described his care for other monks, Aelred prayed for himself as a monk:

Lord, may your good, sweet Spirit descend into my heart, and fashion there a dwelling for himself, cleansing it from all defilement both of flesh and spirit, impouring into it the increment of faith and hope, and love, disposing it to penitence and love and gentleness. May he quench with the dew of his blessing the heat of my desires, and with this power put to death my carnal impulses and fleshly lusts. In labors, and in watchings, and in fastings may he afford me fervor and discretion, to love and praise you, to pray and think of you. (Orat past, ch. 5, pp. 111–12)

Aelred may have lacked such words when he entered Rievaulx in 1134, but they still sum up his purpose and intentions. He sought love, self-control, the renewal of his being, and union with God, all within a community of men. In a new brotherhood he would find the loves he needed.

6

worst habit and best friend

AFTER FOUR DAYS in the guesthouse at Rievaulx, Aelred was presented to the community and then allowed to enter the *probatorium*, or novitiate. According to medieval practice, he would have to remain there for a year before he could take final vows and become a monk. Nowadays candidates for monastic life first take temporary vows, and the process that ends with solemn vows can take five to seven years. In the Middle Ages life expectancy was shorter; there was not so much time to dabble and doubt. Also there were fewer choices available. To aristocratic sons, brought up with respect for authority and heroism, the monastic life did not seem so outrageous as it might today.

The guestmaster at the time was named Simon. He was still alive when Walter wrote after Aelred's death. By then Simon was abbot of Wardon in Bedfordshire. This house was also known as Sartis, a daughterhouse of Rievaulx from 1136. Walter Daniel called on Simon as his witness to the truth of Aelred's commendable behavior during his novitiate. In this "testing place," "old vices" are stamped out. "In the days of his young manhood when the heat of the blood so often erases the mind and clouds the feelings and burns away the energy" (WD, pp. 16–17), Aelred excelled. He distinguished himself for his service and concern for the other novices. His charity was outstanding and selfless, so he fulfilled the saying of Christ about the greatest love of all.

Walter did not provide many details here. He claimed, in his typical rhetoric, that he did not want to tire his readers, and so he moved quickly over to Aelred's profession as a monk. But later he mentioned a practice Aelred apparently initiated while he was a novice, cold-water immersions:

I should not omit to tell how he had built a small chamber of brick under the floor of the novice-house, like a little tank, into that water flowed from hidden rills. Its opening was shut by a very broad stone in such a way that nobody would notice it. Aelred would enter this contrivance, when he was alone and undisturbed, and immerse his whole body in the icy cold water, and so quench the heat in himself of every vice. (WD, p. 25)

This brief section has been noticed only as an indication of how Aelred continued a practice known from Celtic monasticism. But Aelred surely was not concerned with the historical background for this form of asceticism. As Walter had indicated, the novice Aelred was of an age when he was subject to sexual temptation. The freezing waters, which perhaps came from the springs that emerged from the hills above Rievaulx and provided the monastery with its water supply, cooled down Aelred's bodily impulses. Such practices surely helped bring on the severe arthritis which plagued his last years.

The content of everyday life for northern European Cistercians in the twelfth century, with only a single heated room in the entire monastery, probably also contributed to Aelred's later condition. For Walter it was quite natural that Aelred dealt with his sexual impulses by cooling down his body. Aelred himself described this harsh regime when he wrote to his sister. There he used a literary device apparent in Saint Paul. For humility's sake, the writer tells of himself in the third person:

I know a monk who at the beginning of his monastic life was afraid of threats to his chastity from the promptings of nature, from the force of bad habit and from the suggestions of the wily tempter, and so declared war on himself, was filled with savage hatred for his own flesh and sought nothing more than what would afflict it. Accordingly he weakened his body by fasting, and by depriving it of its lawful due suppressed its simplest movements. But when he was forced by weakness to allow himself more, the flesh came to life again and upset the tranquillity which he thought he had acquired. Often he plunged into cold water and stayed there for some time singing psalms and praying. Frequently too when he felt forbidden movements he rubbed his body with nettles and so, by inflaming his bare flesh, overcame the inflammation of lust. (Inst Incl, ch. 18, pp. 66–67)

I have quoted this passage in full because Aelred put into context something at which Walter Daniel only hinted: the new monk of Rievaulx felt obliged to do everything he could to stop "the inflammation of lust," a phrase that probably hints at the erections that especially for a young man can be quite involuntary. Aelred found that if he practically starved himself to death, such troublesome physical phenomena stopped.

Aelred insisted on total control over his bodily responses, especially his genital ones. It might seem inappropriate to look at him in this way, but such an interpretation of Aelred is based on information that he himself gives us. He wanted and needed to tell about himself, how he went almost out of his mind in his campaign for chastity!

When all this proved of no avail and the spirit of fornication still harassed him he applied the one remaining remedy and, prostrate at Jesus' feet, he prayed, wept, sighed, implored, besought, insisted that he either kill him or heal him. He cried out repeatedly: "I will not go away, I will not be quiet, I will not let go of you until you bless me." He was granted some temporary relief but refused lasting tranquillity...My God, what crosses, what tortures that wretched man then endured, until in the end he came to find such joy in chastity that he conquered all the pleasures of the flesh that can be experienced or imagined. But then also it was only for a time that he was delivered, and now when sickness is added to old age he still cannot flatter himself that he is safe. (Inst Incl, ch. 18, p. 67)

Aelred was probably in his fifties when he wrote these lines. By medieval standards, he was old. Certainly he was ill and suffering from arthritis. No reduction of these lines to the language of Saint Paul or the hagiographical images of Pope Gregory the Great in describing Saint Benedict can take away their personal application to Aelred. He wanted his sister and through her an audience to know that he as a young monk had had great problems in controlling his body.

In the terminology of our age, he forced himself to stop masturbating. It may seem like an oversimplification to be so specific with a word that Aelred himself never used in order to describe his problem. Such vocabulary covers physical acts and ignores the richness of Aelred's own considerations. Nineteenth- and twentieth-century words can hardly be sent back in a time machine to the Middle Ages without misrepresenting our spiritual ancestors.

Aelred had set out to reorient his whole way of life and to live without any form of active sexuality. This concern explains why he followed up the account of his own unfinished battle by angrily pointing out how other men deceived themselves into believing they were old enough no longer to have sexual temptations. They would live together, even sleep in the same bed, embrace and kiss each other, "and yet declare they have no fear for their chastity because their body has grown cold and their members are powerless to commit sin" (Inst Incl, ch. 19, pp. 67–68).

Aelred took some of his language here from a well-known letter by the church father Jerome to the girl Eustochium. Here he had warned her against a similar practice, according to which a saintly man and woman lived together and even shared the same bed. The idea was that by remaining chaste, they could assert their victory over temptation. Just as Aelred altered Augustine to fit his own experience, Aelred now changed the context of Jerome in order to describe two males who in old age chose each other's company.

Aelred intended to use this example as a warning to his sister so that she "never rest secure but always be afraid" (Inst Incl, ch. 20,

p. 68). Thereby he thus revealed his own insecurity and fear. His mention of such a practice also hints that as late as his fifties, Aelred felt attracted by the thought of living together with one other man. In this fantasy, he would share everything, but without having a physical sexual relationship.

Cutting himself off from any form of genital sexuality and investing himself completely in the community of the monastery, Aelred especially in his first years apparently had difficulties in living up to his own requirements. But an all-encompassing love of God embraced him and saved him from himself:

I had grown accustomed to filthy pleasures and he drew me to himself and led me on by the taste of interior sweetness. He struck off the unbreakable shackles of bad habit. He rescued me from the world and welcomed me with kindness. (Inst Incl, ch. 32, p. 95)

The bad habit, *mala consuetudo,* of which Aelred here and elsewhere wrote, is an Augustinian phrase that clearly has a sexual connotation. In Augustine it concerned his need for sexual release through union with an unnamed mistress, who was ever loyal but for whom he never admitted anything more than a physical need. In Aelred, the habit was not clearly associated with another person. It came from within. As he prayed for himself:

...against the vices and the evil passions which still assault my soul, whether they come from past bad habit [*antiqua consuetudine mea pessima*] or from my immeasurable daily negligence, whether their source is in the weakness of my corrupt and vitiated nature, or in the secret tempting of malignant spirits, against these vices, Lord, may your sweet grace afford me strength and courage; that I may not consent thereto, nor let them reign in this my mortal body, nor yield my members to be instruments of wickedness [Rom 6:12]. (Orat past, ch. 5, p. 111)

Aelred's language, here as elsewhere when he describes sexual temptation, is at one and the same time precise and vague. He does not specify the exact problem, but he describes it in terms of a "worst habit." Using Pauline language about giving way so that the parts of his body should become "instruments of wickedness," Aelred supplied everything but the medieval Latin technical term for masturbation, *mollities corporis.*

The language of the church fathers, whether of Jerome or of Augustine, allowed Aelred to be suggestive without being offensive. As he wrote to Bernard of Clairvaux in the first book of the *Mirror of Charity* in dealing with the subject of sexual sin:

I pass over in silence many arguments suggested to my mind against this vile plague, through respect for your modest eyes, my most loving and beloved friend, for whom I intend this little work. At what I have written, I seem to imagine a blush, that mark of modesty, spreading over your features and the gentlest lowering of your eyes summoning me to be silent.

(Spec Car, 1.26.76, p. 131)

Aelred either forgot or did not know that Bernard himself could be quite graphic when describing illicit sexual behavior. His Bernard was the understanding and insightful abbot that he found on the way to Rome at Clairvaux in 1142, and to whom he shortly before had entrusted his worries and concerns. Now this Bernard had ordered him to write about the rigors and trials of monastic life, and Aelred could not leave out sexual difficulties. Aelred came closest to being specific about his difficulties with a habit of masturbation a little later in the *Mirror of Charity*, in the same passage where he had described his sexual temptations at the court of King David. On entering the monastery, he still found sexual temptation:

I was swept towards you, only to fall back into myself again. Those things I used to experience pleasurably in the flesh kept me shackled, as it were, by force of habit, although what my spirit proposed by force of reason pleased me more....Anything I gazed at turned worthless to me, but habits of sensual pleasure oppressed [me]. (Spec Car, 1.28.81–82, pp. 135–36)

Aelred came to see his problem with controlling his own sexual impulses as by no means a unique one. As he wrote to his sister, "I have known a man who in his youth through force of habit was unable to contain himself" (Inst Incl, ch. 22, p. 69). Once again Aelred's exact meaning is not clear, but the most obvious explanation is that the youth, like Aelred, had trouble in resisting the desire to masturbate. The monastic literature of the period frequently brings up the problem. In the *Life of Godric of Finchale*, a twelfth-century peddler and later a hermit whom Aelred knew, a young monk is said to have approached Godric. He explained that he spoke on behalf of another monk who could not control a habit of sexual sin. Godric saw through the monk and realized he was talking about himself. Later when the monk became a Cistercian abbot, Godric recalled the story (Godric, ch. 141, pp. 270–72). Chronologically the story cannot be used to make Aelred Godric's subject here, but the tale emerges from the same milieu as Aelred's, in all the enthusiasm — and fanaticism — of the Cistercians in the first period of growth.

Aelred's mixture of frankness and reticence about his sexual dilemmas is typical for an age when self-conscious literary language allowed a degree of individual expression. In drawing on the writings of church fathers in order to describe himself, Aelred could distance himself from his own experiences. But he wanted to make it clear to his audience that his first years as a monk were difficult. He did not come to the monastery and live happily after. He brought the baggage of the self with him, and in discarding what was undesirable, he had to cut deep into his habits.

Aelred could make this change because he could turn to fellow novices and to some of the monks at Rievaulx. Walter Daniel "watched him attentively wait upon all the novices with whom he lived" (WD, p. 17). Walter was also probably present at Aelred's monastic profession. Here he compared Aelred to the Old Testament king David, "ruddy and withal of a beautiful countenance and goodly to look at" (1 Sam 16:12) so that "he gave great delight to the eyes of those who looked upon him" (WD, p. 18).

From the time Aelred arrived at Rievaulx, he was drawn into friendship with two monks, Hugh and Simon. Hugh later became prior, probably at a daughterhouse of Rievaulx, but at the time Aelred met them, both Hugh and Simon were at Rievaulx and were close friends. In the early 1140s, when Aelred was writing his *Mirror of Charity*, Simon died. Aelred concluded his first book by writing a lament for his beloved Simon. Thus he provided a glimpse into the emotional involvements of his first years at Rievaulx. Like his model, Bernard of Clairvaux, who a few years before had written a similar lament for his dead brother Gerard, Aelred addressed the dead friend:

I loved you because you welcomed me into friendship from the very beginning of my conversion, showed yourself more familiar with me than with the others, linked me with your own Hugh in the inner depths of your soul. So great was your love for both of us, so similar your affection, so single your devotedness, that as I seem to have gathered from your words to me, your attachment preferred neither one to the other, though unbiased reason would have preferred him to me because of his holiness.

(Spec Car, 1.34.109, p. 154)

Such a passage helps explain how Aelred in his mid-twenties was able to stand the harsh ascetic requirements of reformed monastic life. He had entered into a world of friendship where all the erotic intensity of men could be transformed into agapetic joy. Instead of finding himself excluded from a particular bond already established between Hugh and Simon, he sensed their willingness to open themselves to him.

There was no question of overtly physical love. Everything became spiritualized and harmonized into the life and requirements of the monastery: "I embraced you, dear brother, not in the flesh but in the heart. I used to kiss you not with a touch of the lips but with attachment of the mind." Simon was the kind of youth with whom Rievaulx apparently abounded: "a frail young boy, distinguished by birth, remarkably handsome" (Spec Car, 1.34.100, p. 149). Aelred saw him as being led by the boy Jesus, who introduced to him "the manger of his poverty, the resting place of his humility, the chamber of his charity."

Rievaulx brought together boys around the boy Jesus and let them become deeply devoted to each other. Aelred visualized how a friend such as Simon could be everything to him, son, brother, father (I.34.104). Roles are combined in the sweep of biblical friendship, but nothing can express what Aelred felt for Simon. Like everyone who has loved and lost, Aelred could not imagine life without the presence of the friend:

> What a marvel that I be said to be alive, when such a great part of my life, so sweet a solace for my pilgrimage, so unique an alleviation for my misery, has been taken away from me. It is as if my body has been eviscerated and my hapless soul rent to pieces. And am I said to be alive? O wretched life, O grievous life, a life without Simon! (Spec Car, 1.3.104, p. 151)

However much Aelred missed Simon and felt pain in losing him, he made sure to point out that this bond did not weaken his attachment to the monastic life. It strengthened it. One of the best-known passages in the lament for Simon concerns how the very glimpse of him during the monastic day comforted and encouraged Aelred and enabled him to maintain the discipline required. Words were not necessary: "The authority of our Order forbade conversation; his appearance spoke to me, his walk spoke to me, his very silence spoke to me" (1.34.107, p. 153).

Aelred's lament can be — and has been — taken apart piece by piece in order to show its debts to Bernard of Clairvaux and to the writings of church fathers such as Ambrose of Milan. It belongs to a great literary tradition, but this background need not obscure the fact that Aelred here described his own feelings. He made no attempt to idealize the relationship, for he admitted that during the last year of Simon's life, the friend had distanced himself from Aelred. He had withdrawn into himself, and Aelred had felt hurt. At the end, Aelred was not with him, though he wanted to be: "Why did you not want me present at your departure?" he asked the dead Simon (1.34.109).

Aelred assumed that his audience would understand his conflicting feelings for Simon: his desire to be with him, joy in his peaceful death, regret that he would never see him again in this life, and his need to express love and even bitterness. The naturalness and matter-of-factness with which this lament develops shows more than a familiarity with literary forms. Aelred's celebration of his friend and their friendship hints that it was considered acceptable for a monk to have a special love for another monk and to make that love known to his fellow monks. Aelred went even further here than Bernard, who, after all, was expressing devotion to a man who first was a brother in the flesh before he had become his fellow brother in the spirit. Aelred was not related to Simon but had become both brother and lover to him. Lover in every sense of the word except one.

Again like Bernard, Aelred saw that some readers or listeners might misunderstand the nature of his relationship with Simon and how it affected the common life of the monastery. Aelred protested that he was able to share Simon with the other monks. Their bond did not cut them off from the rest of the community:

Look at how my own Simon was loved by everyone, embraced by everyone, cherished by everyone! But perhaps some stalwart persons at this moment are passing judgement on my tears, considering my love too human. Let them interpret [my tears] as they please. But you, Lord, look at them, observe them! Others see what happens outside but do not heed what I suffer within.

(Spec Car, 1.34.112, p. 157)

Aelred had neither hesitations nor regrets. He could publicize the fact of his love and feel free and innocent about it. Only the Lord, he added, can know what goes on within us (Heb 4:12). Returning to his concern for Simon, he asked that any guilt or sin imputed to his friend be placed on his own shoulders: "I shall pay for everything" (1.34.113, p. 158). Again he borrowed a concept from Bernard, which originally came from the Rule of Saint Benedict itself, that the abbot takes responsibility for the monks under his charge. Bernard and Aelred went further by taking on the very identities of those they loved.

Aelred's lament in the last chapter of the *Mirror of Charity*'s first book itself becomes a mini-biography of Simon, a kind of *Vita Simonis*. In these pages Aelred conveyed the concerns and the intensity of his first years at Rievaulx. His interior sexual inclinations were modified not only by the harsh physical regime of Rievaulx but also by the rich friendships in his life. "He did not spare the soft skin of his hands, but manfully wielded with his slender fingers the rough tools of his field-tasks to the admiration of all" (WD, p. 22). He worked hard, but his labor was probably made easier by the companionship of other young men who had deliberately given up the pride and obsessions of aristocratic life to humble themselves — and to live in common.

During these years Rievaulx was thriving. It had enough recruits to send communities to Melrose in Scotland and Wardon in Bedfordshire in 1136, and then in 1142 to Dundrennan in Scotland and Revesby in Lincolnshire. Finally in 1146, Wardon sent monks to Rufford in Nottinghamshire. Aelred could not have helped being aware of these new foundations, for novices with whom he grew up at Rievaulx would have been sent to them. Melrose may have been of special interest to him. It was a house that revived an earlier monastic tradition at the site and showed how the Cistercians were bringing new life to monastic institutions in Scotland.

We know little about Aelred's daily life during these years. But he probably had more than enough in the routine of the monastic day to keep his thoughts occupied. Like everyone else, he had to get up in the middle of the night for vigils. Since the church was under construction (the nave dates from 1135–40), the brothers may have stumbled their way from temporary huts along the river to some makeshift construction.

The great numbers of brothers must have been both inspiring and inconvenient in practical terms. To this day some brothers at Gethsemani Abbey in Kentucky remember how it was in the late 1940s, when there were so many novices that tents had to be put up in the courtyard. Rievaulx must have been similar. So many recruits came that there was hardly room for them all. At Rievaulx in the 1140s, like Gethsemani in the 1940s, the solution was to found daughterhouses as quickly as possible, and to hurry on with the building program.

In the midst of the commotion created by many bodies in a limited space, Aelred was finding his own spiritual way. Walter heroicizes him as the "soldier of Christ, unsubdued," who "found life and nourishment in these exercises and virtues" (WD, p. 23). He was like a busy bee who filled the hive with honey, oil, and butter: "the honey of contemplation..., the oil of piety..., the butter of compassion for his neighbor" (WD, p. 22). Walter's imagery, however heavy, conveys a truth: Aelred managed to combine inner spiritual growth with outer involvement. He did not enter the monastery in order to escape from his fellow human beings. He went in order to seek out like-minded men with whom he could share his need for the love of God and the love of other men. Rievaulx was the place.

7

the politics of peace

*t*HE GIFTED YOUNG AELRED was not allowed to remain for long as one of the choir monks. Perhaps about 1140, Abbot William decided to make use of Aelred's practical abilities, which had been already demonstrated in Scotland. Walter Daniel's reference does not make it clear whether or not Aelred was made a member of the monastic council, which Rievaulx, in accord with the Rule of Saint Benedict (ch. 3), probably had. But it is evident that William decided to make use of Aelred's skill in human relationships and diplomacy, because he sent him to Rome on the difficult case of the York election (WD, p. 23). After he returned, Aelred was made novicemaster, a task he held for only a year or two before being elected as abbot of Rievaulx's daughterhouse at Revesby.

These were difficult years for England. After the death of King Henry I in 1135, a dynastic struggle led to civil war. The resulting conflict was devastating particularly for the north of England. In the words of Walter Daniel, "It was hard for any to lead the good life unless they were monks or members of some religious order, so disturbed and chaotic was the land, reduced almost to a desert by the malice, slaughters and harryings of evil men" (WD, p. 28).

Scotland became involved, and in 1138 Aelred's beloved King David sent a force into Northumberland. He was opposed by Aelred's close friend and patron Walter Espec, as well as by the archbishop of York. In 1138 there was a confrontation not far from Rievaulx, at Northallerton, which has gone down in chronicles as the Battle of the Standard. At some point afterward, Aelred wrote what might be called a meditation on the men who participated in the battle and their motives. His work was not an account of the battle itself, to which he devoted only a few lines. Aelred was concerned with the personalities and the clash of ideals that led to the actual confrontation, and how it might have been avoided.

Aelred's composition of *The Battle of the Standard* has traditionally been placed in the mid-1150s, but at least one historian has chosen an earlier date, the early 1140s. Whatever the correct date, Aelred in 1138 must have been painfully aware that two groups of men, both of whom he loved, were in mortal conflict with each other. He did not criticize King David for the invasion but tried to excuse the cruelties shown by David's men by ascribing them solely to the "barbaric" men of Galloway, who were almost impossible to control.

Aelred showed how the confrontation might have been avoided. He described a speech by Robert Bruce to King David in which Robert urged his lord to keep from attacking. Robert pointed out the friendship and assistance once given him by Walter Espec and other Norman lords. It was the Picts, especially the Galwegians, who were the Scottish king's real enemies. He had virtually become their prisoner (Stand, PL 195:710).

Such a speech emphasizes the role of friendships among male aristocrats. These men, especially Walter Espec, had founded new houses for monks and thus had spent their time and money in a far better way than they could have done on the battlefield. In Walter Espec's speech, Aelred has him tell how he would rather play chess than fight. But he was proud of the Norman conquests and considered his present involvement to be just and right. For Aelred each side had good and brave men, but the Normanized Scots were being pushed on by the wildmen of Galloway and the Highlands. Walter Espec in the speech Aelred gave him described these men, with their "rumps half-bare" in their kilts, as being not men but beasts. They were not afraid to fight without arrows, Walter warned (PL 195:707). Later when they charged and met a shower of arrows, Aelred made use of a line from a martyr's life to describe the Galwegians stuck full of arrows coming to look like porcupines (PL 195:711). He seemed impressed by the savage courage of these men, but his real heroes were the Norman leaders who insisted on protecting the North from Scottish invasion and reestablishing a rightful alliance with the king of Scotland, who in their eyes was one of their kind.

For Aelred, as for other monastic historians, the writing of history was an exercise in showing the workings of God's power among men. It was never easy to find God in the morass of human events, but in the Battle of the Standard Aelred found a meeting of two parts of his life: the Scottish court, with its good king now led astray by overzealous warriors, and the Norman aristocracy established in the old Northumbria, now triumphant in a new alliance. Though Scotland and England would continue for centuries to harass and abuse each other, Aelred saw in the events of 1138 a tragic confrontation between two groups of men who had every reason to be each other's friends. Aelred separated the barbarian Picts and Galwegians from the civilized Scots and insisted that these had been led astray. His hope was that an earlier unity of Scot, Norman, and English under Henry I now could be reestablished.

Aelred believed in the possibility of reconciliation. Inside the monastery he had not lost touch with or cut himself off from the world outside. As part of a new monastic generation, he was involved with the older brothers, fathers, and uncles of the monks who had come to Rievaulx from Norman or Old English families and who had every reason to worry about the effects of the Anarchy. Later as abbot of Revesby (1143–47) Aelred seems to have actively encouraged the aristocracy to hand over lands to the monasteries in order to gain prayers for their souls, for the life expectancy of a warrior was not great during those years:

And so he desired that land, for which almost all men were fighting to the death, should pass into the hands of the monks for their good; and he knew that to give what they had helped the possessors of goods to their salvation, and that, if they did not give, they might well lose both life and goods without any payment in return. (WD, p. 28)

Walter Daniel may here have been writing from the vantage point of the late 1160s, by which time the Cistercians were being harshly criticized for their acquisitiveness. But in starting the *Battle of the Standard* by mentioning the new monastic houses founded by the aristocracy, Aelred years earlier may have been making the same point: it was better to hand over land to monks who could make good use of it, instead of fighting to the death for it and ending up in hell.

Monastic prayers in exchange for aristocratic lands were the commerce of everyday life in a period of civil war. But Aelred was not out to get land as if the lay world and its leaders were mere objects to be manipulated for monastic acquisition. He believed in the possibility of peace and reconciliation among families, especially the royal family. His work on the *Genealogy of the English Kings* is a bold and careful statement of how to reshape the scattered bonds of the past in terms of families and their ideals. Writing after King David of Scotland's death on May 24, 1153, and before King Stephen of England's death on October 25, 1154, Aelred hailed the grandson of Henry I, Henry duke of Anjou, as the coming king of England. Aelred foresaw the end of the Anarchy and a new period of peace and reconciliation.

The *Genealogy* belongs to the early period of Aelred's abbacy at Rievaulx, but it reflects the ideals and hopes he had cherished since his youth in Scotland. He addressed Henry as the son of Matilda, or Maud, queen of the English and daughter of the queen of the Scots, Margaret. Through her, Aelred opened the door to the English line, where he went back to Egbert of Wessex (829–39), then Ethelwulf (839–58), remembered for his charity and his pilgrimage to Rome. But the greatest king was Alfred (871–99), for whom Aelred formulated a speech to his army that saw the invasion of the Danes as the wrath of God and encouraged them to fight for their wives, their daughters, their church. "Behold the eyes of the Lord are again upon you, and his ears to our prayers" (Gen Angl, PL 195:721). Aelred had King Alfred use the language of the Psalms and made him into a new king David, ready to defend what is right. In time of peace he did not grow lazy but translated "sacred writings into the English language" (PL 195:722). He wrote and published "most Christian laws, in which his faith and devotion to God, his care for his subjects, his mercy towards the poor, and justice to all is clear to all who read them." He started a school for Anglo-Saxons in Rome, gave money to the patriarch of Jerusalem, and was especially noteworthy in Aelred's mind for his generosity to the church of Durham.

Alfred was a just king who provided an example to his successors. Aelred shows ability at using anecdotes to illustrate character, and his thumbnail portraits warrant the remark of Aelred Squire that "none of Aelred's writings can have cost him more thought and care." To borrow a phrase from Norman Cantor, Aelred was inventing the Anglo-Saxon past, picking out the facts and reigns that fitted in with his thesis of piety, devotion, and harmony. One or two kings were indeed lecherous or incompetent, he admitted, but he saw for the most part a line of good men concerned for their people.

The longest royal speech that Aelred invented in order to characterize a king's policies was put into the mouth of "Edgar, the king of peace" (959–75). His sermon was delivered to the clergy of the realm. Here he claimed it was a royal concern to make sure that priests lived up to the duties of their offices. He criticized them for negligence in "getting together for the solemnities of mass more in order to play than to pray" (Gen Angl, PL 195:727). The houses of clerics, he charged, had become beds of whores and gathering places for actors, while the clerics themselves were caught up in food and drink (728). The only hope for the clergy was to seek the highest standards in their lives. Otherwise the king would force them to do so: "I have the sword of Constantine, while you have that of Peter in your hands. Let us join our right arms, let us join sword to sword, to throw out lepers from the camp and purge the sanctuary of the Lord."

In using the language of the Old Testament, Aelred gave to Edgar an authority to reform the church and especially its clergy. The speech outlines what might be called Aelred's grand design for the functioning of church and state in the coming reign of Henry II. Aelred saw an ideal alliance in the cooperation between Dunstan as monastic founder and archbishop of Canterbury and Edgar as bringer of peace and material provider for the church. Edgar was not head of the church, but he did take initiatives, such as encharging the archbishop of Canterbury "that by episcopal censure and royal authority those who live in a base manner be thrown out of their churches and those who live in an ordered manner be brought in" (Gen Angl, PL 195:729).

Regardless of almost a century of controversy between church and state, Aelred's model took its point of departure in an older dream of harmony that could unite king and archbishop in a common effort to clean up the church. The archbishop of Canterbury at the time Aelred wrote, Theobald (1139–61), may have had a similar view. Our understanding of church-state relations is distorted by the later conflict with Becket. Aelred died before Becket arranged his martyrdom. The abbot of Rievaulx could believe in the possibility of peace and mutual aid.

The real subject of the *Genealogy* up until Edgar is not the development of English monarchy. It is Aelred's interpretation of the guidance and assistance given by the kings to the growth and development of the church. Turning to Margaret of Scotland's grandfather Edmund Ironside, king of England in 1016, he described the perfect warrior:

Against enemies he showed the savageness of a lion, while towards his own he had the simplicity of a dove. No one was stronger than he, nor was anyone gentler. No one bolder, no one more careful. No one more secure in adversity, but none more reserved in success. (PL 195:730)

Even Edmund, however, could not defeat the Danish Canute. In an amazing speech about the futility of war when no one wins, Edmund declared himself willing to engage in single combat with the Danish leader. In the end, Aelred says, Canute's victory was due not to his military skill but to a traitor who cut down Edmund when he was answering the call of nature. Aelred fantasized about what it could have been like if Canute and Edmund had lived to rule together:

Putting down their arms, they rush to kiss each other, with each army rejoicing, and the clergy too. They cry out the hymn "Thee God We Praise." Then as a sign of the pact they exchange their clothes and arms and return to their people with instructions on how to maintain friendship and peace.

(Gen Angl, PL 195:733)

Just as much as Aelred wished for peace and reconciliation, he condemned the treachery that led to war and conflict. He saw the conquest of England by the Normans as the result of Harald's broken oath of loyalty to Duke William. What mattered most of all was loyalty. Concerning King Malcolm Canmore of Scotland, Aelred told a story that he had from the king's son, David. Malcolm found out that a nobleman was planning to betray him. The king invited the man on a hunt. When they were alone, Malcolm confronted him with what he knew of the plan:

Behold, he said, now you and I are alone with each other. . . . There is no one to see us, none to hear us. . . . If then you can, if you dare, if you have the heart, carry out what you have planned, hand me over to my enemies as you have promised; if you think I am to be killed, when would be better, more convenient, more easy? (PL 195:735)

The king continued in the same vein, almost taunting his potential murderer. There is something of a proto-Hamlet story here, the hesitation that arises when the possibility of carrying out a long-contemplated act is at last present. In Aelred's story the man got off his horse and fell at the king's knees. When treachery was met head on, it dissolved. Aelred admired greatly men who were not afraid, who faced facts and showed courage.

He skipped over the sons of William I in order to follow the English-Scottish line to his own day, with Matilda, or Maud, wife of Henry I, daughter of Queen Margaret of Scotland, and grandmother of Henry II. Matilda's piety and concern for the sick were an inspiration for her brother David of Scotland, the David who took on Aelred and with whose son Henry Aelred spent his childhood and youth. With the future King Henry II of England, David shared descent from the royal house of England. In the coming Norman monarchy with its Angevin lands in France, the blood of the English kings would be united with the blood of their former Norman enemies.

Everything was as it should be. From the vantage point of the early 1150s, it was possible to believe in lasting peace and cooperation between the royal houses of Scotland and of England, so enmeshed in one another. It would no longer be necessary to distinguish Norman from English, for they were one and the same in the king of the English people. Aelred could hail King Henry II as the hope of a new age.

At Rievaulx Aelred never forgot the importance of politics and dynasties. Although almost all the letters he wrote to important figures of his day have been lost, he did not hesitate to make use of his social connections and literary abilities to assert the importance of peace and reconciliation.

When the bones of Edward the Confessor, the last great Anglo-Saxon king, were translated at Westminster Abbey in 1163, the abbot there, Lawrence, asked Aelred to write a new account of Edward's life. Already in 1138, in an attempt to obtain papal canonization, a monk of Westminster, Osbert of Clare, had written a biography. With such a recent biography and little new evidence of saintliness, it might seem that Aelred could do little but alter the style in accord with the tastes of his day. In fact he did much more, transforming Edward from a provincial and isolated saint-king into a classic Christian ruler.

In Edward, Aelred showed how "God recognizes his own people"

(V Edw, ch. 1, p. 20), choosing those whom he wants for the gift of his grace:

Surely no one else was born with such an advantage in all these matters, for he had a model of all kinds of holiness in the most saintly and worthy kings from whom he traced his physical descent. (p. 21)

The idea of Edward as a example of holiness (*exemplum sanctitatis*) is vintage Aelred, an echo of his *Genealogia* with its line of kings who had served the interests and needs of the English church and people.

Aelred gave color to episodes from Edward's life by turning them into exchanges of dialogue, as when the bishop of Winchester is supposed to have had a vision of Saint Peter (V Edw, ch. 4, p. 27). Aelred also made use of biblical quotations and phrases from the Rule of Saint Benedict in order to liven up Osbert's flat description. Instead of repeating Osbert's physical description of the king, he started with a quotation from the book of Sirach: "Have they made you prince? Be not proud but remain among them as one of them" (32:1). To show Edward's fairness to the people, Aelred borrowed from Benedict's phrase in the Rule (ch. 2) and claimed that Edward made "no distinction among persons" (p. 34: *nulla apud eum personarum acceptio*). Cistercian emphasis on the inner life of the person also served Aelred well:

His body itself was illuminated by his inner spirit of holiness, and you could see in his face an unusual mildness, dignity in his walk, straightforwardness in his affection. (V Edw, ch. 6, p. 34)

Here as elsewhere Aelred gave Edward much more interiority than Osbert allowed him. Aelred's king thinks, prays, and acts. By showing the king's outer concerns, Aelred intended to penetrate his heart and mind. His legendary chastity was not only a matter of his behavior but also of his quality of mind. Osbert was concerned with the incorruptibility of royal flesh after death, while Aelred was much more interested in how the king had been in life, faithful to his wife without having sexual relations with her:

Their conjugal affection remained, without their conjugal rights, and their affectionate embraces did not rupture her chaste virginity. He loved, but was not weakened; she was beloved but untouched, and...warmed the king with her love but did not dissipate him with lust; she bowed to his will but did not arouse his desires. (V Edw, ch. 8, p. 40)

Aelred could not visualize a marriage in which genital love combined with spirituality. But he did conceive of a bond of affection in which a man and a woman could love each other in non-sexual ways. He projected his own experience of monastic life in deep friendship onto the relationship of king and queen.

None of this fantasy came from Osbert, who avoided such intimate reflections. But for Aelred there was no difficulty in imagining how the choice of chastity could enhance an affectionate bond. Aelred's Edward has thoughts and feelings that are much more developed than Osbert's Edward, who is basically just a miraclemaker and a sacred relic. The new Edward also has more of a political dimension than Osbert's, for the Westminster monk had done his best to stay away from politics. Aelred blamed the family of Earl Godwin for the Norman Conquest and turned them into the story's traitors. Just as in the *Genealogy*, he assumed that good kings are rewarded with a stable rule, but only so long as they are not betrayed by their own people.

Aelred enjoyed making his heroes come alive through the invention of dialogue for them. He put speeches into men's mouths in his *Battle of the Standard, Genealogy of the English Kings,* and also in the *Life of Edward the Confessor.* He was following the tradition of classical historians such as Sallust, who made use of speeches to show character and policies. When King Edward was preparing to go off to Rome to fulfill a vow, he made a long exposition of his motives and ended: "God will be the one who guards and protects all; he will preserve the peace he has given; he will travel with me and remain with you, will protect you and bring me safely home" (V Edw, ch. 10, p. 46).

In the scene that follows, Osbert described how the clergy and magnates had warned that the Danes might return in Edward's absence. But in Aelred it is the common people as well who objected to Edward's plans:

The populace came to hear of it, and there followed protests and riots, the island awash with tears as if the fires were burning already. You could see the poor now holding their hands up to heaven, now falling again to the ground; their thoughts were but of graves and burial, as if they would all die of hunger as soon as the king departed. (V Edw, ch. 10, p. 47)

The people got their way. Edward remained in England.

So aware of his own emotions, Aelred was a master at describing emotional states of mind, whether for the individual or the crowd. Without access to more information than Osbert, the abbot of Rievaulx used his knowledge of people, admiration of kings, and attention to the inner life of the individual in order to draw a more lively portrait of King Edward. The substance of the two Lives is the same, but Aelred changed the form and gave Edward flesh and blood. Aelred projected on Edward his own concern for friendship, for contacts among people, and for dreams and visions.

Aelred saw good kingship as a resolution of the problems of the church and of the people. In his Eulogy for King David of Scotland he praised a man whom he had known well. He saw in his reign the restoration of stability to his kingdom. Aelred did not try to excuse him for the cruelty and violence of some of his soldiers. But a king like David could improve the quality of life for everyone. As Aelred wrote in an address to Scotland:

He calmed your barbarian ways by the Christian religion. He brought marital chastity, which you had not known, to you, and he gave you priests for a better life. He persuaded you to go to church, to be present at mass, and did so by word and example. He judged what offerings were owed to priests and what tithes were to be paid. (Eulog, ch. 9, p. 279)

Such praise has long influenced the evaluation of David by historians, even in our time. However much we would like to think of ourselves as having greater insight than our medieval ancestors, Aelred's description is not so very far from that found in recent textbooks. Their language indirectly provides the same positive evaluation:

The Scottish Church was diverse, unorganized and in some important respects markedly different from the Church of most of western Europe. It was the aim of Alexander I and David I to give it uniformity.... Much progress was made in dividing the various dioceses into parishes, and to help the clergy in this work the king... commanded tithes to be paid to parish churches.

Aelred believed in kings who had the best interests of the church at heart. He wanted them to cooperate with reforming bishops and abbots in order to make sure that old privilege no longer could dominate the religious landscape. The priesthood had to be celibate in order to make its members more concerned for the people of God and less devoted to their own families. The people had to think of themselves as belonging to a parish church, which they were to attend and support.

Aelred's historical works show how during his Rievaulx years, his concerns stretched far beyond his Cistercian vocation. He never completely abandoned the world of his youth at the court of King David. He continued to observe intensely the quality of kingship and the interaction between magnates and church, peasantry and clergy, the married and the celibate. For Aelred kings were loyal servants of the Lord and were to uphold the bonds of society. Thinking of the Anarchy's ravages in England during the 1130s and 1140s, he wrote to the people of Scotland:

The trials of the English people should teach you to have faith in kings, and maintain mutual concord among yourselves, or else outsiders will devour your region before you and it will be destroyed by the enemy's attack.

(Eulog, ch. 9, p. 279)

Aelred's historical works are more statements about ideals of kingship than they are records of events. These writings reveal Aelred as a political human being, concerned with communities and their workings and dedicated to Christian life both inside and outside the monastery. He knew that the Cistercian experiment could not succeed without sympathetic patrons and stable societies. Even if the Cistercian cliché posited a desert as the monks' home, monks had to deal with their neighbors. From 1142 to 1147 Rievaulx coped with another monastery so close that the monks of the two houses could hear each other's bells and were often confused about the monastic hours. A settlement was finally reached, but another crisis arose when Aelred's friend of youth, Waldef, tried to unite his Augustinian house at Kirkham with Rievaulx. A draft of a settlement that was never implemented is found in the Rievaulx charters. Instead Waldef left Kirkham and came to Rievaulx for a brief stay before his election as abbot of Melrose.

Even a thriving community such as Rievaulx lived precariously so long as monastic foundations competed for room and for privileges. Even more dangerous was the situation of the period 1135–1154. Aelred's election as abbot of Revesby in 1143 shows that the Cistercians considered him to be an able candidate to balance conflicting interests during a dangerous time. Already in 1141, Abbot William of Rievaulx chose to send Aelred to Rome. As Walter Daniel wrote, William "discovered that Aelred was ten times as wise and prudent as he had supposed" and showed "unexpected ease in the solution of hard, difficult and important problems" (WD, p. 23). For Aelred there was apparently no division between inner life and outer involvements. Unlike Bernard he did not complain overmuch about the demands of "business" but took his turn in stride, ever confident in the possibilities of peace, negotiation, and reconciliation.

8

making love's mirror

ELRED RETURNED FROM ROME, probably in 1142, to be named novicemaster. It used to be thought that during this brief period before he became abbot at Revesby in 1143, he composed his *Mirror of Charity*. It was begun now but was a long time in the making. Recent studies of this work, the greatest of Aelred's writings in terms of theological and personal insight, confirm Aelred's own explanation that he composed it on the basis of notes that he had already sent off to his friend Hugh, now prior of another Cistercian house. In an excellent introduction to the new English translation of the *Mirror*, the Aelred scholar Charles Dumont has pointed out some of the segments sewn together in the text we have.

I agree with Dumont that Aelred could not have finished this lengthy treatise made up of three books while he was novicemaster but continued working on it as abbot of Revesby. A medieval monastic author had good conditions for making revisions and additions to his work, thus frustrating many a modern editor who has to decide at what stage it was "finished."

Aelred would have felt that the *Mirror of Charity* was never completed, so long as he continued to learn how monastic life and the expression of Christian love combine with each other. In a letter that was attached to the text as a justification for its existence, Bernard ordered Aelred to show "as in a mirror what charity is, how much sweetness there is in its possession, how much oppression is felt in self-centeredness [*cupiditas*]" (Spec Car, p. 71). Aelred replied by writing in the first book about "the excellence of charity," also in terms of self-centeredness; in the second book he answered the "complaints of certain people"; in the third he intended "to show how charity should be practiced" (p. 75).

The completed work contains the fullest exposition we have of the new Cistercian claim that the ascetic life in community was an excellent way of living the two great commandments. Like Augustine, Aelred wanted to love and to be loved. Only in the context of the right attachments (*affectus*), however, was it possible to love God and one another in a harmonious manner. Otherwise obsessions take over: the human person becomes attached to goods that are limited and that cannot give the consolation they seem to offer:

But what is more tranquil, you ask, than to love and be loved? If this is in God and for God I do not disapprove....But if this is according to the flesh or the world, realize how many acts of envy, suspicions, or stinging lashes of a jealous spirit banish peace of mind. (Sp Car 1.25.71, p. 128)

Aelred made the same type of observations as Augustine had done centuries earlier. In his position as novicemaster he was obliged to form his program in a way that was teachable for young aristocrats. These came from a world in which pleasures of the body and exercise of power were theirs by right. Aelred insisted that lack of restraint in such matters brought a total loss of control:

Goaded by the fiery spurs of debauchery, loosening all reins of decency, drunk and disorderly, it [the mind] is driven into every kind of disgraceful action. When the inferno of a passion once conceived is extinguished, it must be enkindled no less in another with greater intensity. In such yearning, then, it is quite absurd to look for rest for the rational mind.

(Spec Car, 1.26.75, p. 131)

For Aelred the individual seeks a spiritual sabbath in which rest and tranquillity are reached. These are only possible in a kind of spiritual circumcision: the novice had to make it possible for God "with a divine scalpel" to cut away the part of himself that encouraged lust, gluttony, and anger (Spec Car, 1.17.50, p. 115).

In order to encourage his novices and fellow monks, Aelred used the experience of his own life. At the same time he faced in the second book the objections he met as novicemaster. He acknowledged complaints that in coming to the monastic life, some men lose a sense of closeness to God that they had experienced while they were in the world. It was as if the move to the monastery brings nothing but aridity instead of the sweetness, the tears, and the yearning that were the very reason for leaving the world:

Why is it, you ask, that when I lived in a rather more lax way, when I enjoyed richer food, relaxed a bit with good drink, indulged in a little more sleep and did not weaken my body by hard work or irritate it with such rough garments, and when I was not restricted to so much silence, I felt so much compunction, I was so affected, and so open to a certain sweetness of mind? Yet now, in this strictness, I go along so dry and parched that I cannot, even by force, wring any tears from my eyes? (Spec Car, 2.7.17, p. 175)

Aelred dismissed such feelings as deceptive. So far as he was concerned, the shedding of tears and the sense of being close to the love of Jesus in themselves are nothing. If the person is "engulfed in a monstrous whirlpool of vice" and has "no horror of any flagrant acts," then

his religious impulses are not genuine. Aelred may have been recalling his own state of mind before he entered Rievaulx. Then he had
been deeply taken by the Jesus he found in the Gospels. "By a wonderful attachment to the sweetness of Jesus' love," Aelred then felt Jesus'
embrace of him (2.7.18, pp. 175–76). But this sensation was all in
vain, as empty as the experience of the monk Aelred knew who "after
idling away the whole day gossiping and drinking in the company of
worldlings, both men and women, came back to the monastery late
and burst into such tears and sighs that he offended the ears of many
brothers with his troublesome groanings" (2.7.19, p. 176).

Aelred here distinguished between what we might call emotional
highs and genuine religious feeling. He knew the sensitive, enthusias-
tic young men who came to Rievaulx. If they were in their late teens
or early twenties, many of them would still have been subject to adolescent fits of depression or exaltation. His task as novicemaster was
to talk to them, encourage them, but not to hide from them the rigors
of the path they had chosen.

Using his own experience in order to admit what was involved,
Aelred answered brothers who might have objected to his idealization
of spiritual rest in the monastery. Aelred admitted that he could feel
tempted and distressed. He also sensed tensions in human relationships, in spite of the benefits of monastery environment, because of
self-centeredness:

When a thoughtless word escaped me a while ago, a very dear friend of mine
took it so badly that he even betrayed the hurt on his face, and when I fell
prostrate at his feet, was in no hurry to lift me up. (Spec Car, 1.29.83, p. 136)

Aelred blamed himself for being too familiar with the friend and taking
it for granted that he could accept an "idle word." At every turn the
monastic life had ambushes and small defeats. The monk, who after
all was often an aristocrat brought up on arrogance and self-assertion,
had to prostrate himself and ask for forgiveness.

Aelred saw that many men came to the monastery in thinking that
the new form of fellowship would make it easier for them to express
the intensity of their own desire for God. Instead they often found
dullness, sourness, and meaninglessness in many of the exercises and
requirements. Even if a person only experiences pain, Aelred warned
against abandoning the monastic life (2.16.40, p. 192). We know from
Jocelin of Furness in his *Life of Waldef* that even so outstanding a
candidate as the young Waldef faced this problem. All the ascetic observances of the monastery at one stage became a burden to him. In
Powicke's summary:

Waldef had periods of depression and misgiving. He was repelled by the in-
sipid food, the rough garments, the hard manual labour and the incessant

round of offices and saying of psalms. As his mind went back to the years which he had passed at Nostell and Kirkham, he seriously considered whether it was not his duty to return to a life which, if less austere, was better adapted for the discipline and salvation of the soul. (WD, pp. lxxiv–lxxv)

Aelred described one conversation he had as novicemaster with a brother who clearly came from Waldef's type of privileged environment. This man told him how in his former life he had laughed and told stories:

Having freedom of my will, I enjoyed the company of my relatives and amused myself in conversations with my friends. I attended sumptuous dinner parties and did not shrink from drinking. I caught up on my sleep in the morning as I liked and stuffed myself with food and drink far beyond the limits of necessity. I say nothing of the stabs of anger which sometimes spurred me on, of the quarrels and disputes, or my cravings for worldly things, on which I was as intent as I could be. (2.17.42, pp. 193–94)

Coming to Rievaulx, the brother had entered a completely different regime: "My food is scantier, my clothing rougher, my drink comes from the well, and I often get my sleep over a book" (2.17.43, p. 194). With an opportunity to speak only with three people (abbot, novicemaster, and confessor), he had to give up his own will and put himself in the hands of others. The brother concluded that this way of life was infinitely better than his earlier one, for now there were no conflicts or enmities. Aelred warned him, however, against idealizing what he saw. Unlike Walter Daniel, Aelred was careful not to romanticize the requirements and discipline involved in growth in the monastic life.

The vision of unity in the cloister is always tempered by the fact of human limitation and self-deception. Aelred warned his novices not to mistake their tears for genuine fervor. The love of God was not to be mixed up with outer manifestations of love and sorrow. The ease with which we are moved by dramatic narratives shows nothing about the depth of our attachments:

If someone hearing these things being sung or listening to them being recited is moved by some sort of attachment even to the point of weeping, would it not be terribly absurd on this basis of worthless devotion to make some inference about the quality of his love? Could it be claimed that such a person loves one of the characters in the play, for whose rescue he would not be willing to spend even a tiny part of what he possesses? (2.17.50, p. 199)

Here Aelred again concerned himself with the way human attachments settle on worthless objects of affection and how the emotions lead one astray. Like Augustine in his admission that the excitement of the hunt still could titillate him, Aelred pointed out to his novices that the mere name of Arthur could excite visions of gallantry and excitement. Piece by piece he inspected the baggage with which his novices came from their aristocratic world, and he exposed to them its falseness:

Bringing a heart full of pictures even to our place of rest, we pass sleepless nights because of this utterly absurd nonsense. In the most idiotic kind of daydreaming, we depict battles of kings and victories of dukes as though they were before our eyes, and we straighten out all the affairs of the kingdom with our idle ramblings, even as we sing psalms or pray. (2.24.72, p. 214)

As elsewhere in his writings, Aelred was probably describing himself and his own disposition as much as he was telling his novices about themselves. Like them, he had been brought up to be curious, ambitious, and playful. Aelred realized how hard it was to replace the encouragement of individualistic passions with respect for the needs and norms of community life. The novice from an aristocratic background who managed to become a monk could continue to dream of past possibilities and make problems for his brothers:

Unable to bear the flame of his ambition once kindled, he gasps, seethes and is so tortured that his bitterness is apparent in his silence and his indignation in his speech....If by chance...a senior is caught in some fault, this fellow then seizes the occasion to avenge what he considers an injury to himself. He raises his eyebrows, wrinkles his forehead, and opens wide his lips in uncivil uproar. (2.26.76, p. 217)

In such a description, both precise and hard-hitting, Aelred revealed that he wrote on the basis of his own experience and observation. His point of departure is Augustine, but the materials and approach are different. Augustine presented in his *Confessions* the portrait of one man in his search for God. Aelred expanded this description to cover an entire religious community. Never forgetting the involvement of the individual monk in his own process of self-knowledge, Aelred remained faithful to Augustine's insights. But just as the *Confessions* express the individualistic ethos of Late Antiquity, so the *Mirror of Charity* celebrates an especially medieval pattern of community formation. There is nothing collectivist in Aelred's sharp individual portraits, but his goal was to reshape the novices in his care into the harmony of a community based on love rather than on power.

Aelred's most complete expression of this vision is to be found in the third book of the *Mirror*. He organized his teaching on human attachments (*affectus*) into a vision of inner growth. Returning to his image of the spiritual sabbath, Aelred begins with the love of self that, when rightly ordered, creates in the person a "marvelous security" that turns into joy and even jubilation in the praise of God (3.3.6, p. 225). But the person must move out of his "secret chamber" and embrace other people, first blood relatives, then "those who are linked to us by a bond of special friendship or bound to us by an exchange of services" (3.4.9, p. 227). Other involvements concern people in the same profession or way of life. Finally comes the love of all "those who are outside . . . pagans and Jews, heretics and schismatics" as well as one's enemies (3.4.10, p. 228). Only a person who encompasses all these loves will be able to enjoy fully "the sweetness of brotherly love" in the sense of Psalm 132 (133), where it is "good and pleasant for brothers to dwell together in unity," one of the most popular formulae for community harmony that medieval monks used.

Aelred moved from this assertion of brotherly love into an analysis of the attachments behind loves. In the physical type (*affectus carnalis*), he saw either attachment to beauty or to harmful pleasure. It is acceptable, he insisted, to be drawn to certain people because of their pleasantness, good looks, or virtue. Aelred did not ask that his novices deny a human tendency to be attracted to those who were easy and pleasing to be with, so long as vice was not involved. Reason and attachments need to be balanced. In mutual love, mutual need and concern for each other's interests could arise.

As far as physical presence is concerned, friends naturally seek each other. Aelred used the New Testament example of Paul and Timothy to show that this desire is not always reasonable. In all forms of natural attachment, control is essential. Aelred's Latin word is *modus* (measure), a word of central importance also in his *Spiritual Friendship*. Taking the words of Christ about hating mother and father (Luke 14:26), Aelred interpreted them not as a requirement to leave family and friends completely behind, but to consider such bonds in terms of reason (Spec Car, 3.26.60, p. 261).

Another form of attachment that needs to be guided by reason is *officialis affectus*, translated as "dutiful attachments," the type of bonds that abounded in feudal society. Such attachments required that services, gifts, and gestures are reciprocated. Aelred was wary about what such reciprocity might involve: "We must be careful about the attachment that moves us toward someone from whose kind deeds we derive benefit or by whose deference we are aided" (3.25.58, p. 260).

Simple, spontaneous affection for a person because of his position, generosity, or physical attractiveness can be allowed but must always be kept in check. Aelred proposed a register of emotional control, according to which everyone was to be loved in God and for the sake of God (3.26.63, p. 264). He believed in the exercise of temperance and moderation, but he also feared what happens when attachments get out of control:

If only those who govern the Church would chastise their own attachments according to this rule! Many of them surround their relatives with an all

too human attachment.... To enter the homes of some of our bishops —
and still more shameful, of some of our monks — is like entering Sodom
and Gomorrah. Effeminate, coiffeured young men, dressed up like courtesans,
strut around with their rumps half bare. (3.26.64, pp. 264–65)

The last phrase, in Latin *seminudis natibus,* is the same one that
Aelred used in his *Battle of the Standard* to describe the Galwegians
in kilts (PL 195:705). Aelred's vision of cute, half-undressed young
boys indicates his own inner turmoil as much as it describes the
churchmen of his day.

Here as elsewhere, Aelred intended to show how the privileged life
of the aristocracy, whether in the church or in the world, distorted lawful attachments and ended up in self-indulgence. "The hunting dogs
and hawking falcons and lathered horses," which also appeared in the
environment of pretty boys, meant that it became impossible to distinguish between aristocratic decadence and ecclesiastical habits. Carnal
and dutiful attachments were mixed up. With everything invested in
family attachments, anything that did not threaten family interests
was allowed. The whole scene reeked of self-indulgence.

However much he worried about such attachments, Aelred was
not willing to throw out physical bonds completely. Unlike some of
the Egyptian desert Fathers, whose sayings in the Latin *Lives of the
Fathers* were popular reading for medieval monks, Aelred did not re-
quire that his monks tear themselves away from all forms of human
affection. Provided there was "some degree of moderation," physical
attachment was acceptable, at least by those who were in control of
their bodies (Spec Car, 3.27.65, p. 265).

Aelred was aware that such bonds might develop an element of
forbidden sexuality. He described how good men sometimes took on
youths in the religious life and rejoiced in their great progress, only to
discover that they themselves had become emotionally and physically
attached to them. Before they knew it, their self-control was replaced
by desire. Such men, by whom Aelred must have included novice-
masters and whoever else in the church were charged with the care of
the young, found themselves "tormented by a vice-prone attachment":

Those who, ... would not countenance others equally guilty of that crime, but
far more would cast them with the greatest horror from the bosom of their
nauseated soul — these very modest, very sober men, these serene men with
perhaps even maidenly decorum, whom no unchaste person could glance at
without shame for his own hopeless condition — could scarcely keep company with them [those of tender years] without some titillation of vice.

(3.28.66, pp. 266–67)

Again I think Aelred here described himself as much as anyone
else. His honesty is intentional and not a literary facade. He knew that

it is difficult to distinguish between physical and spiritual love. And yet he did not forbid all attachments. He found some consolation in the phrase from the Epistle of Titus (1:15) "To the pure all things are pure." He believed in moderation, not in absolute prohibition. Despite an ever-present risk of sexual attraction, experienced men could take on as disciples and friends those younger than themselves. It was a natural human trait to seek out beauty and intelligence and to remold them into the image of Christ. Aelred was not afraid. In his awareness of what was at risk, he trusted himself and his self-knowledge in the Lord.

Few observers of Aelred have tried to interpret exactly what he meant in the above passage. Surely he was describing the same process of attraction indicated long ago in Plato's *Symposium*, and one that everyone who works with young people must consider. The American medieval historian Norman Cantor, who has become something of a scourge of academic historians, has pointed to a similar disposition perhaps in our century's finest monastic historian, David Knowles:

During his mid-thirties he almost inevitably became emotionally involved with these beautiful, refined young men to whom he gave spiritual and educational counseling as novice master. This homoerotic disturbance in his life, sweeping aside his overly developed superego and making its way into his ego personality, was manifested in the signification of his wanting to run away with the young monks and found a new monastery. There is nothing novel or astonishing about such an outcome, the withdrawal and romantic flight motif in the history of monasticism. It is especially explicit, with precise homoerotic overtones, for instance, in the writings of Aelred of Rievaulx, the mid-twelfth century English Cistercian abbot, with which Knowles was very familiar.

I would not necessarily use the Freudian vocabulary that Cantor applies here, but his interpretation is a helpful one for understanding what was at stake for the attentive, sympathetic novicemaster. One reservation remains, however: the "romantic flight motif" is present in Walter Daniel's description of Aelred, but not in Aelred's life as we can see it from his own writings. Nevertheless, Cantor has come close to capturing the special quality of tenderness and intimacy that makes the role of novicemaster both attractive and dangerous, whether in the twelfth century or in the twentieth. How can one live in such close contact without developing either strong attractions or repulsions?

Aelred had no qualms about conceding the pitfalls, while it has taken our own age a half century even to begin to admit the forces at work in the life of a modern monk like David Knowles. Even now, Cantor's interpretation is being either deliberately ignored, or ridiculed, or fiercely challenged by historians at Cambridge and elsewhere who are devoted to the memory of Knowles. Aelred also has defendants who suppose they can forbid considerations about his psychology or ban speculation about his sexuality.

Aelred did not write the *Mirror of Charity* to discuss his own sexuality or that of other clerics. But in describing the degree and type of human attachments, he found it natural and inevitable to bring up the question of sexual attraction and involvement. His keen awareness of other men, and his talent for getting attached to them, are well attested in a story from Walter Daniel that, like the above passage from the *Mirror*, has generally been ignored. It concerns a difficult novice in Aelred's charge. In Walter's phrase, for once succinct, he was "a man with no mental stability." He told Aelred that he wanted to leave the monastery, and Aelred forbade him to do so. Nevertheless, the brother went his way. Wandering all day long, he found in the evening that he had gone in a circle "and suddenly found himself within the monastic wall" (WD, pp. 24–25).

So far the story is a familiar one, almost like a folk tale, concerning the person who cannot run away from his "fate." But in monastic terms, it is the tale of a weak novice and a wise novicemaster. Aelred's response, when he came upon the man, recalls the father greeting the prodigal son:

His prophet, he who had begged God for his soul, catching sight of him, ran to meet him, put his arms round his neck, kissed his face, and exclaimed, "Son, why hast thou thus dealt with me? (Lk 2:48) I have wept many tears for you today. And as I believe in God, I believe that, as I have sought from the Lord and have promised you, you shall not perish." (WD, p. 25)

Aelred failed to tell his abbot at Rievaulx that the brother under his charge had disappeared. Walter does not say it, but this oversight was a potential breach of the Rule of Saint Benedict, for all things (and people) were in the abbot's care. Thus a runaway must be reported immediately. Aelred knew that if the abbot were told, the man might be expelled. As novicemaster he took on the fate of the brother as his own responsibility.

This incident was only the beginning. The brother apparently went to Revesby when Aelred became abbot in 1143. Walter does not say so, but Aelred himself might have chosen to take with him the troublesome novice, who by now must have been a monk. Here the monk made the same type of objections to the requirements of the Cistercian observance that Aelred outlines in the *Mirror of Charity:*

I cannot endure the daily tasks. The sight of it all revolts me. I am tormented and crushed down by the length of the vigils, I often succumb to the manual labour. The food cleaves to my mouth, more bitter than wormwood. The rough clothing cuts through my skin and flesh down to my very bones. More than this, my will is always hankering after other things; it longs for the delights of the world and sighs unceasingly for its loves and affections and pleasures. (WD, p. 30)

The brother was again preparing to leave. At this point Aelred again departed from normal procedures and showed how much it meant to him to keep the unstable monk. He told the fellow that he would go on a hunger strike until the man returned. Aelred withdrew into his tears, but not before his subcellarer, who is described as being a kinsman, showed up and tried to talk some sense into him: "Why on earth do you cry out your eyes for that wretched creature?" Aelred told the subcellarer that the matter was none of his business: "What is it to you?"

Just as Aelred's relative at Hexham once found that he could not get hold of the relics he wanted but was driven back, so too Aelred's monk at Revesby discovered that he could not move in the direction he wanted. The air at the open gate of the monastery held him back. When the monk finally gave up and returned to Aelred, who was thus spared missing any more meals, the abbot's remark was: "Truly, my God, who has brought you back safe, has had compassion on me" (WD, p. 32). It is remarkable that Aelred here praised the Lord for his mercy not on the difficult monk but on himself. It is as if he thanked God for saving him from the suffering and worry experienced by a person who loves someone else but finds the loved one walking out of his life. Walter Daniel underlined this event by concluding, "Let all true lovers of Aelred read this miracle over and over again." As far as Walter was concerned, Aelred by his willpower and prayer was able to keep the man in the monastery. This was the miracle, but in describing how it came about, Walter revealed the strength of Aelred's attachment to the monk.

A final mention of the troublesome monk belongs to the time after Aelred's return to Rievaulx as its abbot. Aelred sent him on a mission together with others, including Walter's father, Daniel, to an abbey that had been under the observance of the Order of Savigny. In 1147 this Order was incorporated into the Cistercian Order, so the events narrated here must have been from about this time, shortly after Aelred's election.

The night before the monks were to return to Rievaulx, Aelred had a dream in which it was revealed that his difficult monk soon would die. In the early morning Aelred was told that the monk had arrived at the gate and wanted to speak to him. Aelred "kissed him tenderly and, thinking of the vision, shed many sweet tears over him" (WD, p. 35). He warned the wayward monk of approaching death, but the man either could not or would not understand. Instead he returned to his familiar theme of the deadliness of monastery life. He asked Aelred's permission to visit his family for a month.

Aelred refused and informed the monk that he, Aelred, could no longer live without him, just as the monk would not be allowed to die without Aelred. He lured him back into the monastery, where he became ill after a few days. Walter describes the scene of Aelred's care for the dying monk. Aelred forgot that he had learned from the vision that the monk would die in his hands. When he did remember, the monk could die: "He, as the abbot touched his head and uttered the name of the saint [Benedict], immediately breathed his last in Aelred's hands" (WD, p. 36).

In contrast to the two previous episodes with the troublesome monk, Walter added no further comment here. With a "let us proceed," he generalized about Rievaulx as a "stronghold for the sustaining of the weak, the nourishment of the strong and whole" (WD, p. 36). In describing Rievaulx under Aelred, Walter probably was inspired by the praise of Clairvaux under Bernard that his friend William of Saint Thierry formulated by about 1150 in the first book of Bernard's biography. In literary terms, Walter did not manage to incorporate the story of the wayward monk into his version of a favorable description of a monastery with a good abbot. Walter wanted to illustrate Aelred's great concern for his monks. But Walter ended up in revealing Aelred's humanity and emotional involvement in another monk when he described how Aelred told the subcellarer at Revesby, his own kinsman, to mind his own business.

A similar narrative of emotional involvement with a difficult monk is available in the *Life of Saint Anselm* by Eadmer, written in the early years of the twelfth century. There is no special evidence that Walter knew this account, but he might have been aware of it. Here Anselm, as prior of the monastery at Bec in Normandy, is described as making special provisions for a wayward youth, Osbern, who refused to conform to the requirements of monastic life. Instead of punishing him, Anselm gave him the same kind of leeway that Aelred did with his difficult novice. A difference, however, is that after giving Osbern privileges, Anselm gradually became stricter on him and finally demanded more from him than from anyone else in his charge. Anselm seems to have tried to wean himself of his affection for Osbern, while there is no evidence that Aelred distanced himself from his unnamed monk. In fact, the last episode with Aelred's sending of the man on an important mission indicates that he had given him a position of responsibility.

In both instances, Anselm with Osbern and Aelred with his wayward monk, beloved youths died at an early age, much to the sorrow and concern of their abbots. Both Anselm and Aelred obtained divine information about the state of their friends' souls. In Anselm's case,

his concern can possibly even be documented by a letter written to Osbern's mother after the boy's death. There is no doubt here that both
Anselm and Aelred became caught up in an attachment that went beyond the novicemaster's or prior's obligation to take responsibility for
those under them, as prescribed in the Rule of Saint Benedict.

For both Anselm and Aelred it was essential to make sure that their
friends remained in the monastery, come what may. The early deaths
provided fulfillment for the hope of deliverance and release from the
immediacy of emotional demands. Nowhere else in Anselm's life or
letters do we find him losing his heart so completely to another monk.
Nowhere else in Aelred's life or writings do we find him crying out in
anger and pain, "I am tormented in this flame and unless help comes
to my son, I die" (WD, p. 31). Can we not conclude, in the most generous way possible, that Aelred, like Anselm before him, had fallen in
love with the novice and could not imagine life without him, unless he
got an assurance that the man's soul and body were safely in the monastery? Such emotional bonds, of course, were precisely those against
which Aelred warned, but his own awareness of his attraction made it
all the more possible for him to write about what was needed in order
to live a life of well-ordered attachments.

There is no need to sentimentalize such bonds and to think of Aelred in modern terms as a frustrated homosexual, afraid of admitting
to himself what his true feelings were. He probably was aware of what
was going on inside of himself and did his best to cope with his feelings in a way that his own moral and monastic standards could allow.
In doing so he did not deny the fact of his attachments. Aelred sought
to integrate his feelings for the man into his, and the friend's, identifi-
cation with the community. So long as individual loves and bonds did
not threaten the stability of monastic life, then they were acceptable.
Aelred had every right to tell his kinsman the subcellarer to mind his
own business!

At the same time as Aelred dealt with the impulses of his own
sexuality and his joy in beautiful, sensitive, religious men, he acted in
a competent, forceful way as abbot of the new house at Revesby. Here
any patronizing vision of the abbot as "poor, driven Aelred" does not
correspond to Walter Daniel's portrait, one that is confirmed in Aelred's writings. Aelred made use of his charm, gentleness, and warmth
of personality to draw people to him, either so that they would enter
the monastery or be materially generous to the new house. In Walter's
description:

Bishop, earls, barons venerate the man and the place itself, and in their reverence and affection load it with possessions, heap gifts upon it and defend it
by their peace and protection. The bishop orders him to preach to the clergy
in their local synods and he does so; to bring priests to a better way of life,

as he does not fail to do; to accept grants of land from knights in generous free-alms, and he obeys. (WD, p. 28)

All this may be idealized and is impossible to check because of the lack of records from Revesby, but it corresponds with what we know about Aelred's later activities at Rievaulx. He made himself invaluable both to his monks and to their aristocratic relatives. To the latter he could preach as he had done to his novices:

There exists a natural order. That is, if a person who has not committed illicit actions so chooses, he may make use of everything licit, provided [he does so] licitly. For example, eating flesh meat and drinking wine are licit, as are also the use of marriage and the possession of riches.
(Spec Car, 3.32.77, p. 273)

Aelred appreciated the importance of such a way of life. He criticized it only when its content clashed with the requirements of Christian love and duty. It was good for a man to keep faith with his lord, but if he did so only "to grasp glory or avoid dishonor," this was foolishness (3.27.101, p. 293).

Aelred ended his *Mirror of Charity* with a celebration of the bonds of friendship as they can develop in human and especially in monastic society. He wrote of those joined "by the sweetest bond of spiritual friendship," who were to be "more pleasantly hidden in the innermost and secret recesses of our breast" (3.38.106, pp. 295–96). He took Cicero's words on friendship and transformed them into a Christian observance, as he would later do in greater detail in his treatise on the subject:

It is no mean consolation in this life to have someone with whom you can be united by an intimate attachment and the embrace of very holy love, to have someone in whom your spirit may rest, to whom you can pour out your soul....

Alone you may speak with him alone, and once the noise of the world is hushed, in the sleep of peace, you alone may repose with him alone in the embrace of charity, the kiss of unity, with the sweetness of the Holy Spirit flowing between you. Still more, you may be so united to him and approach him so closely and so mingle your spirit with his, that the two become one.
(Spec Car, 3.39.109, p. 298)

Is Aelred's lyricism about a kind of spiritual marriage reserved for the human state after death, in a kind of paradise for friends? His language reaches the heights, but he was aware that it might be misinterpreted:

Lest someone think that this very holy sort of charity should seem reproachable, our Jesus himself, lowering (Himself) to our condition in every way, suffering all things for us and being compassionate towards us, transformed it by manifesting his love. (3.39.110, p. 299)

Aelred referred here to the love Jesus showed for John the Apostle, who was especially favored as the only one of the twelve who was a virgin and who had the privilege of putting his head on the "virginal breast" of Jesus.

Aelred made use of a language here that hardly had any heirs in the twelfth century or later in the Middle Ages, except in terms of meditations on the sufferings and body of Christ. In terms of friendship and union among men, he remained alone in his boldness of expression and fervor of imagination. Before ending the *Mirror*, he provided one last warning so that he would not be misunderstood:

Let us enjoy one another in sanctification, so that each may know how to possess his vessel, that is to say, his own body — in sanctification and honor, and not in the passion of desire. (3.40.112, p. 300)

The *Mirror* was complete as a series of prescriptions showing how to match the impulses of the individual monk with the requirements of community, the baggage of family background, and the challenge of union with Christ. Ever the optimist, Aelred trusted that this very intimate expression of his own experience would be acceptable to the formidable Bernard: "It is sweet and pleasant to converse in spirit on this sort of thing with someone very dear who is absent" (30.40.113, p. 301).

We do not know whether Bernard liked the result or not, but enough monks did so that the work was preserved and used. The next monastic generation, however, abbreviated Aelred's text. They removed his personal references, in accord with a new intellectual partiality for analysis and abstraction. But in the original text, the novicemaster lives on with his loves and attachments, making a mirror for all who wanted to embrace love.

9

ABBOT HATED
AND LOVED

AELRED WAS ABBOT, either at Revesby or at Rievaulx, for almost twenty-five years of his relatively short life of fifty-seven years. Modern descriptions of his way of governing Rievaulx sometimes indicate that he was too tolerant with people unfit for the monastery. This view is associated with Walter Daniel's description of how Aelred allowed the monks to sit on his bed and hold hands with each other (WD, p. 40). He emerges from such sketches as something of an overkind abbot, who let matters get out of hand. As Powicke has pointed out, Walter Daniel himself was aware of such criticisms. He wrote his Life of Aelred "in part as a passionate refutation of the suggestions that he [Aelred] was ambitious, a wirepuller, fond of luxurious living, a successful prig who in his time had been no better than he should have been" (WD, p. lxvi).

I will consider in chapter 12 the aftermath of Aelred's abbacy, but here our main sources are Aelred's own writings together with Walter Daniel's remarks. As before, Walter provides much interesting material, but it is Aelred who gives us a clear picture. I will first consider Walter's descriptions and then turn to Aelred, especially in his sermons to the monks. My impression is that Aelred enjoyed very much his position at Rievaulx. There he could combine practical abilities with a perennial need for human affection and closeness.

Walter Daniel takes the bull by the horns in his description of Aelred's election at Rievaulx:

There are some who think that ambition brought him to the headship of this house. Every good man knows that this is false. That his virtue provoked jealous men to lie is not surprising — virtue never fails to stir envy — and how many jealous busybodies this man of peace had to endure! (WD, p. 33)

The literary genre of hagiography, the writing of a saint's life, often includes the theme of the detractors who jealously run down the person in question. Walter could borrow his combative stance from the standard hagiographical work of the West, the *Life of Martin of Tours* by Sulpicius Severus. At the same time, Walter comes across as an aggressive personality, impatient with others, as Aelred portrays him in the last two books of the *Spiritual Friendship*. Here Walter appears as one of the participants in Aelred's dialogue on friendship and is seen as using every opportunity to cut down another participant, the monk Gratian.

The combination of Walter Daniel's fervent desire to be Aelred's interpreter and the presence of Aelred's critics may explain why Walter at this point in his biography was so defensive on Aelred's behalf. He accounted for Aelred's privileges in terms of food, drink, and baths in the monastery as a necessary regime for his illnesses of gallstones and arthritis:

One day, after no less than forty visits to the bath, he was so incredibly exhausted in the evening that he looked more dead than alive. And you dare to talk about the bathings of Aelred! Do you suppose that he took delight when there was so much frustration? He, himself a friend of the sick, the physician who used to relieve them so manfully in their imperfect state and to cure so many! (WD, p. 34)

Walter's anger here may have been directed toward critical monks at Rievaulx who, after Aelred's death, began openly to speak against him. The source of some of the resentment seems to lie in the fact that Aelred, especially in the last decade of his life, moved to a hut where he could get special treatment for his ailments. Here he allowed a relatively large group of monks to have access to him:

Every day they came...twenty or thirty at a time, to talk together of the spiritual delights of the Scriptures and of the observance of the Order. There was nobody to say to them, "Get out, go away, do not touch the Abbot's bed"; they walked and lay about his bed and talked with him as a little child prattles with its mother. (WD, p. 40)

There is nothing more dangerous for the reputation of a leader in a fellowship whose members are in daily contact with each other than to bestow special privileges on one segment of the community. During these very years after Aelred became abbot, the first Cistercian lay brother revolts were taking place. The lay brothers protested that they were what we might call second-class monks, cut off from the choir monks in terms of concessions on food and other privileges. We do not know if the lay brothers at Rievaulx were also restless, but Walter's defense of Aelred indicates that his particular attention to some of the monks alienated others.

Walter does not hint at community resentment concerning Aelred's partiality to one or two monks. Here Aelred seems to have maintained his intimate friendships in harmony with the requirements of the common life. The problem was the existence of what looked like a clique that had access to the abbot's room and whose members could talk freely with him. Walter's later "Letter to Maurice," a polemic against those who criticized Aelred, revealed the intensity of at least one monk's anger against the abbot. This episode concerned a physical attack on Aelred in his hut by a monk who is described as being mentally ill:

He came to where Aelred lay. Bellowing cruelly and gnashing his teeth he seized hold of a side of the mat, with the father lying on it, tossed them both up with all his might and hurled the father of at least a hundred monks and five hundred laymen into the fire among the cinders, shouting, "O you wretch, now I am going to kill you, now I am going to destroy you by a hard death. What are you doing, lying here, you impostor, you useless silly fellow? You shall tell no more of your lies, for now you are about to die."

(WD, p. 79)

Walter Daniel was an eyewitness to the attack and described how he defended his abbot and tried to get the man under control. Walter and his friends would have probably given the monk a thrashing, but Aelred stopped them by insisting that the man was sick and should be handled with love, not anger:

Taking his head in his hands, the most blessed man kisses him, blesses and embraces him and gently sought to soothe his senseless anger against himself, just as though he himself felt no pain from his own sickness and had been touched by no sadness because of the injury done to him. (WD, p. 80)

Aelred refused to allow the man to be punished. Combining Christian forgiveness with the language of feudal society, he insisted that the man had acted only against his person, not against monastery discipline. Therefore he, Aelred, could choose whether to seek revenge or not, and he would not.

Walter made use of the episode in order to show that Aelred's charity was greater than any miracle. Today we can interpret the incident in terms of Aelred's instinctive understanding of mental illness and its effects on human behavior. Aelred's loving response to the man by his embrace of the poor fellow points also to spontaneity and lack of concern on his part that such contact would be misunderstood. Twelfth-century monks like Aelred could allow themselves much more physical contact with each other than their nineteenth- or early twentieth-century successors.

At the same time, however, the monk's accusations may have been more than the ravings of a madman. He accused Aelred of being a hypocrite and a liar. His anger may reflect the feelings among a group of monks who felt that they were kept outside the privileged zone of friendship and contact that Aelred, especially in his last years, established around himself.

Another indication that Aelred's way of being caused resentment is found in Walter's story in the *Life of Aelred* about the abbot of a daughterhouse of Rievaulx who came there on a visitation. He and Aelred did not get on. Walter blamed the resulting quarrel on the visiting abbot, who clearly was dissatisfied with Aelred's criticism:

He burst out upon our father and, violently attacking him with darts of cursing and cruelly pursuing him with the arrows of many blasphemies, moved his spirit to indignation against him and deservedly roused him to anger upon him. His unjust presentation of his case turned the dispute against him.

In his frustration, Aelred cried out to God that the man was falsely accusing him and asked that he quickly be freed from this evil. King Henry II said something similar a few years later, leading to the murder of Archbishop Thomas Becket. In the *Life*, Walter saw Aelred's words as leading to the man's speedy death, but in the "Letter to Maurice," he had second thoughts about Aelred's willing the man's death and toned down the story (WD, p. 68).

Such an episode may indicate the very opposite of what Walter had intended. Aelred is shown here to have been furious and even vindictive with an abbot under his care. When the man left Rievaulx, Aelred refused to give him his abbatial blessing. Walter adds that this happened "to the great indignation of all the brethren at Rievaulx" (WD, pp. 44–45). The reaction of the Rievaulx community shows that Aelred's decisions and actions were not always popular. In many situations Walter described Aelred as a peacemaker, such as the time shortly before his death when he made a visitation to a daughterhouse in Galloway and reconciled warring parties in the region (WD, p. 46). But in his own monastery Aelred could have difficulties in winning the support of all the monks.

Aelred managed to attract swarms of people to the monastery, and he ended up paying a high price for his accessibility. There were also many more lay brothers and lay workers who came to populate the monastery and its environs. Any administrator would have had a hard time in dealing with the inevitable factions and dissensions, and it is no wonder that Aelred sometimes met opposition. Behind his charm was a strong will, and at some moments, as with the visiting abbot, a very human anger took hold of him.

This impression of Aelred as a capable, conscientious abbot who sometimes was challenged and criticized is confirmed by a review of his sermons. In them he often referred to his position in the monastery and his responsibilities. The most complete statement that I have found in Aelred comes in a sermon for the feast of All Saints (November 1), which begins by considering the brothers' desire to share the society of the saints. In order to do so, they have to remember the per-

secutions that the saints underwent. All who want to live in Christ
will suffer (cf. 2 Tim 3:12). Aelred here turned to the pain he suffered
as abbot:

It is a great persecution to have to care for all, to grieve for all, to be sad when
someone is sad, to be afraid when someone is tempted. How intolerable a
persecution it is, as sometimes happens to us, when some one of those whom
we have nurtured and guarded and loved like our own being is conquered by
the devil to such an extent that he even departs from us, or lives in such a
perverse and lost manner that we have to expel him from ourselves!
                                                    (Serm 26:18, p. 214)

Aelred's words here conflict with Walter Daniel's statement that in the
seventeen years during which he was under Aelred at Rievaulx, "he
did not expel a single monk" (WD, p. 40). Walter admitted that four
left "without his knowledge, but the Lord led them all back, save one
follower of Satan." Could Aelred have been referring to lay brothers,
whom he did send away, as opposed to monks, whom he did not?
Aelred, in his own words, seems to have been a stricter abbot than
Walter made him out to be.

In his sermon on All Saints, Aelred appealed to his monks to consider the burdens of his office. The monks' awareness of the abbot's
concern for renegade monks might encourage the rest of them to live
in a better way:

Brothers, if you are sorry or sad when such things happen, you who are
monks, how much sadness do you think we have, who are both brothers
and fathers and guardians, we who took them in [to the monastery] to render
account for them? Surely, brother, you ought to have great compassion on us
and give us joy in your good way of life, for in so many other matters we
experience sadness. (Serm 26.19)

Aelred's exhortation can be interpreted in various ways. He was referring to the warning in the Rule of Saint Benedict (ch. 2) that the
abbot at the Last Judgment must render account for all the souls entrusted to him. But this is merely his point of departure in appealing
to his monks. Was he using emotional blackmail or simply baring his
heart? He said, as it were, to the brothers, that they had to behave,
because he as abbot needed support and encouragement. As the historian Caroline Bynum pointed out in her landmark *Jesus as Mother*,
Aelred, like other Cistercian abbots of the twelfth century, at times reversed the usual image of the abbot as father and preferred to describe
himself as mother. Here he went even further, practically asking the
monks to look after and mother him.

Aelred's reply to his own doubts and insecurity lay in an assertion
of the unity of community. Each of the brothers, he continued in his
sermon, "before he came here, had one soul that was only his own."

But in the conversion to God in the monastic life, the brothers had given themselves over to the Holy Spirit, whose fire consumed their souls, "and from all your hearts and souls he has made one heart and one soul" (Serm 26.43, p. 220). Aelred here made use of the Acts of the Apostles 4:32 with its assertion of unity in the first Christian community at Jerusalem, a point of departure for any idealization of monastic life. But he went further, claiming that the virtues of the good community approached that of the angels. In chastity and charity, humility and obedience, the monks competed with the angels.

Instead of ending this sermon with the angels, Aelred returned to the brothers who were weak and sick "and cannot do such things as the others can." He encouraged them "not to be sad or despair." The only danger was that through "laziness or negligence" a brother may fail to offer to the others what he was capable of giving (Serm 26.46, pp. 220–21). In such a community everyone depends on everyone else. No one is to be praised more than any other. The goal is unity: "If there are true unity and charity among you, without doubt whatever one does, it will be [the doing] of all and whatever all do will be [the doing] of each one." Every community member, whatever his talents or limitations, participates in its wholeness and individuality. The only outsider is the person who puts himself outside, either by leaving or by creating dissension within.

All this might seem straightforward, but the very simplicity makes it into a magnificent statement of the dynamics of community life. Aelred took as his model the harmony of the saints and the memory of the first Christian brotherhood. He reflected upon the words in Acts about how everything was shared, but he went further, describing how members with different talents each made their own contributions. Here we have an idealization of a society that was supposed to have arisen with Communism but relatively quickly has come to nought. New forms of human organization will continue to pursue this dream of living together in harmony, giving each according to need, not according to what he or she produces or manipulates. Aelred visualized a voluntary union of persons with different backgrounds but with the same purpose of praising the Lord.

Aelred encouraged his monks not only by idealizing the harmonious community but also by describing quite frankly what could and does go wrong in daily life. In one sermon, he portrayed three habits of mind that can block the solitude that a monk must develop. These are wanderlust, suspicion, and curiosity. In the first category Aelred described the monk who could not sit still in one place but "now goes out and now comes in, so that he can hardly spend an hour on the same task or in the same place":

If he starts to sing, he can scarcely bear it once he has sung through one verse or two [of a Psalm]. If he begins to read, before he has finished a page, he gets up, and if he cannot leave the cloister, at least he goes to another part of the cloister. (Serm 43.25, p. 342)

The restless monk finds some excuse to speak with the prior and goes from one room to another. He uses sign language to find out where the prior is and indicates a great need for him.

If he finds him, he makes a sign and enters a room where speaking is allowed [auditorium], prostrates himself, asks forgiveness, imagines that he has done this or thought that, not so much because of sorrow for sin but because of desire to speak. (Serm 43.26, pp. 342–43)

There is a dash of humor in Aelred's description of the monk who just cannot sit still. Anyone who needs to concentrate on a task that can be repetitive or boring can recognize Aelred's description. He continues the exposition by turning from bodily wanderlust to spiritual, "when the monk keeps himself bodily in one place but mentally wanders here and there." This type includes the suspicious person, who "always has his eyes turned outside himself, so that he never pays attention to himself, but is always suspicious of the life and habits of others and has the worst thoughts of them":

If he happens to see some individuals speaking with each other or using sign language, he always thinks that they are talking about himself or that it is evil. He cannot keep silent, but always is judging and detracting. Similarly the one who is curious, who always has his ears erect for rumors and pointless confabulation, his eyes ever open to investigate what another might be doing or saying. (Serm 43.27, p. 343)

Aelred's ironic description of the restless monk reveals his powers of observation and his frankness with his monks. He knew what it was like to live in a community with different types of people and to have to deal with pettiness, jealousy, self-righteousness. The only possible response was "tranquillity of body and of spirit." "We must keep quiet, so that we can remove from our mouths and hearts all empty things, all forms of suspicion and all detractions" (Serm 43.28). This response is possible only through the process of loving, which reaches beyond the self, to others and to God.

Aelred interspersed his sermons with such direct examples from the everyday lives of the brothers. He did so not only in his sermons for feast days but also in the sermons he gave on Isaiah. Here his passages devoted to moral exposition of the prophecies of Isaiah often touched on the life of the monastery. One can imagine the brothers, sleepy in the morning chapter after hours of wakefulness from the time of vigils, perking up with the same attention that any preacher gets when referring to something familiar, and perhaps painful or funny, taken from the everyday lives of the listeners.

The literary heights and sophisticated imagery of Bernard's *Sermons on the Song of Songs* were not Aelred's goal. Much of the time, he was more an old-fashioned exegete, going line by line through the language of Scripture and bringing out the various meanings: historical, allegorical, moral. But he added his own experience and that of the brothers in the monastery and so left us with another mirror, reflecting the thoughts of an abbot who loved his monks and at times felt frustrated by the task of molding and maintaining a loving community.

Regularly in these sermons, Aelred linked his own difficulties with those of his brothers. How did this personal dimension influence the monks? We do not know precisely, but Walter Daniel claimed that anyone who came to Rievaulx "in his weakness" not only found "a loving father in Aelred" but also "timely comforters in the brethren" (WD, p. 37). Aelred may well have created what we would call a supportive atmosphere, so that problematic monks received encouragement.

The Rule of Saint Benedict makes the abbot's disposition and leadership the very center of monastic organization. Even if the Cistercians had added their brilliant superstructure of government upon the monasteries, each abbot still had decisive influence in his own house. Thus an abbot like Aelred could make an immense difference in the way the monks dealt with each other. One can imagine the effect of a passage like the following, preached to the brothers on the feast of Mary's Purification (February 2):

The more I love you, the more I desire your progress and the more I am afraid of your failure. I am not saying this as if I distrust any of you. Certainly, brothers, I distrust none of you. Whoever says to me, "I am weak," I believe him. But, my brothers, I warn not only you, but also myself, that we do not have too much faith in ourselves. For know, dearest ones, that the flesh is deceptive and, unless we act prudently, often deceives us.

(Serm 24.23, p. 284)

Aelred said to his brothers, as he had written to his sister, that they were never to feel secure, but always to be afraid. In one moment of sin the achievement of a lifetime can be lost. Each monk balanced on the brink between heaven and hell, and the abbot was very much there with them:

Behold, brothers, sweetest ones, in all that I live, in all that I know, I offer for your betterment and devote to your use. Use me, as you like, and do not spare me in my work, wherever it can serve your progress.

(Oner 16, PL 195:422)

Aelred explained at the start of this particular sermon that he had been away from the monastery for a long period and felt happy to return to his monks. He spoke of his hunger for their presence, but at the same time warned them that there is "no security" (*nulla securitas, fratres mei, nulla securitas*), so long as the enemy sleeps and has not perished (PL 195:426).

The enemy was, of course, the devil, and Aelred did not try to hide his fear that even in the monastery the enemy attacked monks with sexual images and temptations. His sermons are by no means full of warnings against sexual temptations. These are merely one of the many pitfalls the monk experiences. On the feast of Saint Benedict, Aelred contrasted the saint's self-control with the monks' lack of it. This inability showed that the monks had not left the world in the same way Benedict had done:

What was Saint Benedict? Without doubt a man as you are, as another man is, as I am. That one is flesh, you are flesh. . . . What then could he do that you cannot? He when still a boy, fresh and delicate, left the world, fled from his parents. But you being great and wise and prudent still dream of the world and sigh for your parents. If you complain that you sustain grave temptations, he too, as you know, was gravely tempted. He resisted in a manly way, while you succumb in a weak manner. (Serm 37.3, p. 300)

Aelred did not recommend here the kind of bodily mortifications that Benedict inflicted on himself, but he did warn the brothers against "the familiarity of and conversations with women." Benedict counsels the monk "never to be unoccupied, never to wander about, never unstable, never dissolute in words." The monk must mortify his body "in abstinence, vigils, manual labor," and maintain his heart "in good meditation, in prayer, in compunction and devotion" (Serm 37.10, p. 302).

These admonitions are standard advice for monks, and it is important to realize that Aelred, especially in his sermons, was usually quite traditional in his language. It is only occasionally, for example, when he compares the brothers to the crucified Christ, that he could be innovative in intensifying the expression of religious experience:

As a crucified man cannot move his hand or feet or other members, so a man who wishes in life to die in the fear of God and his precepts must constrain and refrain all his members from evil acts. All these are to be held on the cross until death. (Serm 36.14, p. 297)

We must nail our bodies to the cross.

Much of the time Aelred spoke about sexual temptation in a generalized manner, as the spiritual father avoiding explicit material for a sensitive audience. But occasionally he became more specific, such as in his sermons on Isaiah, commenting on the passage, "I shall visit evils on the cities" (Is 12:11). Here he spoke of a "pestiferous evil" that resulted in the destruction of good attachments "defiled by base loves and sordid thoughts. Good Jesus, when will you see to it that you restore my soul from that malignity?" (Oner 13, PL 195:412). Continuing in this vein in the next sermon, he reflected on the destruction of Sodom and Gomorrah as the end of Babylon's delights, the result of "that horrid and hateful sin against nature." Only man of all creatures defies the order of creation in committing such a sin "in contempt of God, in shame for himself, to the injury of all things ... so that all which God instituted, which reason has approved of, which usage has confirmed, he is not afraid to pervert" (Oner 14, PL 195:413). This hellfire and damnation sermon contains vivid portrayals of the punishments in store for the one who sins against nature. Aelred rarely allowed himself such a tirade, but beneath the loving surface of his addresses to the monks, there is fear of homosexual acts.

This concern becomes much more specific and detailed in a sermon preached to the clergy at Troyes in Champagne, not far from Clairvaux and perhaps on Aelred's way to or from the Cistercian General Chapter. It is as if Aelred assumed that homosexual behavior was rampant among the secular clergy: "Truly these [men], corrupt in mind and body, ... confound the order and use of the sexes" and thus make their bodies filthy by acts of "monstrous lust" in which they "abuse themselves by every form of filth" (Serm 28.28–29, p. 237). Aelred's term is "sodomites," making his meaning unmistakable. Once again he went into detail about the horrible punishments such sinners could expect.

Aelred's section on clerical homosexual practices, however vivid, makes up only one part of a rather long sermon. Even if we extricated all the passages in his sermons in which he dealt with sexual matters, they would probably take up less space than similar sections on the vice of pride. Aelred was keenly aware that the men who came to the cloister were brought up to act in an arrogant and assertive manner. Pride is the vice almost inborn in the new aristocracy of blood and spirit. In the fall of Lucifer, foreseen in the words of Isaiah, "I will be like the Most High" (14:14), Aelred traced the fall of the monk who entered the monastery full of promise:

Beware of pride, most beloved brothers, beware. For how many are there, something I say in sorrow, who ... deserve to have the name of Lucifer, so that in the morning, that is in the beginning of their monastic life, they are considered to be brighter than the others who share the same life, and at first get puffed up with a hidden purpose, despise their superiors, and accuse them of naivety and ignorance. Then, when they are concerned with temporal matters, they deride and criticize them, and look upon all as being inferior to

them. [Such monks] always have before their eyes whatever they can find in
others that is reprehensible. When they can find nothing, they make it up.
(Oner 17, PL 195:429)

Aelred apparently knew what he was talking about, for a monastery
such as Rievaulx would in his day have been recruiting young men
of the type who in a later generation went off to Oxford and Paris in
order to show their abilities. But in the first decades of the twelfth century, such ambitious youths felt attracted by the Cistercians and came
to Rievaulx with high expectations. The sight of the low-born abbot,
buckled over by health problems and speaking a traditional theological
language distant from that of the modish French schools, might have
been a letdown. Aelred imagined their reaction:

What are you saying? "What is he or who is he, that he is placed over us?
He is an unlettered man with no schooling, a man who spends all day long
concerned and devoted to worldly matters, a man neither outstanding for his
eloquence, not trained in Scripture, not accomplished in his work, nor skilled
in spiritual matters." (Oner 17, PL 195:429)

Aelred here may have echoed criticisms he thought were being voiced
behind his back. In Walter Daniel as in Aelred's Sermons we are given
direct access to the grumpy world that the monastery can be when its
members have gone sour on each other and turn their anger against
the abbot as the source of the trouble.

Aelred's approach to his monks centered on his awareness that
people are different and have different needs. Each brother has his
place, whether as a cloister monk, an obedientiary (with a special office), or a prelate, with the direct exercise of power over some or all the
monks. The cloister monks were to watch out for curiosity and sensuality and were not to be too concerned with what was going on in the
world. When they do pay attention, they get big ideas: "Then some
plot in their hearts and imagine and say, 'Oh, if I were abbot, or prior,
or cellarer, or gatekeeper, I would not get mixed up in worldly matters but would do this or that'" (Serm 17.9, p. 136). Such complainers
have to learn to find a secure place to hide from temptations:

We must consider and carefully explore the quality and nature of each person who flees the world. What can harm the one more, what the other, by
what spirit is the one tempted, by what attachment is he upset? We must
provide for each individual an appropriate place of hiding, either from vices
or from demons, or from himself or from nature, from corruption or attachment, from habit or the companionship of a certain person, when he is in
danger of being attacked either by suggestion or by example. Some are to be
protected from all exterior occupation, others from contact and cohabitation
with certain people. Others are to be placed under the shadow of silence, to be
kept from anger and rage, others through limitations on consumption can be

well protected from natural urges. Still others are hidden under the shadow of labors and vigils from a wandering heart and unstable spirit. Again, some by psalms and prayers, by meditation, prayer and spiritual reading are defended from ambush. (Oner 29, PL 195:485–86)

Aelred saw a need to adapt the discipline of monastic life to each monk's background and requirements. If his sermons have one dominating theme, it is concern for his monks as persons who had joined themselves to a collective life but still required personal attention for individual growth.

Aelred knew that this process of adaptation was not easy, especially for beginners. He spoke to their pain and reminded those who were more advanced what everyone must go through:

I speak to the experienced. At the beginning of our monastic life, amid hard temptations of body and mind, when the spirit of fornication sometimes eats us up, when anger flares up, when appetite stimulates the palate, it might seem almost impossible to bear it all, especially when youth's instability and temptation's cunning diversity show how easy it would be to fall from weakness. What then shall we reply to the spirits that suggest such things? What shall be our hope and our refuge? [Ps 90]. (Oner 23, PL 195:453)

Aelred consoled his monks that, as Paul promised, they would never be tempted beyond their abilities (1 Cor 10). He recognized the insecurity of young recruits to the monastic life and did not want to scare them off. At the same time he told them that he too, in spite of his age, continued to be plagued by temptations, especially sexual ones. One of his sermons on Isaiah turned into a prayer in which he asked Jesus how long he would continue to suffer in this way: "How long will Moab [the flesh], whom I thought I had avoided in the start of my conversion, revive and continue to make war on me?" (Oner 27, PL 195:473).

Here Aelred cried out in a way that recalls the language of the Psalmist who felt abandoned and in desperate need of help:

> How long, O Lord, will you forget me?
> How long will you hide your face?
> How long must I bear grief in my soul,
> this sorrow in my heart day and night?
> How long shall my enemy prevail? (Ps 12:1–3)

As with the sermons of Saint Bernard, we can never know if what we find in written form was actually spoken in the chapter room. But Aelred's sermons reflect the concerns apparent in his other works or in Walter Daniel. The sermons, because most of them have not been translated and some of them not edited, remain the last great frontier of Aelredian studies. Here I have merely touched on a few passages in order to show one dimension they contain: Aelred's use of his own experience combined with biblical texts in the context of the feasts of the church year in order that he could show the way for his monks.

The content of the sermons reveals Aelred's conception of his functions as abbot. He did not find it an easy task to lead a monastery, and at times a certain fatigue shows through. But for the most part he seems to have enjoyed the job, watching his monks, talking to them, reprimanding them, and seeing them change and develop as persons. He saw that all the aspects of monastery life are important. He knew that it was inevitable that some monks would complain about his regime. It was impossible to satisfy everyone. But as we shall see, Aelred still felt relaxed enough with his monks to draw a few of them to himself as his friends. Here his own need for intimacy did not conflict with a position that necessarily put him at a distance from everyone else.

10

Living Friendships

ELRED'S BEST-KNOWN WORK, the *Spiritual Friendship*, was probably written in two stages. The first book, dedicated to the origin of friendship, is set at a daughterhouse of Rievaulx, probably Wardon in Bedfordshire. On a visitation Aelred took off time to discuss friendship with a friend, Ivo. He is apparently the same monk at whose request Aelred wrote his *Jesus at the Age of Twelve*. This dialogue could have taken place shortly after Aelred became abbot at Rievaulx, in the late 1140s. In the second book, which, like the third, takes place at Rievaulx, Aelred talked of the growth of friendship with Walter, assumedly his biographer Walter Daniel, and another monk, called Gratian. At the beginning of the second book, Aelred remembered Ivo as a beloved friend and claimed that years had passed since he had begun his work on spiritual friendship:

Indeed, the fond memory of my beloved Ivo, yes, his constant love and affection are, in fact, always so fresh to my mind, that, though he has gone from this life in body, yet to my spirit he seems never to have died at all. For there he is ever with me, there his pious countenance inspires me, there his charming eyes smile upon me, there his happy words have such relish for me, that either I seem to have gone to a better land with him or he seems still to be dwelling with me here upon the earth. But you know that very many years have passed since we lost that bit of paper on which I had written his questions and my answers on spiritual friendship. (Am Sp, 2.5, p. 70)

It is important to note that Aelred included in an exposition of the theory of friendship a memorial of actual friendship. He did so not only in portraying Ivo, but also, at the end of the third book, with an extended description of the two most important friendships of his life. Whether or not the settings first of Wardon with Ivo and later of Rievaulx with Walter and Gratian reflect literary convention or historical fact, Aelred intended to write about real friendships. However indebted he was to the classical heritage in Cicero and to the church fathers in Ambrose, Aelred here as in his other works drew on the experience of his own life.

One indication of the passage of time from the writing of the first book to that of the second and third books is an apparent change of mind on Aelred's part. In the third book, which is mainly concerned with problems in maintaining friendship, Aelred admitted that an immature friendship among the young, which he calls carnal, can be acceptable as a point of departure for deeper bonds:

This friendship except for trifles and deceptions, if nothing dishonorable enters into it, is to be tolerated in the hope of a more abundant grace, as the beginnings, so to say, of a holier friendship. By these beginnings, with a growth in piety and in constant zeal for things of the spirit, with the growing seriousness of maturer years and the illumination of the spiritual senses, they may, with purer affections, mount to loftier heights.

(Am Sp, 3.87, pp. 113–14)

In the first book Aelred had warned against carnal friendship as leading to "mutual harmony in vice." He saw an alliance of the senses concentrated on "beautiful bodies or voluptuous objects" leading to a pact that "after they have entered upon such a deplorable pact, the one will do or suffer any crime or sacrilege whatsoever for the sake of the other" (Am Sp, 1.38–39, p. 59).

Interestingly enough, Aelred here is very close to the description of friendship found in the Roman historian Sallust's depiction of Catiline in his conspiracy against the state, which led him to create a "community of like and dislike." In the third book, Aelred drew on Augustine's description of the friendships of his youth, which depicted in a much more innocent way the enjoyment that young people can have in each other's company. It is not clear why Aelred softened his view of such friendships, but in any case this change of interpretation indicates that his work on friendship was written in stages and also that toward the end of his life he remained faithful to his youthful enthusiasm for friendship.

Aelred's amazing optimism about friendship needs to be put into the context of a deep-seated monastic skepticism about the value of close bonds in the monastic community. This attitude is linked to a fear of the body as a hindrance rather than a help in bringing the individual to God. The desert Fathers left behind in their Sayings a veritable arsenal of warnings against too close contacts, while John Cassian, who brought much of the desert wisdom to the West in his writings, pointed out the danger that friendships in the monastery could turn into cliques that would challenge the abbot's authority. Even though the Rule of Saint Benedict contains lyrical passages about the harmony of the brethren, it has several warnings against preferential bonds, as in its prohibition against one brother's defense of another (ch. 69).

Aelred chose not to deal with this negative tradition. He went behind it, to Cicero and the church fathers, but especially to the Bible itself. In the descriptions of David and Jonathan's friendships, Aelred had rich material to replace Cicero's references to classical friends. In Jesus' befriending of John the Apostle, Aelred found a special attraction. The first book closes with Ivo's referring to John as the friend of Christ and taking his words (1 Jn 4:16) to say that if God is love, then God can be friendship. Here Aelred moved theologically as far as possible in making the ideal and the experience of friendship into an essential part of Christian monastic life.

Aelred came closest to his own experience in the third book, which especially deserves our attention. He started here by contrasting Gratian's generosity with Walter Daniel's crankiness. The book opens with Aelred and Gratian's waiting for Walter to arrive and his comment that Walter "is quicker in grasping things, better at questioning, and has a better memory, also" (Am Sp, 3.1, p. 91). When Walter arrives and Aelred tells him about Gratian's friendly remark, his only comment is that this is typical for Gratian: "How could he fail to be my friend, since he is everybody's friend?"

This dart of hostility underlines a tension between Gratian and Walter already present in the second book. Gratian, in accordance with his name (*gratus*, pleasing), does try to please, and the more he does so, the less pleased becomes Walter Daniel. Aelred may have wanted to interject an element of humor and pleasantry in his dialogue, but he also probably intended to reflect the atmosphere of a monastery, where there are different personalities. Walter represents the combative intellectual, out to make his point and prove his case, while Gratian is a more easygoing fellow, too much so for Walter.

Walter concluded the second book with a prickly warning against Gratian's being late the next morning. In the third book it was Walter who was tardy the next day, not Gratian, but Walter conceded nothing. Instead of apologizing, he attacked Gratian. Aelred ignored the barb and went straight to a new formulation of friendship, which has its foundation in love. But his presentation of conflicts of personalities underlines what might be called an acceptance of dialectic in monastic life: out of the tensions come harmony, out of the differences come likeness; out of conflict, understanding. In this context we can consider one of Aelred's most frequently quoted descriptions of what he saw around him at Rievaulx:

The day before yesterday, as I was walking the round of the cloister of the monastery, the brethren were sitting around forming as it were a most loving crown. In the midst, as it were, of the delights of paradise with the leaves, flowers, and fruits of each single tree, I marveled. In that multitude of brethren I found no one whom I did not love, and no one by whom, I felt sure, I was not loved. I was filled with such joy that it surpassed all the delights of the world. I felt, indeed, my spirit transfused into all and the affection of all to have passed into me, so that I could say with the Prophet: "Behold, how good and how pleasant it is for brethren to dwell together in unity" [Ps 132:1]. (Am Sp, 3.82, p. 112)

However idyllic this passage, Aelred did not here claim that everyone at Rievaulx loved everyone else without problems. He referred exclusively to his own loves and the loves he sensed in return. At the same time, the description has to be seen in the context of the third book, which is almost a case study of difficulties in friendship. Aelred expected problems, but he was hopeful that in the end they would be worked out and most friendships could continue.

Balancing between realism and idealism, Aelred dealt with Saint Jerome's categorical statement that "friendship which can end, was never true friendship" (Am Sp, 3.48, p. 103). Aelred provided a method for making sure that the people chosen to be friends could remain so. First they must be selected, then tried and tested; thirdly they could be admitted, and fourthly one could live with them in harmony (3.8, p. 93). How could Aelred have imagined that it would be possible to choose one's friends? What happens to the spontaneity of friendship when it is turned into a such a rational, deliberate process? Aelred's reply would be that in the monastic life, as well as in the Christian life in general, everything is a choice. In removing the barriers that separate individuals, one must proceed "with extreme caution."

Aelred warned against various personality types that create difficulties in friendship: the irascible, the fickle, the suspicious, and the garrulous (3.14, p. 94). Instead of limiting himself to generalizations, however, he referred specifically to a friend of his who was known for being difficult. Here Gratian provided the description:

A few days ago that friend of yours, whom many think you prefer to all of us, was, so we thought, overcome by anger, and said and did something that everyone could see displeased you. Yet we do not believe or see that he has in any degree lost favor with you. Hence we are not a little surprised that, when we speak together, you will not neglect anything that pleases him no matter how trivial it may be, yet he cannot bear even trifles for your sake.

(Am Sp, 3.18, p. 95)

Gratian's words provide us with a window to the inner life of a monastery: the abbot's every word and every nod to one monk or another are noticed by everyone. When he seems to favor someone, all are aware of it and discuss their observations with each other. Here Gratian was practically accusing Aelred of showing preferential treatment. The abbot let the difficult monk make special demands on him but did not expect anything reciprocal.

Aelred's reply is calm and balanced, perhaps calmer than it would have been if he really had been challenged. Yes, he was attached to the man. Since he had become his friend, he had to love him. The loyalty he owed him meant that Aelred yielded to the friend's will, "since there was no question of any dishonor being involved, and as confidence was not violated, or virtue lessened" (Am Sp, 3.20, p. 95).

Just as in the first book of the *Mirror of Charity*, Aelred made his argument much more vivid by referring to an incident from monastery life. There he had mentioned a monk whom he inadvertently had offended. Here the problem was a friend whose demands on him were great. It does not matter whether or not such a friend existed in the flesh; what is important is that Aelred replaced a theoretical discussion of the problems involved in friendship with a practical exposition, taken from what could and perhaps did happen in monastery life.

After further discussion about the various difficult types of persons to be avoided in friendships, Aelred let Gratian return to the friend in question. Telling the abbot not to be angry, he asked Aelred outright if the man did not seem irascible to him. Remarkably, Aelred admitted that the man was inclined to anger, "but in friendship, hardly at all" (Am Sp, 3.33–34, p. 99). Aelred explained that he was confident that he could keep his friend under control. Because of their bond of friendship, the friend respected a limit. The monk knew that if he kept himself from exploding in public, he could have access to Aelred in private to tell him his thoughts:

Indeed, he about whom we are now speaking, preserves the law of friendship toward me in such a way that I can restrain an outburst at any time by a mere nod, even when it is already breaking forth into speech, so that he never reveals in public what is displeasing but always waits till we are alone to unburden his mind's thoughts. (Am Sp, 3.38)

Aelred expected a remarkable degree of tolerance in his friendship, but he also required control. A distinction between public behavior and private confidence was essential for him. Otherwise it would have been impossible for him to continue as abbot.

Midway in the dialogue, Aelred has more or less conceded the necessity that the individual distance himself emotionally from an impossible friend who makes excessive demands. Outwardly, even if attacked, he should still show loyalty: "As long as the abuses are tolerable, they ought to be endured. This honor should be accorded to old friendship, that the fault should be in him who commits, but not to him who suffers the wrong" (Am Sp, 3.43, p. 101). Here we detect something of the bonds of loyalty in feudal society, where outward appearance is just as important as inward reality. But Aelred added that the individual bond also must be seen in terms of the mesh of commitments that result from living in human society. If the friend hurts others and fails to change his behavior, then he has to be cut off. Aelred was probably reflecting on his own position as abbot, taking the welfare of all members of the community into consideration:

...if your friend has injured those whom you are bound to love equally well, and if, even after he has been called to task, he continued to be an occasion of ruin and scandal to those for whose well-being you are responsible, especially when the infamy of these crimes is damaging to your own good name. For love ought not to outweigh religion, or faith, or charity toward one's neighbor, or the welfare of the people. (Am Sp, 3.46, p. 102)

In such a statement Aelred made a distance between his own teaching and his epoch's growing fascination with romantic love, according to which the beloved alone matters and everything else pales by comparison. In an ordered friendship, directed according to the norms for which Aelred always looked, there could be no conflict with one's social or moral obligations. Unlike the English writer E. M. Forster, who saw genuine friendship almost as an act of defiance to the demands of society, Aelred believed that true love has a respectable name and a rightful place in good human company, especially that of the monastery.

Aelred's recommendations for maintaining friendship in the community context are often specific and concrete. Considering the problem of how to deal with an act or statement by the friend that is unacceptable, Aelred elaborated on his previous statement about waiting for the right opportunity in private to speak to the difficult friend:

If a friend when he is in the midst of others should commit some fault, he should not suddenly and publicly be reproached; but one ought to "dissemble" because of the place.... One ought to excuse what he has done, and wait to administer in secret the deserved rebuke. (Am Sp, 3.112, p. 123)

If the friend is emotional and not susceptible to calm reasoning, then one ought to wait for a better moment.

Such advice might seem almost banal, but Aelred gave it in order to show how friendship functions within the banality of everyday monastic life. He expected and experienced problems in his own friendships and wanted to make clear how carefully friends are to be selected and how reluctantly they are to be cut off from one's life. Friends are worth cherishing, even when they create complications and make what may seem like excessive demands. Aelred felt confident that if he could get away from the press of business and the curiosity of others, he could engage in a dialogue of intimacy that would sort out all the differences. One thinks of the phrase in Andrew Marvell's poem: "If there were world enough and time enough...." We can transfer Marvell's longing for sexual love to Aelred's assurances of the intimacy that grows up in friendship. For Aelred, there are world and time enough.

What Aelred wrote to Ivo at the very opening of the first book, he might also have said to the difficult friend whom Walter and Gratian noticed:

Here we are, you and I, and I hope a third, Christ, is in our midst. There is no one now to disturb us; there is no one to break in upon our friendly chat, no man's prattle or noise of any kind will creep into this pleasant solitude. Come now, beloved, open your heart, and pour into the ears of a friend whatever you will, and let us accept gracefully this place, time, and leisure.

(Am Sp, 1.1, p. 51)

Taking the words of Jesus that where two or three are gathered together in his name, he is with them, Aelred believed in the possibility of friendship within Christian communities.

Aelred concluded the third and final book of the *Spiritual Friendship* in describing his own experience as verification of this possibility. The central friendship of his younger days as a monk was probably with the Simon whose death he had lamented in the *Mirror of Charity*. The second friendship came later, after Aelred had spent many years in the monastery. The first "rested for the most part on affection," while the second was based on reason, though reason was found in the first and affection in the second. Aelred described himself as having changed over the years in terms of needs and desires, but the basic requirement of friendship remained the same:

[On the first friend] I demanded nothing and I bestowed nothing but affection and the loving judgment of affection itself according as charity dictated. The latter I claimed when he was still young to be a sharer in my anxieties and a co-worker in these labors of mine. (Am Sp, 3.119, p. 126)

The first friend was probably the same age as Aelred, or a little older, while the second he brought as a youth "from southern regions to this northern solitude, and first introduced him to regular discipline" (3.120, p. 127). All efforts to discover the identity of this second friend have proven in vain, but I find it of secondary importance to attach a name to the man who provided for Aelred the most complete friendship of his life.

Abbot Maurice of Rievaulx, who headed the monastery for a brief period between William and Aelred (1145–47), is supposed once to have criticized Aelred's youthful friend for going to the infirmary. The early Cistercians worried about the abuse of this privileged area, where sick monks obtained better food and even heating. Maurice apparently felt the young man was not sick enough to need such coddling:

The boy was so ashamed at this that he immediately left the infirmary and subjected himself with such zeal to corporal labor that for many years he would not allow himself any relaxation from his accustomed rigor, even when he was afflicted with serious illness. (3.121, p. 127)

Aelred admired the youth immensely for his stamina and cultivated him as his friend. He describes the stages from "inferior" to "companion" (*socius*), then friend (*amicus*), and finally "most cherished of friends." At this point Aelred, in his role as abbot, appointed the monk subprior. The friend was not pleased at all, worrying that it would create a distance between himself and Aelred. When Aelred refused to reconsider, the monk became even more frank with Aelred and told him "what he feared for each of us, and what in me pleased him but little." Later he told Aelred that he had thus intended to offend the abbot and in this way to avoid a position of responsibility that looked like favoritism.

Aelred's response reveals, perhaps better than anything else in his writings, the person he was and the needs he had:

But his freedom of speech and spirit only led our friendship to its culmination, for my desire for his friendship was lessened not a whit. Perceiving then that his words had pleased me, and that I answered humbly to each accusation and had satisfied him in all these matters, and that he himself had not only caused no offense but rather had received more fruitful benefit, he began to manifest his love for me even more ardently than before, to relax the reins of his affection, and to reveal himself wholly to my heart. In this way, we tested one another, I making proof of his freedom of utterance and he of my patience. (Am Sp, 3.123, p. 128)

This passage can be read in different ways. First of all, it can appear as if Aelred was so much in love with the youth that he did not care what the boy said to him. Aelred would have been pleased with anything the monk said in reply. I do not think this actually was the case, even though Aelred's decision to bring him to Rievaulx and to test him shows that Aelred indeed at some point made a rational decision to invest his emotions in the boy.

A second interpretation takes its point of departure in Aelred's claim that he had decided to develop a friendship with the youth. How, one may ask, can anyone ever decide to make a friendship? Is this not at least partly a spontaneous process, dependent on chance and circumstance, and subject to compatibility of character and interests? Here Aelred answered with the assurance of both classical and patristic writings on friendship: friendships can be made and unmade; they are richer and deeper when they are conscious and intentional; the one friend must seek out and test the other. This development is, in Aelred's mind, what happened between him and his friend in their confrontation. What especially delighted him was the fact that the process of friendship became reciprocal. Just as he had been testing his friend, the friend now tested him.

A third interpretation of Aelred's motives is that when he picked out the youth and brought him to Rievaulx, he knew what he was doing. He recognized his own need for the affection of other men. He had come to the point where he could transfer his sexual energies in this area to a calmer desire for companionship and exchange of thoughts and insights. The question was whether or not the friend could be fitted into the structure and requirements of the monastery. In choosing him as subprior, Aelred publicized his relationship with the man and claimed that he selected him not because he was his friend but because he was qualified for the post. Aelred, as so often in his career as abbot, put his personality and authority on the line and waited for the response. When the monk reacted by showing more openness than ever before, he fulfilled Aelred's deepest desire and goal in the friendship. Thus Aelred's attention to community needs in filling the office, at least in his own interpretation of what happened, only contributed to strengthening an individual bond within the community.

I think all three explanations have an element of truth in them: Aelred at some point, but not when he chose the man as subprior, had probably been infatuated with the youth. Aelred, ever a man of method and interior discipline, believed that he could mold and shape a friendship in a positive manner. Finally, Aelred did succeed to a large extent in getting what he wanted: intimacy, understanding, and the chance to deepen the friendship even more by having practical tasks and concerns in common.

What Aelred does not tell his readers, but what we can assume, is that it was not all that easy. With a hundred pairs of eyes on him, Aelred and his subprior needed to take into account the responses of the individual monks, many of whom would probably have very much liked to share the subprior's favored position. When Aelred wanted to give the man privileges so he would be better able to cope with his health problems, the subprior refused, claiming concern for Aelred's position in the monastery:

... saying that we should be on our guard against having our love measured according to the consolation of the flesh, and of having the gift be ascribed to my carnal affection rather than to his need, with the resultant effect that my authority might in consequence be diminished. (Am Sp, 3.126, p. 129)

Aelred did not add, as we could, that the subprior might also have worried that no one would respect his decisions in the monastery if he were considered the abbot's favorite, an overprivileged monk, able to live an easier life than the others because of his relationship.

In the last sections of *Spiritual Friendship*, the more Aelred seeks to elevate the facts of his greatest friendship, the more we as descendants of Voltaire and Freud might wonder if it was what he thought it was. Here it is important to remember that Aelred saw the friendship as a process, a development, in which each side moved slowly and deliberately:

Thinking that I should at an opportune moment harshly reprove him, I did not spare him any, as it were, reproaches, and I found him patient with my frankness and grateful. Then I began to reveal to him the secrets of my innermost thoughts, and I found him faithful. In this way love increased between us, affection glowed the warmer and charity was strengthened, until we attained that stage at which we had but one mind and one soul, to will and not to will alike. (Am Sp, 3.124, p. 128)

Aelred here combined the language of the Acts (4:32) with that of Sallust, but a Sallust whose definition of friendship was Christianized.

With Aelred's version of the actual friendship, we are left guessing how his friend experienced the bond. Aelred may have needed the friend more than the friend Aelred. In his description of the relationship, Aelred concentrated on how he could resort to the friend, instead of indicating anything about the friend's recourse to him:

He was, therefore, as it were, my hand, my eye, the staff of my old age. He was the refuge of my spirit, the sweet solace of my griefs, whose heart of love received me when fatigued from labors, whose counsel refreshed me when plunged in sadness and grief. He himself calmed me when distressed, he soothed me when angry. Whenever anything unpleasant occurred, I referred it to him, so that shoulder to shoulder, I was able to bear more easily what I could not bear alone. (Am Sp, 3.126–27, p. 129)

One way to understand Aelred's meaning here is by transferring this description of friendship to the view of marriage that began to develop in Aelred's own time. Theologians now discussed marriage as a question of consent and affection. Even in Aelred there are scattered references to a more idealized view of marriage than the one he might have had from his monastic training. If we take his description of the choice of a friend and apply it to the choice of a spouse, Aelred's categories express the new requirement that marriage be a meeting of minds:

Let him choose from among [the many persons] one whom he can admit in familiar fashion to the mysteries of friendship, and upon whom he can bestow his affection in abundance, laying bare his mind and heart even to their sinews and marrows, that is, even to the most secret thoughts and desires of the heart. (3.129, p. 130)

In every sense except the physical one, Aelred's requirements live up to the later medieval and post-medieval idealization of marriage. Here one shares one's being completely with the other person in the discovery of the self. Aelred was perhaps ahead of his time when he imagined such a bond not only between a man and a woman but also between two people of the same sex. But in doing so, Aelred returned to a tradition in the history of the West that went back to Jesus and John and beyond them to David and Jonathan and the intimate friends of classical Antiquity.

Aelred believed that such a complete and all-embracing bond of love can find its way into the monastery. This love was possible, he thought, because the good monastic community provided a taste of paradise, where everything is in harmony. In the world of platonic ascents and descents, which Aelred saw around him (and whose intellectual basis was in the writings of Augustine), friendship was one way of climbing up the ladder to God:

> Was it not a foretaste of blessedness thus to love and thus to be loved; thus to help and thus to be helped; and in this way from the sweetness of fraternal charity to wing one's flight aloft to that more sublime splendor of divine love, and by the ladder of charity now to mount to the embrace of Christ himself; and again to descend to the love of neighbor, there pleasantly to rest?
>
> (Am Sp, 3.127, p. 129)

Was it really so good? Aelred's paean to spiritual friendship here is not isolated in his work. Similar passages are to be found in the *Mirror of Charity* as well as in his sermons. His historical works and saints' lives also contain frequent references to friendship and show that this was one of the major concerns of his life. Walter Daniel's biography of Aelred is also a witness to a friendship, even if Aelred did not seem to share himself as intimately with Walter as the abbot claimed to have done with his subprior. But for Walter the sense of attachment was strong and emotional, as we shall see in his long, detailed description about Aelred's last days and death.

Besides the two or three intimate friendships of Aelred's monastic life, there were also bonds with men outside the cloister. Aelred's portrait in *The Battle of the Standard* of the Norman knight and landowner Walter Espec indicates that a friendship grew up between the two men. Aelred's contacts with such laymen would have increased after he became abbot, while he at the same time would have been able to get to know other churchmen. Here we can return to the monastery at Durham and its monk, Reginald. Reginald of Durham, as we saw in chapter 2, dedicated his *Life of Saint Cuthbert* to his friend Aelred. Probably in the 1170s, Reginald took on another hagiographical project and this time wrote a *Life of Godric of Finchale* (c. 1069–1170), an unusual fellow who had a career as peddler and later became a hermit. After about 1110 Godric had settled on the bishop of Durham's land and thus became associated with the monks of Durham. Roger, then prior of Durham, gave him a rule of life and a bond of confraternity with Durham. He was twice nearly killed, once when the Wear river flooded, and another time, in the fateful year of 1138, when Scottish soldiers attacked him. Reginald wrote several versions of Godric's life: his fellow monks were apparently dissatisfied with the first drafts. In the most complete version, he expressed a great debt to Aelred:

I have not been asked, but forced to write, by several friends who are most dear to me, and especially by the lord Ethelred [Aelred] abbot of Rievaulx. He had me write down what I had heard. What I did not [sufficiently] know about, he had me carefully investigate. (Godric, p. 19)

Here we find the same Aelred/Ethelred who himself wrote the *Life of Saint Ninian* and who had contributed important family stories to Reginald's earlier new *Life of Saint Cuthbert*.

Through Reginald's narrative, we discover that Aelred cultivated a bond of friendship with the eccentric hermit Godric. In several chapters Reginald told stories that Aelred had told him after Aelred originally had heard the anecdote from Godric. Some of these tales concern Robert, abbot of Newminster near Morpeth in Northumberland. This was a daughterhouse of the other great Yorkshire Cistercian house, Fountains, founded in 1137. Robert (c. 1100–1159) was known for his piety of life and became a friend of Godric's.

Just before Robert's death, Godric had a vision of how angels took the soul of Robert to heaven. His spirit was all on fire. The hermit would later tell his friends such as Aelred (who, as we have seen, dedicated his last work to a description of the soul and its functions) that the substance of the soul appears as a round sphere (Godric, ch. 75, p. 171). When, in Godric's vision, Robert was taken into heaven, he heard a voice saying, "Come now my friends, come now my friends" (Godric, p. 172).

Such a vision of the afterlife was probably influenced by the descriptions of Gregory the Great in his *Dialogues* at the end of the sixth century. What is extraordinary here is the way the source reveals an interaction between Benedictine Durham, Cistercian Newminster and Rievaulx, and the special environment of Godric's hermitage. "All these things in the same order in which we have described them," Reginald ensured his audience, "we have verified from the Lord Abbot Ethelred, as told by him" (Godric, p. 173).

In another scene from Godric's life, Reginald described how Aelred once came to the hermit: "They refreshed each other by much spiritual conversation and discussed at length the secrets of God's judgments" (Godric, ch. 87, p. 176). A brother of Durham had accompanied Aelred to the hermitage, but he remained outside the church "while the abbot, with the servant of God, in order to converse more secretly, went inside." When they emerged, Godric saw the Durham brother sitting on a tomb and predicted that the man would soon die. But since he did so in a joking manner, Aelred did not take it seriously. When the brother later became ill, Aelred remembered the hermit's words.

Reginald described how Aelred "called together his more intimate friends" (*secretiores amicos*) and told them what Godric had prophesied. He asked for their prayers for the man. Reginald was interested in the episode as an illustration of Godric's gift of prophecy. Thereby he also showed Aelred together with his special friends, entrusting to them his knowledge and asking them for their help. "These things the lord abbot very often mentioned" (p. 177), Reginald concluded, giving us a sense of lively talk in a monastic environment among those who obtained inside knowledge of visions and prophecies.

Elsewhere Reginald described how Aelred, together with Thomas, prior of Durham, ordered him to go to Godric "as if to find out what I was to write about his life, hoping that I would learn for certain all secrets from his mouth" (Godric, ch. 140, p. 269). Reginald was shocked to hear Godric's evaluation of himself as a terrible person who was "not a hermit but a hypocrite, . . . not an example but a monster." The text sounds better in Latin, and comparison with an earlier version shows that Reginald embellished his rendition of the hermit's tirade. When Reginald persisted in his intention to write about the man and returned some months later he threw himself at the hermit's feet, wept, and kissed him. After several years the hermit finally opened his secrets to him (p. 271).

One of the stories Godric eventually told his biographer I mentioned earlier, in chapter 6. This concerns a Cistercian monk who apparently could not keep from masturbating. Godric comforted him but warned that even though he would be able to overcome the habit, he would continue to be "tortured in the flesh" by impure thoughts (Godric, ch. 141, p. 271). This monk eventually became a Cistercian abbot and, after Godric's death in 1170, came to Durham and told the story to Reginald. Since this happened a few years after Aelred's own death in 1167, the Cistercian involved cannot have been Aelred. I wonder if Reginald altered the chronology in order to protect Aelred's reputation. In any case, the story conveys to us the atmosphere of intimacy and supportiveness behind the saint's uncanny knowledge of people and his prophecies about them. Godric became a close friend to this unnamed Cistercian monk, later abbot, as he did to Abbots William of Newminster and Aelred of Rievaulx.

Godric's world of human contacts, spiritual counseling, and prophetic insight reflects the same environment of intimate relationships in which Aelred functioned. In Reginald's portrait of Godric there is much less sentimentality about such bonds than there is in Walter

Daniel. They are just there, a fact of life, as the "secret friends" that Aelred could call to himself when he needed them. At Rievaulx as at Finchale, Durham, and Rievaulx's daughterhouses, Aelred worked on the spiritual friendships without which he would have found life harsh and empty.

a body in pain and in beauty

BY THE TIME Aelred wrote his *Pastoral Prayer*, a moving summary of his concerns as person, monk, and abbot, he was ill. He could no longer follow strictly the monastic routine and had to spend his time, as Walter Daniel described, in baths and special treatments. Aelred prayed:

Since the weakness of my flesh, or it may be my lack of courage and my heart's corruption, prevent my edifying [the monks] by labors of watching and fasting, I beg your bounteous mercy that they may be edified by my humility and charity, my patience and my pity. (Orat past, ch. 7, p. 115)

The last ten years of Aelred's abbacy were spent in periods of extreme pain, with arthritis and gallstones. The Cistercian General Chapter, in a decision not recorded in the regular statutes and probably made in an informal manner, released Aelred from the requirements of regular discipline (WD, p. 39). He still remained active in traveling. We see him at Rievaulx's daughterhouse, Dundrennan in Galloway, a few years before his death, as active as ever, and blessed by divine help in rainy Scotland so that his bed remained dry in spite of a hole in the roof of a temporary building (WD, pp. 74–75).

Aelred's retreat at Rievaulx to heated quarters and monastic nurses recalls a similar regime followed by Bernard of Clairvaux. But Bernard, as he comes across in his writings and in the portrait written by William of Saint Thierry, resented the care he got and was a touchy patient. Aelred, as Walter reveals him, made use of his weakness and periods of immobility as a means in order to cultivate companionship in the monastery. Some monks got virtually free access to him. The quality of the discussions that took place in Aelred's sickroom was, for Walter Daniel, much more important than the resentment that some of the monks felt because they were not included in the abbot's company.

As Powicke long ago surmised, Walter Daniel probably had medical training, for his descriptions of Aelred's illnesses are almost clinical

(WD, p. xxvii). Walter registered a change in Aelred's behavior in the years before his death. He gave up the special treatments he had allowed himself, stopped drinking wine, and practically stopped eating. In Walter's words:

Throughout those four years before his death, our father experienced what I may call a second circumcision, not by the removal of superfluities which even did not exist, but by depriving himself of necessities very helpful to him in his weakness. He made his little body free of everything that is pleasant in this present life. He sacrificed himself on the altar of unfailing suffering: hardly any flesh clung to his bones; his lips alone remained, a frame to his teeth. (WD, p. 49)

Walter described how Aelred in secret removed food from his mouth and tried to hide the evidence as well as he could. The result of this regime was that as his face grew more emaciated, he took on what Walter saw as an "angelic expression." Apparently in the back of his hut, Aelred had a little room where he could withdraw, his oratory, where "he forgot all about regular hours and about meals." Here Walter was convinced that he lived a life of contemplation, with tears, reading (especially Augustine's *Confessions*), and conversations with heavenly visitors (WD, pp. 50–51).

In terms of traditional hagiography, such passages are conventional. They show the potential saint desiring to be together with God and so separating himself from all that links him to this life. But Walter alters the pattern by showing that Aelred was still involved with the life of the monastery and especially with the inner lives of the brothers. In order to show Aelred's gift of prophecy, he described how Aelred contacted some of the brothers and told them to confess their sins because he had knowledge of actions on their part that could lead to their damnation. An attentive abbot, of course, would be aware of the situation in the monastery and be able to surprise a monk with his knowledge. But this is precisely the point: Aelred remained in contact and, despite his periods of withdrawal, wanted to know what was happening in the monastery and to tell his monks what he knew. Both intimacy and guidance remained important for him.

In one case Aelred commented on an episode in the dormitory in which two monks cried out during the night:

Son, the Devil truly came among the brethren there by night, trying to seduce one or other of them, but was forced to depart in utter confusion; his malice was in vain. Nonetheless, somebody gave way to him a little. (WD, p. 51)

Aelred's awareness of a monk's temptation demonstrates his continuing sensitivity to the members of his community. Another illustration of his attention is contained in Walter's summary of a sermon from the time when Aelred announced to the brothers in chapter that one of them had taken the Eucharist even though he was in mortal sin. The response was probably precisely what Aelred wanted: "The brethren marvelled greatly, especially those who were conscious of some fault in themselves; and when the sermon was ended, went to him and opened to him the secrets of their hearts" (WD, p. 52).

This section of Walter Daniel has gained very little attention from historians of Aelred. For me it underlines Aelred's life-long fascination with other men in terms of their interior worlds, their intentions, and their concerns. If the word "voyeur" had any positive connotation at all, then Aelred would deserve the term. He had to see, to know, to be told. At the same time, however, the monks needed to know about their abbot. Walter described how a monk, apparently during this period, had a vision in which he saw the dead Aelred prostrate before him. Then looking up, he saw Aelred's soul in all brilliance:

The image appeared to float in the middle of the house without any hold or tie from above....It hung in the empty air like a globe of flame in cloud. Indeed, a tiny cloud could be seen near the navel of the image, dim in comparison with the rest, not adhering to its light but, as could be seen at moments, hanging from it. (WD, p. 53)

The monk met someone, perhaps an angel, who explained to him that the image was the soul of Aelred, fulfilling the prophecy that "the righteous shall shine forth as the sun in the Kingdom of their Father" (Mt 13:43). The cloud at the navel was explained as the last vestige of Aelred's bond to the flesh: "He cannot die before that tiny cloud is taken away and his soul is cleared of this reproach" (WD, p. 54).

It is likely that the cloud symbolized Aelred's sexuality. As so often in medieval monastic language dealing with sexual matters, the literal meaning of such a passage remains elusive. But the story shows how the monks of Rievaulx were just as interested in the state of their abbot as he was in his monks' spiritual condition. Aelred's openness about himself may have attracted, confused, and frustrated some of the community's members. He was their man, and yet he lived at a distance from them, lost in his heavenly thoughts and bodily pain. And yet he could take his monks, one by one, and reveal to them the inner dispositions of their hearts.

There is a fine line here between invasion of privacy and spiritual guidance. Even if medieval monks in principle had no right to privacy, Aelred knew well that it would be a grave sin to indulge his own curiosity about the monks. He needed to be on his guard to serve them as a counsellor who gave the help needed. In his *Pastoral Prayer*, he addressed the Lord:

Teach me your servant, therefore, Lord, teach me, I pray you, by your Holy Spirit, how to devote myself to them and how to spend myself on their behalf.

Give me, by your unutterable grace, the power to bear with their shortcomings patiently, to share their griefs in loving sympathy.

(Orat past, ch. 7, p. 114)

For Walter Daniel, there was no instance in which Aelred overstepped the bounds of propriety and wisdom and exploited his position as spiritual guide. The special quality of life at Rievaulx as he conveys it in the biography lies in its combination of intense involvement of Aelred in his monks and they in him with a sense of discipline and order in the monastic life. Walter's frankness by including the vision of the cloud at Aelred's navel shows an admission on his part that Aelred had needed to grow spiritually. At the same time Walter conceded the existence of criticism among the monks of Rievaulx. In such a community, strong bonds of personal friendship and openness about interior life created jealousies and divisions. This was the price of maintaining individual affections within community discipline. For Aelred it could be no other way, but his insight and appeal to the monks' affection did not always have the desired result.

During the last year of his life, Aelred had a dry cough that weakened him greatly. Walter describes how it gave way to fever and an oversensitivity of the nerves that made it impossible for him to stand contact with anything on his body. Walter Daniel tried to relate these symptoms to his own understanding of how the body works:

In my opinion, the suffering in his breast and the difficulty of breathing were all due to an abnormal distemper in the head, producing fresh fever, and this in turn, when his body was racked by the cough, set up irritation together with the coughing. For he felt a weight on his chest, his tongue was rough, his gullet ulcerated and contracted, his jaws burning with great thirst.

(WD, p. 55)

In a note on this passage, Sir Maurice Powicke, ever attentive to such concrete details in Walter, compared these observations to similar ones in Saint Hildegard of Bingen (1098–1179). Powicke was ahead of his generation in an awareness of Hildegard's writings and interest in medical theory. Today she has become almost something of a cult figure in "creation spirituality." But both Walter Daniel and Hildegard bear witness to the twelfth century's desire to understand the workings of the body and to relate them to the soul.

Walter expressed his love for Aelred by articulating his awareness of him. He did not claim to have treated him as his doctor, but it is clear that during this last period he spent a great deal of time with the abbot. On December 24, 1166, Aelred gave a sermon in chapter, where, according to Walter Daniel, he told the brothers that he now wanted to die. The brothers sighed and wept, and Aelred returned to his cell (WD, pp. 55–56). The description of his last three weeks of

life and especially of his very last days takes up about 10 percent of
the biography. This attention is as it should be in terms of traditional
hagiography, where the saint's encounter with death is considered to
be the most important part of his life. But Walter's powers of observation provide the narrative with more than edificatory filling. Walter
gives us a very good idea of what it was like for Aelred to die — and
for him to lose his abbot:

For two hours he lay as though unconscious and half dead; then I came and
saw the father sweating in anguish, the pallor of his face flushed, his eyes
filled with tears, the ball of his nostrils twitching, his lips bitten by his teeth.
I said to a brother, "Of a truth the lord abbot now suffers much, for those
changes in his members are signs of great pain." But he, gazing on me fondly,
for he was so sweet, said, "Yes, my son, yes, yes, just as you say; I am greatly
vexed by the agonies of this sickness; by the will of the Lord Jesus there will
soon be an end to all this trouble." (WD, p. 56)

At this point Aelred may well have believed that it was only a question of hours or days before death came. In point of fact, he held on
for almost three weeks. Even though Walter interpreted Aelred's words
and actions as indications of the abbot's holiness, an alternative explanation is possible. When Aelred reverted to his own Anglo-Saxon
language and cried out, "Hasten, *for crist luve,*" he may well have been
expressing impatience and near-despair that he had to go on suffering,
day after day (WD, p. 60).

Walter's text indicates a progression from a first stage, around the
time of Christmas, when Aelred still could deal with his surroundings,
to a later one in which he was almost beyond reach. In the earlier
period, he refused to bother with the ordinary business of the house,
gave a homily in which he said goodbye to his brothers, and provided
general advice on the choice of his successor. There were many tears,
and everything said and done is edifying in terms of the literary genre
of hagiography and its requirements.

"I desire you all as a mother her sons in the viscera of Jesus
Christ," Aelred is to have said, summarizing his own concerns and
pointing to the new Cistercian attention to motherhood as opposed to
fatherhood (WD, p. 58). The words of a dying saint are always of great
interest for the hagiographer, but Aelred's words do not fit into any
easy pious pattern. They indicate growing impatience:

When I said to him, "What, lord?" he stretched out his hands, as to heaven,
and fixing his eyes like lamps of fire upon the cross which was held there
before his face, said, "Release me, let me go free to Him, whom I see before
me, the King of Glory. What do you linger for? What do you? What are you
to wait for? Hasten, for the love of Christ, hasten." (WD, p. 60)

According to Walter, Aelred in his final days kept repeating these words. He could not die. Walter claimed that it was the strength of his spirit inside the delicate body that kept death away. For Walter the experience was overwhelming:

I tell all of you who may read this that in all my life I have never been so stricken to the heart as I was by those words, so often repeated, so awfully uttered, by such a man at such an hour, by a good man at the point of death.
(WD, p. 60)

The fact of death in a monastery is both banal and overwhelming. Banal because monks or nuns who live their lives together come inevitably to experience each other's deaths. Overwhelming because their religion considers death to be a passageway to new life. Walter, as a medieval hagiographer, naturally concentrated on all that was wonderful in Aelred's last days: his sayings, the reactions of the brothers, his sufferings, a vision given to a sleeping brother in which Aelred predicted the exact day of his death, the arrival of other Cistercian abbots. I cannot help wondering how Aelred actually experienced these final days, surrounded much of the time by monks, with his mind consumed by the fire of fever, and with the horizon of eternity constantly retreating from him.

The day before he died, in the presence of most of the monks and some of the lay brothers, one of the Passion narratives from the Gospels was read aloud. By this time Aelred was "no longer able to speak a word that could be understood" (WD, p. 61). But Walter watched the various changes of expression on Aelred's face and could tell that he was following the narrative attentively. Aelred seemed to be experiencing the sufferings and death of Jesus with the same immediacy he had sought in his own writings and meditations.

At this point physical contact with the dying saint also became possible. The usual prohibitions regulating contact with another monk's body were no longer in force. Just as Aelred once sat with his runaway monk's head in his hands, Walter now could hold his abbot:

I sat with him on that day and held his head in my hands, the rest of us sitting apart. I said to him in a low voice, so that nobody would notice us, "Lord, gaze on the cross; let your eye be where your heart is." (WD, p. 61)

Aelred opened his eyes a little and looked at the image of Jesus. His words now were the first he had spoken in two days: "Thou art my God and my Lord, Thou art my refuge and my Saviour. Thou art my glory and my hope for evermore. Into Thy hands I commend my spirit."

If this had been a saint's biography written in the early Middle Ages, Aelred at this juncture would have conveniently died. But this was the twelfth century, with its realistic powers of description. Walter knew well that he could not move this moment to just before the actual death of Aelred, which did not take place for three more days. There were too many witnesses, too many varying opinions about the abbot, and so he had to stick to the facts.

The facts, however, as they can be gleaned from Walter's account, point to a man who hung on to life for so long that dying became a horrible, perhaps a ghastly process. In spite of Walter's attempt to fit Aelred's words and gestures into the hagiographical mould, something disturbing remains behind in this narrative. Perhaps it is simply the fact of realistic description that comes across behind all the piety. In Walter's precise observations, Aelred can be seen as experiencing all the emotions of elation, regret, sorrow, near-despair, and growing peace through which a dying person can live. Inadvertently Walter conveys in his close description a sense of death as a process whose stages can be long and memorable for the loved ones, and at the same time terrible.

When it was clear that there was not much time left, Aelred in accordance with monastic custom was lifted onto a hair cloth covered with ashes. Here, at last, he died. Walter gave the precise time and date and then described how he saw Aelred's body when it was stripped and washed in the prescribed way:

His flesh was clearer than glass, whiter than snow, as though his members were those of a boy five years old, without a trace of stain, but altogether sweet, and composed and pleasant. There was no loss of hair to make him bald, his long illness had caused no distortion, fasting no pallor, tears had not bleared his eyes. Perfect in every part of his body, the dead father shone like a carbuncle, was fragrant as incense, pure and immaculate in the radiance of his flesh as a child. (WD, p. 62)

Walter later defended this passage. In the "Letter to Maurice," he admitted that he here imitated Sulpicius Severus in his description of the corpse of Martin of Tours (d. 397).

Walter's reply to his critics provides valuable information in the history of hagiography. In his rebuttal and explanation of his method, he indicated how an author makes a *conscious literary borrowing* from a source. But the passage also deserves analysis in terms of what may have been going on in the author's *conscious perception* of Aelred. Finally it might be worthwhile to consider Walter's *unconscious bond* to Aelred.

In the passage quoted Walter twice characterized Aelred's body as that of a child. In terms of weight loss and slightness of build, Aelred's body may in reality have become like that of a child. But his biographer was not only making a physical observation; he was also telling his audience how he experienced Aelred. The dead body, he says, smelled good ("like incense") in accord with the medieval belief that a body with an attractive smell betrays the good life its owner once led. Second, the body shone forth "like a carbuncle," a gem of deep red color. The physical remains of Aelred reflected the virtue and brilliance of his life. One can imagine Walter through his tears looking at the body of Aelred and being hardly able to see it in any other way than that of a vision of light. To translate his images, one can say that he experienced the corpse in terms of beauty (the untouched body), a good smell, brilliance, and boyishness. All these provided signs of Aelred's purity of life and childlikeness. In death Aelred showed how he in life had become one of the children who could inherit heaven.

Some of these images may have passed through Walter's head as he looked at the dead Aelred washed and gleaming before him. We must remember that Cistercian brothers saw each other's naked bodies only when one of them was dead. In other Cistercian medieval narratives, as from the great abbey of Villers in the thirteenth century, we sometimes hear of how at this moment it could be discovered that an abbot's genitals had almost disappeared, a sign of purity of life. One can imagine the fear and fascination that must have driven monks to take a look at the body, to see the flesh that until recently might have been a source of sexual temptation but now had become holy and innocent.

How was the monk who had loved his brother to deal with such a moment and express his feelings? In this crucial rite of passage or liminality (from the Latin *limen*, or threshold), as the anthropologist Victor Turner would call the monastic rituals of stripping and washing the body, the brothers would have been intensely aware of each other's actions. But Walter could not hold himself back:

I was not able to restrain the kisses which I gave his feet, though I chose his feet lest feeling, rather than pure affection, should reproach me; the beauty of one who sleeps rather than the love of one who lies as he lay. Whenever I think of him, then, I am still overcome by joy and wonder at the gracious recollection. And when do I not think of it? When do I not brood on that sweetness, that beauty, that glory? (WD, pp. 62–63)

Walter was afraid that someone might misunderstand his kissing of Aelred's body and think he thereby was showing physical affection rather than spiritual love. Yet there was a physical element in Walter's love. He put his lips at last to what he saw as a beautiful and no longer tortured body. Walter only hints at his feelings, but at this moment of resolution, he may have realized how much he had yearned to touch, to embrace, to enfold this frail body. Now that Aelred's struggle was over, Walter could project his own sense of peace onto the body and see Aelred as perfect in his new state. Walter conveyed to Aelred in death a physical expression of the love he had long felt for him in life.

Was this the gruff, touchy Walter of the *Spiritual Friendship* who baited Gratian? We have only to turn to the "Letter to Maurice" to see this Walter, defending the memory of Aelred and his own accuracy in recording it. But for a moment, in describing the death scene and his own reaction, Walter showed both tenderness toward Aelred and fear of the community's censure. In Aelredian terms, he knew that his affection could be considered to have been "too carnal."

Walter chose, however, to rejoice in the perfect flesh and made it more vivid in the final story contained in the biography: the anointing of Aelred's body by Roger, the abbot of the nearby Cistercian house Byland. The ointment at first seemed to be insufficient to anoint all the parts of his body, but there turned out to be more than enough to cover every place. This narrative allowed Walter once more to dwell on the body that he loved:

He anointed the face of the father, forehead, ears, neck, eyes and nose and the whole of the head, and still there seemed as much [ointment] left as when he began....

...as we were marvelling, the abbot Roger proceeded to anoint the father's hands, and he anointed as freely as before...

In the end we perceived that much of the arms had also been sprinkled by the same; nor was the anointing ended, for the heavenly blessing of the plentiful infusion still hung on the abbot's fingers. (WD, p. 63)

For a group of men that had abandoned the things of the world and chosen to live in a spiritual realm, the Cistercians left behind narratives that show practical sense and awareness of the material world. This observation is true not only in their acquisition of property but also in their descriptions of abbots such as Aelred. Walter followed a European pattern of hagiography in dwelling at length on the passage from life to death, but in doing so, he showed a special Cistercian attention to physical detail.

What was going on in Walter's mind as he came to terms with Aelred's death? In Aelred's corpse, Walter said he saw three qualities: sweetness (*dulcedinem*), beauty (*venustatem*), and glory (*gloriam*). The first word is practically impossible to translate into modern English. Sweetness is for us not what it was for the twelfth century, when sugar and its manifestations did not exist as they do today in the over-abundance of Western society. If we think of sweetness in terms of a person who was immensely attractive to others and link this concept to an inner beauty of character for which Walter used the word *venustas*, we begin to approach his meaning. As for glory, this is the glory of the flesh that Walter was certain would be reconstituted in the resurrection.

Just as in Aelred's approach to the body of Christ, Walter embraced and kissed the body of Aelred when his flesh had ceased to be a reminder of human sexuality but had become a symbol of eternal life. The body of Aelred no longer reminded the observer (as the monk in his vision) that the abbot had difficulty in keeping genital expression under control. Now Aelred's body was a reminder of the joys to come for all those who shared in the risen body of Christ. Years before, in *The Mirror of Charity,* Aelred had recommended that we transfer our attachments from our own flesh to that of Christ: "That he may not succumb to the concupiscence of the flesh, let him extend his full attachment to the attractiveness of the Lord's flesh" (Sp Car 3.5.16, p. 232).

In kissing the feet of Aelred, Walter may well have been remembering a remarkable passage in the abbot's *Rule of Life for a Recluse,* where Aelred demanded from Jesus the right to embrace and kiss his feet. Aelred was recalling the words of Jesus after the Resurrection when he met Mary Magdalene and told her not to touch him. His visualization of the body of Christ was even more vivid than Walter's evocation of Aelred's body:

But, sweet Jesus, why do you keep at a distance from your most sacred feet her who in love desires to clasp them? "Do not touch me" (Jn 20:17), he says. What a harsh command, how intolerable: "Do not touch me." How is this, Lord? Why may I not touch you? May I not touch, may I not kiss those lovable feet, for my sake pierced with nails and drenched in blood?

(Inst Incl, ch. 31, p. 92)

In the contemplative life of the monk, as of the recluse or of any other Christian, physical objects were important as signs of spiritual realities. The question for Aelred, as for Walter and for any monastic writer, was how to distinguish between loving something physical for itself and loving it in terms of its spiritual significance. When Walter limited himself to Aelred's feet, instead of kissing his face, he tried to distance himself from the charge that he was expressing only physical affection. But it was a tricky situation. As Aelred is described, in all the stillness of death, he could have appeared as someone asleep, and Walter in kissing him could have been engaging in an act of sensuality.

In the Cistercian embrace of the body of Jesus, or of the body of a dead brother, there remained a troublesome element of unpredictability. When could the monk know that his devotion was moving from the physical to the spiritual? I do not intend to question the sincerity and devotion of Walter Daniel to Aelred. But in his emotional response to the abbot's death, as well as in his desire to defend Aelred from the charges leveled against him, I find a man who fiercely loved another man. Within his culture and its requirements, there were strictly defined ways in which this love could be expressed. Here in the middle room between life and death, Walter could shed self-restraint and convey his feelings for Aelred.

In writing about his reaction, Walter needed to guard himself and to assure his audience that what he did was acceptable. We are only beginning today to get a sense of the significance and perceptions of the body that medieval people experienced. Walter Daniel's awareness of Aelred's body combines the practical observations of a medical doctor with the literary imaginations of a hagiographer. At the same time Walter was deeply attached to Aelred's body as a physical manifestation of his friend's existence. It would be easy to conclude that Walter felt a homosexual attachment to Aelred, something that could be expressed once Aelred's body no longer was sexual. But such a modern explanation, however appealing in its clear categorization, would by no means account for the content of homoerotic affection opening into an occasion of agapetic union for Walter. In his celebration of Aelred's death, Walter combined erotic with agapetic love in a manner possible only for a monk trained in friendship in a loving, celibate community.

12

after aelreð

HAT WAS IT LIKE for the monks of Rievaulx when their abbot died? Walter Daniel was so caught up in his own reactions to the sight and feel of the dead abbot that he wrote nothing about the community reaction. But at the Cistercian abbey of Swineshead (also called Hoyland) in Lincolnshire, Abbot Gilbert recorded his own reaction on getting the news. Gilbert was in the midst of a sermon dealing with the Song of Songs. He was commenting on the Song for his monks in chapter in continuation of a series of sermons Bernard of Clairvaux had begun on the Song. Gilbert of Hoyland's theme in this, his forty-first sermon on the subject, was Song 5:1: "I have gathered my myrrh with my spice. I have eaten my honeycomb with my honey." He paused at the news of Aelred's death and announced to the brethren: "It seems to me that in his being taken away from us, our garden is stripped bare." Gilbert described Aelred as a honeycomb dripping with sweetness for all to enjoy. He mentioned his knowledge, his speech, his gentleness of speech and movement.

Like Bernard's own sermons, Gilbert's evocation of Aelred, as we have it, was probably a meticulous written expansion of what he said to his monks. It is not of great importance whether or not Gilbert actually received the news of Aelred's death while he spoke in chapter. What matters is that by writing up a sermon on the Song in which he broke off his text to recall the virtues of a dead brother, Gilbert imitated Bernard's own interruption of his exposition on the Song of Songs (Sermon 26) in order to mark the death of his brother, Gerard.

By taking his cue from Bernard, Gilbert extended an immense compliment to Aelred. He made sure to describe Aelred in the language of the Song, but he also told how he himself had experienced Aelred: "I remember how frequently when someone out of turn had interrupted his speech, he would stop speaking, until the other person had given full expression to his need." Only then would Aelred, totally unruffled and without any ill-will, resume his line of speech. In Gilbert's view, Aelred knew how to "speak at the right time and keep silence at the right time." He was a listener, "slow to speak."

130

In expressing his sense of loss in Aelred, Gilbert turned again to the text of the Song of Songs, "Eat, O friends, and drink; drink deeply, O lovers!" (Song 5:1). He could apply these words to the heavenly banquet in which Aelred now participated and in which his brothers soon could join him:

Remember these things, brothers, recall them, and pour forth your souls from yourselves. This memory has been put on fire. Let it melt your soul and be poured forth in delights and desires, when you go over into the place of the tabernacle. (Gilbert, Serm 41.8)

The text's appeal to friends and lovers fits perfectly Gilbert's evocation of a feast of love held in heaven in which Aelred already shared.

Gilbert used allegorical language that is difficult to translate to modern English and that may well sound overdone. But his tribute shows that Walter Daniel was not the only Cistercian monk who felt called on to note in a special way Aelred's passing. Gilbert intended his tribute to Aelred to have lasting value, since he embedded it in a series of sermons that he must have hoped would be joined to those of Bernard. Gilbert certainly got what he wanted. Until the last century, Gilbert's works were traditionally included with Bernard's, as can be seen from the *Patrologia Latina* edition that reprinted the then standard edition of Bernard by Dom Jean Mabillon. Thus the remarks on Aelred gained a prominent place in Cistercian spiritual literature and have been handed down from one generation to the next. Until our own century, Gilbert's description of Aelred has been much more accessible and better known than Walter Daniel's biography, which Sir Maurice Powicke was the first to bring into prominence.

The English Cistercian tradition concerning Aelred is also evident in the biography of Aelred's friend, Waldef, abbot of Melrose. Its author Jocelin of Furness wrote several decades after Aelred's death and must have drawn on stories and descriptions gathered from old-timers. It is not clear whether or not Jocelin knew Walter Daniel's account. But in Powicke's evaluation, "Gilbert of Hoyland and Jocelin of Furness give the salient traits of Aelred's character more clearly than Walter Daniel does" (WD, p. xxxiv). Here is the conclusion of Jocelin's description of Aelred, in Powicke's translation:

He was a man of the highest integrity, of great practical wisdom, witty and eloquent, a pleasant companion, generous and discreet. And with all these qualities, he exceeded all his fellow prelates of the Church in his patience and tenderness. He was full of sympathy for the infirmities, both physical and moral, of others.

The last sentence sounds as if it could derive from Walter Daniel. Jocelin of Furness at least reflects Walter's awareness of Aelred's gentleness and receptivity toward troublesome monks:

Hence it was that monks in need of mercy and compassion flocked to Rievaulx from foreign peoples and from the far ends of the earth.... And so these
wanderers in the world to whom no house of religion gave entrance, came to
Rievaulx, the mother of mercy, and found the gates open, and entered by
them freely, giving thanks unto their Lord. (WD, p. 37)

According to Walter, Aelred had claimed that it was "the singular
and supreme glory of the house of Rievaulx that above all else it
teaches tolerance of the infirm and compassion with others in their
necessities" (WD, p. 37).

In dealing with this and similar passages, Sir Maurice Powicke was
skeptical. He found Walter Daniel's description of Rievaulx as "idealized" (WD, p. 40). The footnote here in which Powicke referred to
a papal charter from the 1170s by Alexander III concerning runaway
monks from Rievaulx has since been noticed by numerous students
of Aelred, with the result that one hears the remark that Aelred's
permissive regime brought repercussions after his death. The Benedictine scholar Alberic Stacpoole wrote that Aelred's successor, Silvain
(1169–84), had a "bitter task in following him, unable as he was to do
other than exact discipline." In the shop talk that takes place among
historians, monks, and nuns at the annual Cistercian Conference at
Kalamazoo, Michigan, the subject of Aelred is regularly stopped dead
by mention of the "chaos at Rievaulx" after his death.

If we look at the papal charter contained in the Rievaulx Cartulary,
the one piece of evidence for difficulties in the aftermath of Aelred,
it addresses "all persons of the archdiocese of York," asking them not
to receive any runaways from the abbey of Rievaulx. "If they have removed the habit of religion and have been living in the secular state,
you are to denounce them as excommunicate and carefully avoid them
and wholly expel them from your parishes." The letter is thus addressed especially to parish priests and may have been drawn up at
the request of Abbot Silvain.

In order to understand this papal letter properly, it is important to
realize that by the 1170s Cistercian houses were regularly going to the
papal court in order to get confirmations of their privileges. In 1178,
for example, the chancellery of Alexander III issued to the Cistercian
abbey of Esrum in Denmark, like Rievaulx a daughter of Clairvaux, a
bull that enumerates all the privileges of the monastery and contains
a warning against runaway monks: "We also forbid that any of your
brothers after they have made their profession in the same place, because of any lack of seriousness, without the permission of their abbot,
depart from the same place." No other church institution is to dare
give lodging or residence to such monks, unless they have obtained
special permission to leave their monasteries.

The wording here is not as harsh as in the Rievaulx document, but the Esrum privilege shows that by now it was becoming standard procedure in papal privileges to threaten runaway monks and institutions that housed them. With hundreds of monks and lay brothers, Rievaulx may have had a special problem, but its difficulties were by no means unique. The Rievaulx Cartulary indicates in another charter that the monastery was involved in problems in legal disputes and subjected to acts of violence from some of the magnates of Yorkshire, another sign of troubles that were hardly Aelred's fault but that may have encouraged monks to leave the monastery.

In general, this period of the last decades of the twelfth and the first of the thirteenth centuries was a traumatic one for the Cistercian houses that had established themselves in the previous decades. The Cistercians had been the darlings of the church, a fashionable new monastic order that had received in abundance both vocations and gifts from the aristocracy. Now sons and grandsons, as well as nephews, of the original donors were having second thoughts and trying to get back their lands from the monks, or leaving the monasteries they had joined.

At the same time, monasteries such as Rievaulx were in great need of the incomes derived from their properties. It was at this time, around 1200, that the southern range of the cloister was rebuilt, so that a huge refectory and kitchen were erected at right angles to the cloister. This extension was but the first stage of an ambitious building program that also included an enlargement of the eastern part of the church. The elegant Gothic curves of the choir, for visitors today the very symbol of Rievaulx, put the monastery into debt.

This building program was not Aelred's. So far as we know, he was satisfied with having the monks and lay brothers living in temporary buildings and making do with what they could. Walter Daniel's concentration on the natural beauty of the site and his silence about the buildings themselves shows the original Cistercian pioneering spirit, satisfied with simple architecture. The difficulties that Rievaulx experienced after Aelred's death reflect more the development of the Cistercian Order itself than the legacy of Aelred: expensive projects, intervention from lay magnates, a greater need for papal protection, and resentment in clerical circles against the monks' success.

One of the harshest critics of the Cistercians was Walter Map, a cleric who tried to make himself comfortable at royal and episcopal courts in England. His talent was for telling stories, and he picked up some nasty ones about the Cistercians. He heard how two Cistercian abbots had told the bishop of London, Gilbert Foliot, about the miracles of Saint Bernard. This was the same Gilbert who in the early 1160s received a letter from Aelred, dedicating to him his *Sermons on*

Isaiah. According to Walter Map, one of the abbots admitted that he had been a witness to a failure on Bernard's part to perform a miracle:

A certain man from the borders of Burgundy asked him to come and heal his son; we came, and came upon him dead; Master Bernard bade the body be carried into a private room, and "shutting everyone out he lay upon the boy," and after a prayer arose; but the boy did not arise, for he lay there dead.

At this point Walter says he made a comment that made everyone laugh, except for the abbot, who blushed: "He was surely the most unlucky of monks; for never have I heard of a monk lying down upon a boy, without the boy arising immediately after the monk."

The translation by the antiquary M. R. James does not make it clear what the laughter was about. But Walter Map's meaning is clearer in the Latin: he implied that monks had a reputation for putting themselves on top of boys and giving them erections. This sexual slur may well reflect only the resentment of the secular clergy that the Cistercians had been doing so well for so long. But it also could indicate the skeptical reaction of some churchmen to the intense personalities of monastic leaders such as Bernard and Aelred.

A much more subtle hint of sexual impropriety can be found in the Rievaulx legacy of Aelred. Here we find a monk named Matthew, who probably joined the monastery after Aelred's death and eventually obtained the office of subchanter. He spent some of his time writing second-rate poetry. He celebrated friendship, but in a much more secular language than Aelred had done. Matthew wrote the following lines about Aelred:

Illustrious Aelred, endowed with the aroma of his ways.
He was the honeycomb's honey and sweetness for the monks.
In the flower of youth he cherished the king's royal affairs;
Some harmful things he removed far from his mind and his hand.
[*Queque nociva procul animoque manuque removit*]

The first two lines are evocative of the sermon of Gilbert of Hoyland on Aelred's death. The third line could have been derivative of Walter's account. The final line stands by itself as enigmatic. But the language provides a broad hint at what Aelred himself called his "worst habit," his lifelong battle against sexual temptation, whether it was in terms of feeling physically drawn to other men or wanting to masturbate.

Despite this hint, it is impossible to know exactly what Matthew was indicating. More significant is the fact that his evaluation of Aelred is much less warm and positive than a previous address to the first abbot, William, which concludes: "Sweet father, greetings; protect our place, for which you are also the first architect, and founder and guide." Only in terms of honey-like sweetness did Matthew indicate similar enthusiasm for Aelred.

The clearest evidence that there were problems in maintaining Aelred's reputation comes from Walter Daniel's "Letter to Maurice." Here we learn that after he wrote his biography of Aelred, two unnamed churchmen objected strongly against some of his descriptions and pointed out that Aelred at the court of King David had by no means lived as a monk, as Walter had claimed. Walter in his reply provided further evidence and named witnesses to Aelred's miraculous powers. He also explained what he had meant about Aelred's living like a monk at the Scottish court. Aelred there acted like a monk in terms of humility, not chastity. Walter defended himself with great vigor but at the same time indicated how upset he was by the attack on the reliability of his biography:

The two prelates...strive to becloud what I have done in the mists of uncertainty, and use the force of their authority to cast it into the pit of their suspicion and besmirch it as untrustworthy. (WD, p. 66)

Powicke thought that the Maurice may have been the prior of a nearby house of Augustinians at Kirkham and not the Maurice who had been Aelred's predecessor for two years at Rievaulx. Powicke saw Maurice of Kirkham as "an inquisitive man, full of fussy learning," who "might well have interested himself in the miracles of his former neighbor at Rievaulx" (WD, p. xxxi).

Whatever the identity of Maurice and the two hostile churchmen, Walter's response indicates a growing demand in the twelfth-century church that miracles be documented and saints investigated. Walter could not get away with applying time-worn hagiographical phrases about Martin of Tours to Aelred. He had to provide witnesses and confront the gossip that was circulating concerning the sexual adventures of Aelred's youth, his laxity as an abbot, and the relative paucity of miracles associated with him.

Walter's defense of Aelred's reputation calls to mind a passage in the *Spiritual Friendship* that also points to attacks on the abbot's reputation. Here it is Gratian who was speaking to Aelred, in reply to the recommendation that potential friends first should be tested:

Just now I call to mind that friend of yours across the sea, whom you have often mentioned to us, the one whom you proved the truest and most faithful friend by a test of this kind. When certain individuals bore false witness against you, he not only did not relinquish his faith in you, but was not moved by any hesitation whatsoever; something you did not think you could presume upon even from your dearest friend, the old sacristan of Clairvaux.

(Am Sp, 3.67, p. 107)

The friend named here is probably the one that Aelred mentioned at the end of the *Spiritual Friendship*, the friend of the south, brought across the sea, perhaps from Clairvaux, to be with Aelred. The sacristan of Clairvaux has been mistakenly identified as Bernard's brother Gerard, but Gerard was cellarer, not sacristan, and was already dead by the time Aelred first visited Clairvaux.

Whatever the exact identity of the friend who came to Aelred's aid, it looks as though even at Clairvaux rumors circulated concerning Aelred. There is nothing quite as delicious as gossip when speech is severely rationed, and monks in all periods of their history have been superb at telling about each other, for better and worse. Aelred apparently arrived at Clairvaux in the early 1140s with a reputation that had preceded him. It is not unlikely that he was under suspicion for his life in Scotland, and the sincerity of his conversion to the Cistercian Order could have been questioned. Bernard of Clairvaux would have put down all this talk. He chose Aelred as his man to write the *Mirror of Charity* and wrote to him as someone snatched "from a whorehouse of death and the filth of depravity" (Spec Car, p. 71). These phrases of Bernard probably reflect Clairvaux gossip as well as Aelred's accusations against himself. Bernard reversed them and made the best possible use of them!

Bernard understood Aelred's person, his background, and his talents. The generation that followed Bernard and Aelred was apparently less sympathetic to their special combination of personal intimacy and theological insight. The epitomes of Aelred's *Mirror of Charity* and *Spiritual Friendship* that appeared by the end of the century removed many of the passages where Aelred had spoken of himself. In trying to systematize Aelred's thought, monastic writers castrated it. A new age had begun for monks, in which they were strongly affected by the success of school methods that left out individual experience in seeking universality.

As so often in history, even in the Middle Ages styles and tastes change quickly, and we should probably be grateful that so much of what Aelred wrote has nevertheless been preserved. Both during his life and after his death, Aelred had to deal with monks and churchmen who questioned his motives, his illness, his past, his monastic life, and his leadership of the monastery. It could have been no other way for the head of one of the most powerful monastic houses in Britain, who had been welcomed many places as a negotiator and had drawn attention to the success of his monastery.

At Rievaulx there may have been monks who felt their abbot had become involved in too much that had little to do with the office of a Cistercian abbot. At least in terms of historical writing, Aelred's successor at the end of the twelfth century, Ernald, tried to make sure that no Rievaulx monks imitated him. He contacted William, an Augustinian canon at nearby Newburgh, and asked the man to write a history of the times. As William wrote in his preface to Ernald: "This, I perceive, arises from your kind desire to spare, in this respect, the members of your own society, who are so fully occupied in the duties of monastic service." Ernald seems to have believed that it was important for churchmen of the North to continue Aelred's work, but he apparently did not want monks of his own monastery to get involved in the political interests that Aelred had shown.

William of Newburgh's *History* is one of the best medieval historical works that we have, both in terms of the clarity of his descriptions of events and people and in his factual accuracy. We find superb portraits of people important in Aelred's life, such as King David of Scotland and the hermit Godric of Finchale. William, like Aelred before him, visited Godric and was greatly impressed by him:

In this manner he lived, even to decrepit old age, and was bedridden some few years before his death, by the failure of his aged limbs; and for many days supported the scanty remains of life in his decaying body by a moderate draught of milk. At this time I had the good fortune to see and speak to him, as he was constantly lying down in his own oratory near the holy altar; and then he appeared, in a measure, almost dead in all parts of his body, yet he spoke with ease, perpetually repeating those words, so familiar to his lips, "Father, Son and Holy Ghost." In his countenance also, there was a surprising dignity, and an unusual grace.

Aelred and Walter Daniel would have recognized such a description and probably have applauded it. Like them, William emphasized the importance of an ascetic life, as well as the way a man reflects his inner life by his outer bearing. Also like Aelred, William was grateful for the coming of Henry II to the throne in 1154, bringing peace after the terrible civil war: "The ravening wolves fled, or were changed to sheep; or, if not totally changed, yet they dwelt harmlessly amid the flock through fear of the law." William of Newburgh was sensitive to the spread of monasticism in England during the second quarter of the twelfth century. He is the first historian to point to the paradox of a great number of foundations at the same time as civil war raged. He dedicated a chapter to the founding of Rievaulx and Fountains, and another one to nearby Byland, while Gilbert of Sempringham, Aelred's friend and the founder of an English order of canons, also gets a chapter. William of Newburgh even described a visit of Gilbert to Bernard at Clairvaux and the good advice Bernard gave Gilbert in approving his proposal for double houses containing men and women. William praised Gilbert's work, in spite of the fact that the end of the century was much less open to such religious experiments than the earlier period:

He excelled much in the education of males; but by the divine grace accorded to him, he far surpassed in his skill in training females to the service of

God. In this respect, indeed, according to my judgment, he bears away the palm from all who have applied their religious labors to the education and discipline of women.

In dealing with the coming of Henry II, with the hermit Godric, with Gilbert, with early Cistercian foundations in Yorkshire, and also with the dispute over William of York as archbishop, William of Newburgh touched on subjects intimately bound up with Aelred's life and concerns. Yet Aelred is not even named. This omission is remarkable and, I think, indicative of a deliberate choice on William's part. In writing to honor a request of Aelred's successor Ernald, William may have sensed that the abbot of Rievaulx did not want Aelred's name included.

I argue here from silence in a source, and so such an observation can only be a suggestion. But the eerie omission of Aelred in a Yorkshire historian who wrote of Aelred's part of the country and contemporaries cannot be dismissed as a matter of chance. William's reticence is matched by another silence that seems odd in view of Walter Daniel's information about Aelred's miracles. There is no evidence of any twelfth- or thirteenth-century attempt at Rievaulx or elsewhere to secure the canonization of Aelred. Only in 1476 did the Cistercian General Chapter, apparently at the request of English abbots, authorize a celebration of the feast day of Aelred. The decision mentions "new and ancient miracles" and probably acknowledged a local cult of Aelred in Yorkshire. It is possible that a Carthusian devotional revival centered on Mount Grace Charterhouse and strong late medieval interest in Aelred's spiritual writings lay behind this request to honor him. But in the immediate aftermath of Aelred's death, even this limited form of recognition was still three centuries distant.

I can only conclude that Silvain, who came from the daughterhouse at Dundrennan to take over at Rievaulx in 1167, and Ernald, his successor from 1189, did not try to get Aelred canonized and may well have actively discouraged such an effort. Walter Daniel's biography of Aelred did not become a document used in contacts with Rome but remained at the monastery as a defense of an abbacy that some monks wanted to forget.

Aelred had by no means died in disgrace. The monastery did not fall apart after his death. There were problems, but probably no greater ones than other monasteries were experiencing at the time. But something had disappeared with his passing: a personal, intimate quality of life. Rievaulx became more regimented, lost some of its members, tried to build better accommodations for those who remained behind, and had to defend itself against those who threatened monastery lands. Everyday life had taken on the banal, routine quality that any stable monastery knows and on which it thrives and survives. The father who had also been brother and lover was now gone. For the time being, the abbots of Rievaulx preferred to tend to business and not concern themselves with Aelred's memory.

Saints are not born. They are usually made by institutions whose members need them in order to establish their own identities in society. Rievaulx at the end of the twelfth century did not want to equate its identity with Aelred's life and work. His writings were kept and were distributed in a modest way, mostly in England, but to a certain extent also in Cistercian houses of the Clairvaux lineage in France. But Aelred sank out of sight, his bones submerged in the chapter house floor close to the reliquary reserved for his less controversial predecessor William of Clairvaux. We know nothing of any later medieval removal and translation of his body. Aelred remained where he was until the Reformation and its destruction of the monastery. Now his physical remains are scattered forever in the soil of Yorkshire. Only his writings bear witness to his life, along with the ruins in the church nave and the chapter house that date to his period. And yet he lives on, more so today than ever before since the twelfth century.

13

approaches to aelred

C HRISTIANITY MEANS in my definition a faith based on the love of God and neighbor in Jesus. In spite of the importance of interpersonal bonds here, the history of spirituality in our culture often has limited itself to the individual's search for God in seeking escape from other people. Today's fascination with what is thought to be mystical experience provides a form of relief from all that is awful around us: from dysfunctional families to new forms of nationalism and crime both violent and subtle. In the total submergence of the individual in God, there is a desire to reach beyond fears and limitations and find, as it were, a zone of protection.

This process of flight to an all-embracing God and denial of other people also took place in Western Europe during the medieval centuries. Both women and men time and again turned to a demanding God in order to conclude that everything here below is trash and can be treated as such. But sometimes we find spiritual writers and genuine mystics, such as the nuns of Helfta in the thirteenth century, who were different. Gertrude the Great and her sisters experienced God in each other, shared their doubts and hopes with each other, and could not imagine the spiritual growth of the individual person without interpersonal relationships.

Gertrude and her sisters emerge from a Cistercian contemplative monastic tradition that took shape more than a century earlier. In the Cistercian way, part of a larger Benedictine approach to community, the desire for God allies itself with a desire for other people. This, of course, is nothing more than a response to the challenge issued by Jesus himself. But a study of medieval history convinces me that it took ten centuries for a group of Western Christians to understand this message in such a way that the links between love of God and love of neighbor became clear and firm. The Cistercians claimed that they were doing nothing more than following literally the precepts already set down centuries earlier in the Gospels and the Rule of Saint Benedict. But in making communities based not only on discipline but also on mutual love, the Cistercians contributed to a revolution of sentiment that to this day continues in a world context.

The spiritual leader of the twelfth-century Cistercians was Bernard of Clairvaux. It is no accident that he invested his literary efforts most completely in a commentary on the Old Testament Song of Songs, a love poem of physical love that the Middle Ages interpreted in spiritual terms. The power of the imagery of this poem, in which the lover seeks her beloved, finds him, and refuses to let him go, became for Bernard and generations of Cistercians a statement of the soul's search for Christ: "I will find him whom my soul seeks. I will find him and not let him go."

Aelred was also fascinated by the language of the Song of Songs. In his commentary on the Gospel reading concerning the twelve-year-old Jesus in the Temple, Aelred returned several times to the text of Song 8:1: "Who will give you to me, my brother, sucking the breasts of my mother, so that I might find you outside and kiss you?" Aelred here visualized the sighs and yearnings of the boys of Jerusalem, hoping to be able to embrace the boy Jesus. His language is innovative and surprising in view of the near-absence of an exegetical tradition concerning this episode in the life of Jesus. But Aelred's emphasis on love and the desire for union is typical for his life and writings. He looked not to a lonely meeting between Christ and the individual soul; instead he envisioned a coming together of many people in their common pursuit of the love of Jesus. In the communities of men and women that formed around Jesus in the Gospel narrative, Aelred saw the need of people in his own time to form communities to love and serve the Lord.

Aelred wanted to be with Jesus as his lover and beloved. He was certain that only in the embrace of Jesus' body can we be free from all forms of vice (Iesu, ch. 27). The language Aelred uses to describe the physical person of Jesus can seem exaggerated and even embarrassing:

I think that the grace of heaven shone from that most beautiful face with such charm as to make everyone look at it, listen to him and be moved to affection. See, I beg, how he is seized upon and led away by each and every one of them. Old men kiss him, young men embrace him, boys wait upon him. (Iesu, ch. 5)

Aelred lived in an age that saw the physical world as a reflection and manifestation of the spiritual one. Thus physical forms of union could express the fact of spiritual union. Aelred's desire to touch the body of Christ was also a desire to be together with him always. In meditating on scenes from Christ's life, as he did in a vivid manner, Aelred reached out in thirst for the presence of God himself.

In Aelred's time it was common to fill the mind with images in order to seek the presence of God. This *via positiva*, as it is known, was the dominant approach to the contemplative life in the twelfth century. In the later Middle Ages, some spiritual writers recommended emptying the mind of images in order to make space for God, the *via negativa*. Aelred and his fellow Cistercians had faith in the power of images. For them the contents of the contemporary world and their thoughts about people, stories, and human events could lead them to a sense of God's presence.

A contemporary approach to understanding Aelred's quest for God and for the body of Jesus has been to define him as a homosexual male, a man who felt physically attracted to the bodies of other men, more so than of women. I used to discuss this possibility with my students in the 1970s, but it was only with the appearance of the historian John Boswell's landmark study in 1980 that Aelred came to be seen in academic discourse in these terms. Since then, a harsh debate has taken place about Aelred's sexual identity. The evidence of the sources is such that neither side has been able to provide definitive proof for its interpretation of Aelred. As the discussion has dragged on, often with vituperation, it has been sad to consider how one of the most lovable and agreeable people to emerge from medieval history could turn into a point of departure for so much anger.

In the preceding pages, I have interpreted Aelred as a man who felt physically and mentally more drawn to other men than to women. He probably had sexual experience in his youth, but in entering the monastery, he transferred his search for male contact into the spiritual sphere. In doing so, he found much peace and happiness. But Aelred never forgot or denied where he came from. Sprinkled through his writings, he left hints about his sexual drives. Much more importantly, his message was one of love, not of hate, of union, not of division, of understanding, not of rejection.

In 1988, in a book on the tradition and experience of friendship in medieval monastic culture, I characterized the special contribution of Aelred. I concluded that Aelred's emphasis on the centrality of friendship in the monastic life places him outside the mainstream of the tradition. In writing a special treatise dedicated to friendship and indicating that he could not live without friends, Aelred outdid all his monastic predecessors and had no immediate successors. Whether or not his need for friendship is an expression of Aelred's sexual identity, his insistence on individual friendships in the monastic life meant a departure from what is implied in the Rule of Saint Benedict. Here the totality of love in the community is more important than individual attachments.

Aelred's exceptional position in the tradition of medieval monastic friendship makes him important for our times. Following the classical tradition of friendship in Aristotle and Cicero, Aelred insisted on the need of every human being for one or two close friends. For him community bonds alone were insufficient. As heirs of the romantic tradition, which flourished in the nineteenth-century but actually goes back to the twelfth, late twentieth-century people have every reason to look to Aelred's quest. In asserting a need for friendship and love, Aelred legitimized the physical and spiritual embrace of other human beings. At the same time he believed it possible for this union to take place in the context of a flourishing and healthy community.

Aelred does not anticipate nineteenth century romantics, who saw a constant tension and even enmity between individual loves and community demands. The heroic pair of lovers fighting the cynicism of society has no place in Aelred, where all individual loves are reconciled in the love of Jesus and at peace in the love of community.

Aelred's belief in the power and possibilities of human love sets him apart from almost all his medieval predecessors. In 1963 Sir Richard Southern distinguished between the idealized friendships of Anselm, abbot at Bec and later archbishop of Canterbury (d. 1109), and Aelred's bonds: "His [Anselm's] friendships are far from those of romantic love. They are not even very near to the sentimental friendships of the cloister to which the example of Aelred of Rievaulx gave a certain authority and charm." Although Southern has written little else in which Aelred is specifically mentioned, he belongs to what might be called the Oxbridge school of historians, which in the period 1940–70 made an important contribution to the study of Aelred as a representative of medieval Christian humanism.

One of Southern's teachers at Oxford, Sir Maurice Powicke, published back in 1922 an essay on Aelred that he later developed into a rich introduction to the medieval biography of Aelred by Walter Daniel. In 1940, David Knowles, first a Benedictine monk and then professor of history at Cambridge, included in the first of his volumes of monastic history a superb sketch of Aelred's life and its significance. Knowles's inspiration may have encouraged an Oxford student whose own monastic odyssey would make a chronicle in itself, Aelred Squire. His 1969 biography of Aelred drew on careful manuscript work and preliminary articles published in the Cistercian journal *Collectanea Cisterciensia*. In London, another scholar, Charles Hugh Talbot, edited Aelredian texts and kept a close eye on the results of other researchers.

On the Continent, another group of scholars, mostly monks, concentrated especially on Aelred's spiritual writings, providing excellent translations in the *Sources Chrétiennes* series and getting ready the first volume of Aelred's writings for the respected *Corpus Christianorum, Continuatio Mediævalis* edition, which appeared in 1970. Here the Benedictine Anselm Hoste was the main contributor.

Since 1970 British interest in the interpretation of Aelred has continued. Historians such as Derek Baker, formerly at Edinburgh, have made many valuable contributions to the appreciation of Aelred's so-called historical works. The circle of scholars around the Ecclesiastical History Society, which has a yearly conference in which papers dedicated to Aelred often appear, has taken up, as it were, where Aelred Squire and Alberic Stacpoole, another English monastic scholar, left off in the early 1970s. The center of interpretive studies on Aelred has, however, probably moved to America, especially to the annual Cistercian Studies Conference at Western Michigan University in Kalamazoo. Under the inspiration of the Cistercian Institute there, the spiritual works of Aelred have been translated into English, culminating with the *Mirror of Charity* in 1990. New papers on Aelred are given almost yearly at the conference, some of which have been published in the series *Studies in Cistercian History*, now unfortunately discontinued. Scholars such as Marsha L. Dutton have used literary methods to reinterpret the works of Aelred. Except for an occasional paper, the Cistercian group at Kalamazoo has not shown great interest in Aelred's historical and hagiographical writings, such as *The Battle of the Standard* and *The Saints of Hexham*, while the relatively new Haskins Society, made up of both American and British scholars, has returned to these materials with new relish.

On the European Continent a continuing interest in Aelred is now being encouraged by two central figures, the formidable monk Charles Dumont at the Abbey of Scourmont in Belgium, and the gentle priest and philosopher James McEvoy, now at the University of Louvain-la-Neuve. The publication in 1989 of a first volume of Aelred's sermons, by Gaetano Raciti of Orval Abbey on the French-Belgian border, revealed some additions to the known canon of Aelred's works. Here a manuscript originating from Clairvaux has greatly increased our knowledge of Aelred's sermons preached to his monks on feast days. The continuation of these volumes in the *Corpus Christianorum* series is eagerly awaited and hopefully one day will include Aelred's historical works.

In the past few years, significant new contributions to the study of Aelred have appeared. These are no longer limited to an elite group of dons or to a few isolated monastic scholars on the Continent. Nor can it be said that America has completely taken over Aelredian studies. Today Aelred attracts attention and scholarship in places as distant from traditional mainstream academia as Mexico and Australia. The spread of Western medieval studies outside of Europe and North America, the publication of Aelred's work in English, and new interest in monasticism have all brought Aelred's writings to a greater audience than ever before.

The popularity of Aelred's *Spiritual Friendship*, the many fresh translations, new discoveries of his sermons, and debates about sexuality and spirituality in Aelred point to a sympathy between his thought and experience and the concerns of our age. Aelred's optimism about the capability of human beings to love each other and to live with each other in good communities reflects the dynamism of twelfth-century life for a privileged aristocracy in Western Europe. For these individuals, anything was possible, so long as the goal was Jesus.

The historian Norman Cantor recently tried to characterize what attracts us in the High Middle Ages, the period from about 1050 to 1250 in northwestern Europe. In his *Inventing the Middle Ages*, Cantor speaks of the romanticism of the period. As a student of Sir Richard Southern, he acknowledges the importance of the growth of learning and studies in terms of new communities of friendship. Cantor also considers the role of monasticism as interpreted by David Knowles in formulating a Christian humanism that has a universal application.

It is in this world that Aelred lived and moved. Just as much as he is an inhabitant of a past culture long dead, he comes to life in his writings and speaks to us about shared human perceptions. Perhaps one of the best ways to approach Aelred is by considering him in the midst of his natural surroundings. Thanks to Walter Daniel we can see Aelred as an inhabitant of a lovely valley, where the sound of water on the rocks creates a joy in nature with which we can identify:

High hills surround the valley, encircling it like a crown. These are clothed by trees of various sorts and maintain in pleasant retreats the privacy of the vale, providing for the monks a kind of second paradise of wooden delight. From the loftiest rocks the waters wind and tumble down to the valley below, and as they make their hasty way through the lesser passages and narrower beds and spread themselves in wider rills, they give out a gentle murmur of soft sound and join together in the sweet notes of a delicious melody.

(WD, pp. 12–13)

Today virtually the same valley can be seen at Rievaulx as in Aelred's day. Even for those who know that the graceful Gothic arches of the choir were erected a half-century after the death of Aelred, the impression of harmony and beauty is overwhelming. At Fountains Abbey on the other side of Yorkshire, the ruins are impressive and instructive in terms of the development of monastic life in the Middle Ages, from simplicity and asceticism to complexity and comfort. But at Rievaulx the details of architecture and landscape are subordinate to the overall impression: a valley of light, with the strength of stone and the sound of water.

For anyone who takes the path from the castle of Walter Espec at Helmsley five kilometers down into the ravine of the River Rye, Rievaulx appears in the distance at the end of a long, narrow valley almost as a vision in a dream. Three times the monks moved the course of the river in order to make room for the monastic buildings. But technical observations are subordinated to the fact of a meeting between light and dark, nature and humankind, water and stone.

Aelred's remains, probably buried in the floor of the chapter house, are gone. The visitor finds only empty graves and the poor remnants of the shrine made for the first abbot of Rievaulx, William. Here at the western end of the chapter house, as at the western end of the abbey church, we are in Aelred territory. Its Romanesque architecture is somber and squat in comparison to the later Gothic arches. When he first came to the valley in 1134, Aelred probably lived with other novices in a temporary hut along the river, while the stone buildings went up.

Any mental reconstruction of the first Rievaulx buildings and the battle Aelred fought with his own body in the freezing water of his bathing device offers little that is sentimental or romantic. Aelred attracts, not because of his ascetic extremes, but because of his ability to combine a contemplative life with involvement in other people. In entering a monastery he did not leave behind or deny the world of his past. He managed to integrate past with present and future and to find what he had been looking for all along, the exercise of love and a sense of harmony in everyday life.

Aelred's experience does not limit itself to the twelfth century. Aelred is alive and well as a presence today for thousands of monks and nuns. Many of these used to call themselves Trappists, in highlighting a seventeenth-century reform that originated from the monastery of La Trappe in Normandy. The historical roots of La Trappe are in the Cistercian Order, which for the last century has been split into two orders, the regular Cistercians (O.Cist.), and the Cistercians of the Strict Observance (O.C.S.O.), popularly known as Trappists. Most monks who use the initials O.C.S.O. would today call themselves Cistercians rather than Trappists, for they want to emphasize their links with the twelfth-century Cistercians.

In the United States, the post-war generation was introduced to the Trappists through the writings of a monk at Gethsemani abbey in Kentucky, Thomas Merton. Father Louis, as the monks who knew and loved him still call him, was himself fascinated by the Cistercian writers of the twelfth century. Merton wrote a life of Aelred of Rievaulx that had to wait almost two decades after his death to reach the light of day. Merton was heavily dependent on Walter Daniel, but he distinguished himself by giving attention to Aelred's historical works as well as his spiritual writings.

Years ago, the great monastic historian Jean Leclercq said to me that the only people who can write properly about monks are those who actually live the life of a monk. If this is correct, then one should read only what is written about Aelred by monastic scholars such as Charles Dumont, Aelred Squire, or Thomas Merton. But in our time, the Cistercian experiment in its twelfth- and twentieth-century forms has taken on importance outside of the monasteries. From every walk of life and age group, Christians of various denominations who live in the world seek out monks and nuns, both living and dead. The writings of an Aelred of Rievaulx and the lives being lived here and now in monasteries in many different countries have become a matter of vital interest in search of spirituality.

The Benedictine-Cistercian experience, both past and present, seems readily understandable to many people, monastic or not. Is this because so many of us live on the fringes of things and feel like outsiders? Unable to identify with much around us in terms of colleagues, communities, or nations, we become marginalized. A monk or a nun is a person who has deliberately chosen marginalization from society. In the quest for God and the desire to live in a community, the monk or nun limits himself or herself and makes stability, celibacy, poverty, and especially obedience a point of departure for the way to God. This very elimination of possibilities is often nothing more than a natural and inevitable response to an inner call that cannot be resisted.

For many who never receive this call in its fullness, the monastic life still offers encouragement and inspiration. Voluntary marginalization is attractive in a world in which so many people involuntarily have had to learn to live on the "far side" and isolate themselves because of family situation, sexual identity, ethnic background, religious conviction, or political alienation. In a world where things fall apart and the center cannot hold, outsiders seem to outnumber insiders. Few people any longer can claim, or want, to belong to mainstream society or a dominant culture.

In this situation, the monastic experience of opting out of false communities in order to become fuller members of a genuine community has great importance. The question that Aelred had to face in entering Rievaulx is the same problem many Christians and non-Christians today consider: how does the individual with his or her special background, traumas of growth, talents, and inheritance in good and evil fit into the larger entity of society? How can he or she move from the biological family, with all its wounding experiences, into some kind of viable social family? How can one choose any exclusive community without shutting out the pressing fact of our all belonging to a world community?

Aelred found his answer in the love of the brethren at Rievaulx. He became brother and lover and so found his life: brother to all in community life, lover to some in his friendships. A typical modern response to such an assertion would be that it idealizes the facts. In truth, was he not running away from himself? In the preceding pages I have tried to show that Aelred knew what he was doing and did not deceive himself. His rigorous physical regime may have injured his health, but Aelred essentially found what he was seeking: a sense of union and completeness with other people that brought him peace and a sense of the presence of God.

Like every medieval Christian, Aelred believed in the dualism of body and soul or matter and spirit. But Aelred's special contribution to spiritual life is centered elsewhere. In him *eros*, the physical attachment of love, moves gently and naturally over into *agapé*, the experience of religious love in community. Aelred did not have a chance to read the works of Plato, but he was strongly dependent on Augustine, who in turn had learned from Plato. Here the erotic is the foundation of the agapetic: the experience of individual love comes before that of the community, on the way to God. There are no absolute boundaries or easy definitions. But one form of love does not exclude another. Indeed, the love of God and the love of individual human beings can and must be experienced together, by the same person.

Aelred insisted on his need for human loves. In doing so, he did not delude himself into thinking that any love could be stable and unchanging. In writing about the attachments that people experience, Aelred tried to be fair in expressing the complexities of human involvements. His response did not consist in some form of mental or spiritual castration, so that the soul of the lover of God was forever freed from any bond with the cumbersome body. Aelred was aware of his own body and the bodies of his fellow monks and considered it his duty to look after them. From the erotic to the agapetic, Aelred was an idealist anchored in the everyday reality of monastic community. The tension and desire for unity in Aelred's experience gave him an awareness of others and made him face his own thoughts and feelings in order to interpret those of other people.

In Aelred the Christian humanism of the twelfth century finds its most convincing and consistent exponent. As we have seen, the generation after Aelred generally ignored him. Even though the Cistercian Order since the end of the Middle Ages has considered him to be a saint, he has never been officially canonized. It is only today that he has a following that loosely can be considered a kind of cult. I have no intention to spread any cult of Aelred. For anyone who reads him attentively, he is too much a human being to be forced into the usual categories of sainthood. Whatever we do with him, he remains elusive.

afterword

aelred in our time

t HERE IS A STORY, perhaps apocryphal, that the *Spiritual Friendship,* then extant only in its Latin original, used to be kept under lock and key at Gethsemani Abbey in Kentucky. Only the abbot himself could grant permission to read it. Whether this story, like some medieval tale, is literally true does not matter. It contains a symbolic truth: until the mid-1960s there was deep suspicion in religious communities of any close bonds between members. These were known as "particular friendships." Superiors rarely told novices what they meant by this term, but it was obviously something unspeakable. As one priest has written of his seminary days:

I remember lectures and regulations and reprimands about the dangers of intimate relationships with fellow classmates. We were forbidden to seek out special companions during our recreation breaks. We were called into the rector's office if some faculty member noticed too close an association with another student, especially of a different grade.

In the surge of reform and renewal that built up in the 1960s, this structure of repression was swept away. Monks, priests, and nuns were no longer warned against friendship. Aelred of Rievaulx was rediscovered, and since the beginning of the 1970s many of his works have been translated and made available to a larger public than ever before in history. The *Spiritual Friendship* has become one of the best sellers at Cistercian Publications. More importantly, it is available on the library shelves of monasteries, whether Cistercian or not, all over the world.

Aelred has become almost an icon of friendship. In the 1970s, when anything seemed possible, he became something of a hero for gay Catholics. A superficial reading of the evidence led in some quarters to the impression that Aelred had continued to be sexually active after he entered the monastery. Aelred became a symbol of sexual liberation for some Catholics and a red flag for others. I remember visiting Cistercian monasteries in the early 1980s and being warned against speaking on Aelred. He was considered to be almost a code word for sexual permissiveness.

Most of the time, I find this interest in Aelred and his life refresh-ing and stimulating. But a reading of the evidence has convinced me that it is not so easy to transfer Aelred from his own day directly into the questions of our own time. Aelred loved men and desired their love in return. When he entered Rievaulx, he embraced a celibate way of life. Aelred's precise sexual identity remains uncertain, even if I in-terpret him as being powerfully drawn to members of his own sex. In admitting this attraction, however, Aelred used his inner needs as a way to reach out for the love and affection of other men.

Sexual awareness was an integral part of self-understanding for Aelred. He engaged in a relentless inner dialogue between his bodily impulses and his desire for spiritual union with other men, with Jesus, and with God. In his search for integration, Aelred faced himself and told his fellow monks what he found.

Aelred was open about himself. Even though his language of self-analysis is vastly different from our own, we can recognize in him a search for self-understanding that did not allow him to run away from facts and feelings. Aelred's courage in making use of his own sense of self within a loving community means that he has a great deal to offer our particular time in history. After the repression and silences of the 1950s, the openings and anger of the 1960s, the hedonism and splits of the 1970s, and the growing fears of the 1980s, Aelred emerges today as a saint not only of love and friendship but also of self-awareness in the context of community life.

At the moment in the Roman Catholic Church, the Vatican has taken a stance against gay people that virtually justifies social dis-crimination against them. Not only do gay people who are sexually active commit sin; they have no right, according to a 1992 pronounce-ment by the Vatican, even to request the same protection against discrimination in society as other minorities.

I find this situation distressing. As a historian I cannot argue moral theology. But I can point to the fact that periods of history in which Rome has demanded total submission in moral questions have created great human problems, even tragedies, for church members. One such period was the so-called Gregorian Reform of the eleventh century, when for the first time popes and their advisors began to insist with-out any possibility of individual considerations that married priests give up their wives. Aelred's father, Eilaf, was a victim of this Roman revolution. It remains an open question whether the resulting require-ment of clerical celibacy improved the quality of religious life in the West. Aelred, as we have seen, felt guilty about his father's sin but defended Eilaf's memory because of his devotion to the saints of Hex-ham. Ever looking on the bright side, Aelred insisted on the unity of his life, even if the reformed church had broken up his family.

The Gregorian Reform, concentrating on the "purity" of the clergy, imposed requirements on secular priests that most of them probably were unable to live up to. Concubinage continued through the Middle Ages and into the modern period. Even now, more than one secular priest whom I have known has experienced at some period in his life a love relationship involving sexual contact with another person.

Celibacy works only when it is exercised in the context of a loving community, where the totality of human relationships creates the same sense of belonging and caring that is found in a good marriage. Monks in the eleventh century had no need of a "Gregorian Reform," because monasticism from its very beginnings excluded individual bonds with sexual relationships. There has never been — or needs to be — any serious debate in monastic institutions about celibacy. It is there as one of the fundamental requirements of living together in community. This is a completely different situation from that of the secular priest, especially today, on his own, serving and daily interacting with lay people, needing their love and affection and yet always having to maintain a physical and emotional distance from them.

With Aelred it was a natural process to go from the confusion of his life in Scotland to the clarification of life at Rievaulx. Instead of running away from himself, he was joining a community where he could face himself and his needs. I think he recognized in himself an attraction to other men and saw that the only way of reconciling this need with the teachings of the Gregorian church was to live a celibate life. In the monastery he could have close friendships as an expression of the person he was and the deepest needs he felt. At the same time he could move closer to the body of Christ, which became ever more for Aelred an object of love.

I see Aelred as a saint important for us because he managed to combine intimate friendships with daily life in the community to which he dedicated himself. In the past decades we have lived through a period in which individuals first challenged and then abandoned communities. Now we seem to have entered a new era, in which people are looking for viable communities with which they can identify. In the religious experience, especially the Benedictine-Cistercian one, the community is a place where the individual obtains a better chance of loving and serving God. It is expected that the presence of other people is a help, not a hindrance, toward that goal.

In the 1950s and 1960s, when communities were oppressive places that often harbored unhappy people terrified of the world outside, it was the attraction of solitary life that brought many men and women to the cloister. Contemplative monks and nuns were even seen to be living as "hermits in community." Such an ethos departs from the very spirit of the Rule of Saint Benedict, where "none follow what seems good for himself, but rather what is good for another" (Rule ch. 72). Benedict insisted on regular, daily contact and exchanges among his people, so that they could "practice fraternal charity with a pure love." Such a requirement precludes withdrawal into some personal mystical journey away from community.

In his pain and guilt, Aelred found an affectionate, ordered community. He did not obliterate his self in it. In fact, Aelred at Rievaulx made good use of talents that at first glance would hardly seem to have a place in the contemplative life. But in being all things to all men in order to save all, to use the words of Saint Paul (1 Cor 9:22), he became a good monk and an excellent abbot.

Aelred found a way to become both a brother and a lover. In his concern for the weak of body and soul, he showed a generosity that was important for him to exercise. In chasing a wayward monk, as described by Walter Daniel, Aelred may well merely have been drawn by his attraction to the man. But instead of projecting his own needs on the monk, Aelred apparently gave the monk the reassurance and security that he needed so that he could remain at Rievaulx.

Aelred had an ability, so often found in holy (whole) persons, to respond to people where and when they needed help. Such a reaction is apparent when a mad monk attacked him. Plagued by severe arthritic pains, Aelred could emerge from his prison of pain and insist, "He is my son, but he is ill" (WD, p. 80). Aelred thought of himself not only as father but also as mother to his monks, as Caroline Walker Bynum has shown in her landmark *Jesus as Mother*. In the mother's functions of giving birth and nurturing her children, Aelred redefined his role as abbot according to the precepts set forth in the Rule of Saint Benedict. He thought of his own body as a source of comfort and reassurance to his monks. He encouraged them not to be afraid of their own desires to touch and embrace each other's bodies. Such physical contact was limited to special situations. But in his very concentration on the physicality of Christ, his wounds, and his sufferings, Aelred made clear that the path to spiritual life leads through an acknowledgment of physical being.

Aelred's attraction to the role of mother provides us with an understanding of his approach to Mary. He experienced her as unique and attractive because her body had formed the body of Christ. As he addressed her in his *Rule of Life:*

O sweet Lady, with what sweetness you were inebriated, with what a fire of love you were inflamed, when you felt in your mind and in your womb the presence of majesty, when he took flesh to himself from your flesh and fashioned for himself from your members in which all the fullness of the Godhead might dwell in bodily form. (Inst Inc 30, p. 80)

Aelred expanded on this understanding of Mary in a sermon on her Assumption, where he explained that we must try to approach Christ as Mary had done, "loving him and thinking of him and as it were seeing in her heart his nativity, his passion, his wounds, his death and his resurrection" (Serm 20:4, p. 156). This process of union between Mary and Christ turns her into the bride in the Song of Songs seeking her lover, and finding him, saying, "I held him and I will not let him go" (Song 3:4).

In this kaleidoscope, one image melts into another and reforms itself into something new. The language of the Bible, and especially that of the Psalms and the Song of Songs, provides ever-fresh formulations and insights. At the same time the vocabulary and categories of the church fathers, especially Augustine, also serve an ever-changing register of thought and emotion. The result, which in stale academia might be converted into warmed-over patristics or classics, reflects twelfth-century lived experience.

Aelred managed to merge his sources and to form his own synthesis. In doing so, he made himself invaluable to his human surroundings. He moved quickly and easily into positions of responsibility, first at Rievaulx as novicemaster, then as abbot at Revesby, and finally as abbot at Rievaulx itself. Here he carried out the customary duties of the head of a large, flourishing community with several daughter-houses. He held visitations, went to the General Chapter at Citeaux, and attended church councils. His abilities as a preacher brought invitations to give sermons outside the monastery. In his last years, when illness racked his body, he traveled as far away as southern Scotland and slept in a shack with a leaky roof, while stories of his miracles spread about the countryside.

Aelred involved himself in the politics of the time. Even though researchers ritually mourn the loss of a collection with three hundred or so of his letters to notables of the time, we do not need these letters to see that Aelred was an active man who, in the phrase of the Benedictine historian Alberic Stacpoole, showed a "public face." Aelred kept in contact with friends on both sides who engaged in the Battle of the Standard in 1138. He went the same year to Durham to witness the resignation of his father, Eilaf, of his properties to the church. In the early 1140s he journeyed to the papal court, almost certainly stopping at Clairvaux and meeting Bernard. Whatever scandalous stories about Aelred's youth had preceded Aelred there, Bernard took care of matters and adopted Aelred as a representative and interpreter of an affective element in the new Cistercian ascetic tradition. As abbot of Rievaulx from 1147 until his death, Aelred apparently attracted men from all over Western Europe, for he became known for his gentleness and tolerance. Rievaulx under Aelred did not depart

from the Cistercian norms of strictness and obedience. Aelred shel-
tered so many monks and lay brothers, numbering in the hundreds,
because he offered them the same immersion in religious experience
and community life for which he himself had come to Rievaulx. In
the last years, in his illness, Aelred gave in to his own need for company and favored a small group within the monastery. But in his final
days, there seems to have been almost free access to him. In Walter's
words:

All of us came together in one, not doubting of the father's passing to God,
and vying with each other in pious zeal in ministering to his needs in his
weakness. There were now twelve, now twenty, now forty, now even a hundred monks about him; so vehemently was this lover of us all loved by us.
Blessed is that abbot who deserves so to be loved by his own. (WD, p. 59)

Aelred at the end of his stay at Rievaulx, as at the beginning, was
both brother and lover. He had fulfilled the stricture of Saint Benedict
(ch. 64) that the abbot was to seek "rather to be loved than feared."
Walter found in Aelred an abbot for whom love was enough.

A standard medieval image of saints is that of martyrs-in-the-
making, persons who cannot find an opportunity to become martyrs
in the flesh and who so torture themselves and deprive their bodies
that they attain a state of martyrdom. There is only a limited amount
of this masochism in Aelred's writings or in Walter Daniel's Aelred.
We find especially in Aelred's sermons to his community that he did
not favor extremes of asceticism. He sought the union of his own self
with the selves of others. He recognized and welcomed different types
of human bonds: those with intimate friends, with the members of
his community, with other people with whom he had only occasional
contact.

Aelred never denied that he enjoyed being with others. His ability to share human company, while at the same time living a life of
prayer and meditation, partly explains Aelred's attractiveness to his
contemporaries. He could be an excellent diplomat and negotiator because he was emotionally at rest and submerged his own personality
in responding to the signals he received from other people. As Gilbert
of Hoyland explained, Aelred was a calm and patient listener but also
one who maintained the thread of his own thought. He was a good
listener, but not a passive one.

What impresses me the most about Aelred is his optimism. He
believed in the possibility of close friendships within thriving communities. He encouraged his monks to seek out such friendships. He
experienced political life outside the monastery as an opportunity for
friendships and loyalties instead of as a demonstration of human enmity and betrayal. In joining the monastery he did not disparage the

secular life he had left. He remembered fondly his bonds of affection at the court of King David and respected men in power and expected the very best from them.

As for women, there were few of them in Aelred's life, but he did not hate or suspect them. Life was too complete with other men to leave much room for women. Aelred had little time for romantic tales in which women appeared, such as those of Arthur and his court. Early in his life he experienced a mother's love, but he transferred his need for maternal love into his relationships with other men. Later generations of Cistercians would turn to women in order to express their religious feeling and human need, but Aelred belongs to the generation of Bernard, when monks hardly thought of women because they concentrated on each other.

As we have seen, Aelred has been rediscovered in our century. Academic disputes about him flourish. There is growing interest in his writings and his special form of what has been called "sensuous spirituality." At the same time, there is a movement among priests and religious who consider themselves to be gay in their sexual orientation to find in historical figures such as Aelred earlier expressions of their own identity. In spite of the growing atmosphere of intolerance and repression in the highest circles of the Roman Catholic Church, some monks and nuns, especially in America, have chosen to remain inside their institutions and to combine religious life with an acknowledged gay identity.

One of the most visible of such openly gay and celibate religious is Matthew Kelty, a monk at Gethsemani. Kelty's own attachment to his community and religious order is expressed in a simple, beautiful essay, "The Land I Love In," which concludes: "My life as priest, as monk, as gay, is not in what I say or even in what I do, but in what I am. And I think that is really all that matters." Kelty, who among other posts has been guestmaster at Gethsemani, is well-known for his ability to listen to others, to put them at ease, and to talk of everyday matters. He is not a man with an axe to grind, and he prefers to de-dramatize his situation:

As a gay monk, I have found life at Gethsemani to be a great gift from God. The context is ideal. No one at Gethsemani makes much of sexual orientation. It is not an issue. No one cares. There are, surely, other gay men in the community, but I do not know who they are. I am not interested. No monk is labelled. There is no gay support group. None is needed. The community is the support group. If there be homophobia, it is restrained. If there is a house with good discipline, and if there is genuine love for God and for one another, then there is no better place to be. Those who would enter Gethsemani are viewed in terms of their call and the ability to follow it. Sexual orientation is not decisive here.

Kelty's description of Gethsemani reminds me of the atmosphere that I have described at Aelred's Rievaulx. What mattered for Aelred was not whether monks came out of a past in which they had been homosexually or heterosexually active. What he looked for in his monks was a willingness to integrate themselves into the life of community, not in denying the past, but in embracing a new way of life. In this sense the contemplative life can never be an escape from self. But it can be a choice for the person who seeks to integrate his or her being in terms of celibate life with affective bonds in a religious community.

Kelty goes so far as to claim that the monastery is an especially good place for gays who are fitted for and who choose celibacy: "For those so endowed, the monastery is a splendid environment." My own experience in speaking with monks is that some of them are gay. The older monks of Kelty's generation who talk about the matter make it of little concern. Younger ones, in midlife, are often more wounded and less certain about their identities as gay members of a celibate community. Some of them, who entered religious life young, have felt a need to experience active sexuality and have left the monastery.

One or two of these monks have joined the courageous Catholic gay organization Dignity and in this way try to link their gay identity with a continuing search for communities of friendship and love. So far as I know, there are no formalized contacts between the Dignity movement and the American Cistercians. Since June 1992 the Vatican has officially discouraged gay people from identifying themselves publicly (paragraph 14 in the Congregation for the Doctrine of the Faith's, "Some Considerations Concerning the Catholic Response to Legislative Proposals on the Non-Discrimination of Homosexual Persons"). Forthright monks such as Matthew Kelty nevertheless continue to stand by previous statements, and one wonders how long this kind of openness will remain possible in an atmosphere of growing repression.

In this dilemma between love and authority, Aelred of Rievaulx's life and works take on greater significance than ever. Fulfilling Kelty's criteria, he led a house "with good discipline" and where there was "genuine love for God and for one another." As far as we know, he did not grill monks on their sexual orientation. There was much more flexibility in the twelfth century to new recruits. Today a battery of psychological texts and careful observation result in what a young novice described to me as "an atmosphere in which we all feel we're under suspicion." Our age, with its knowledge of human personality, has become skeptical about any human being who says he or she wants to choose poverty, obedience, and especially celibacy. We have abandoned Aelred's calm faith that everything somehow will work out, no matter how many come to the gates.

Was Aelred really all that successful in combining his own needs with community life? What about the silence at Rievaulx after Aelred's death? Does this fact show that something was wrong with his administration? The usual criticism of Aelred as being too soft on his monks can be turned around into an assertion that Aelred's successors saw that they could not live up to the special regime that his personality had made possible. The problem may not have been Aelred's permissiveness but these abbots' own lack of imagination and flexibility. They coped, as insecure superiors can do, by pretending that the past had not happened.

It is, of course, dangerous to compare the monastic life of one period with that of another. Monasticism adjusts and changes with the society around it. But some aspects of monasticism are constants: the requirement of discipline, intensity, and regularity in everyday life, the search for God, the importance of silence, and the experience of warm friendship. Aelred probably sought friendship with a passion and intensity that was unusual, even in his time. His successors had their doubts about how such a quest could be combined with the life of the community. But today most abbots would agree that close friendships and a healthy community life need each other and cannot develop without each other.

Aelred in his optimism and grace combined friendship and community. He could not imagine being a good brother without being a spiritual lover to his monks. He embraced Jesus on the cross and told his monks what he experienced. He neither denied nor forgot who he was and from where he came. Accepting his past, his troubles in the present, and his worries for the future, Aelred offered his whole being to God. As he prayed, in perhaps the most moving passage of all his works:

My powers of perception and of speech, my work time and my leisure, my doing and my thinking, the times when things go well with me, the times when they go ill, my life, my death, my good health and my weakness, each single thing that makes me what I am, the fact that I exist and think and judge, let all be used, let all be spent for those for whom you did deign to be spent yourself. (Orat past, ch. 7, pp. 113–14)

Aelred did not exclude any part of his self from his offering. He made himself available, as Jesus had done, giving everything he had, not for the sake of suffering, but for the sake of love. Aelred would thus have included what we call his sexuality, a part of his life with which he still felt ill at ease and which the Rievaulx brothers perceived as a cloud that kept him from becoming full of light.

To transfer Aelred's language to modern terms, he accepted his own identity and decided to use it for the good of those around him.

This involvement naturally covered Aelred's own desire to touch, to embrace, to know his fellow monks. He wrote of the spiritual kisses that come from the good life, and once in a while he also expressed himself in physical embraces.

In seeking self-knowledge, Aelred came to know God in the Augustinian way: "If I know myself, Lord, I will know you." In this awareness he was able to give all that he was in the core of his being to the brothers whom he loved. Aelred merged erotic and agapetic love.

Aelred is a saint for our time, a man who put his life together and lived it with integrity. He saw that the monk's search for God requires the discovery of self through the embrace of one's neighbor. Like Aelred, we his modern offspring can feel confused about sexuality and insecure about identity. But like him we have the possibility of forging communities, whether monastic or not, where we become each others' brothers, sisters, and lovers.

a guíde
to aelreд ín general
(документатíоп)

AS HAS BEEN SUGGESTED in this book, research on Aelred is expanding at such a rate that it is difficult to keep pace. The following titles provide a guide to the work that has been helpful to me and that might provide the reader with further information or inspiration concerning Aelred or his period in history. I will limit myself almost exclusively to works available in English. The best place to start, of course, is with the works of Aelred himself, in the Latin originals or in the translations provided by Cistercian Publications (see the list of Abbreviations at the front of the book).

An invaluable bibliography, which, however, needs to be updated, is Anselm Hoste, *Bibliotheca Aelrediana: A Survey of the Manuscripts, Old Catalogues, Editions and Studies concerning St. Aelred of Rievaulx*, Instrumenta Patristica 2 (Steenbrugge, 1962). Giles Constable criticized some of the references in *Speculum* 39 (1964): 161–62.

Sir Maurice Powicke's hundred-page introduction to Walter Daniel's *Life* still provides the richest bibliographical materials for Aelred's life and writings, even though new research results make updating necessary. Alberic Stacpoole's "The Public Face of Aelred 1167–1967," *Downside Review* (1967): 183–199 has an invaluable addition with tables concerning Aelred's written works and field of travel (318–25).

The most complete biography of Aelred in terms of his intellectual and theological development remains Aelred Squire, *Aelred of Rievaulx: A Study*, first published in 1969 and reprinted in its original form in 1981 (Kalamazoo, Mich., CP). In a brief Bibliographical Note (p. 153) Squire points out that C. H. Talbot's *Christian Friendship* (London, 1942) "is perhaps still the most engaging of any of the English versions of a complete work of Aelred." Other Aelred experts would agree, but it is almost impossible to obtain copies of the trans-

159

lation, which virtually disappeared as the result of a World War II warehouse bombing.

Before writing his book, Squire concentrated some of his most interesting research in three important articles, contained in the Westmalle (Belgium) Cistercian journal *Collectanea Ordinis Cisterciensium Reformatorum:* "Historical Factors in the Formation of Aelred of Rievaulx," *Collectanea* 22 (1960): 262–82; "Aelred and King David," ibid., 356–77; "Aelred and the Northern Saints" *Collectanea* 23 (1961): 58–69. I am greatly in debt to Squire, and especially to the first two of these articles.

A fine portrait of Aelred remains that by David Knowles in his landmark study, *The Monastic Order in England* (Cambridge: Cambridge University Press, first published 1940, 1966), 257–66, developed into a separate essay in *Saints and Scholars: Twenty-five Medieval Portraits* (Cambridge: Cambridge University Press, 1962), 34–50. Knowles is, however, almost too one-sidedly positive about Aelred.

The classic work on Aelred's theology is still Amédée Hallier, *The Monastic Theology of Aelred of Rievaulx,* trans. Columban Heaney (Shannon, Ireland: CP, 1969). At the moment James McEvoy of the University of Louvain-la-Neuve, Belgium, is at work on the theology of Aelred and has recently made an important contribution on the *Mirror of Charity* at a conference held in 1992 at Scourmont under Charles Dumont. See McEvoy's excellent "Notes on the Prologue to Saint Aelred of Rievaulx's *De Spirituali Amicitia,* with a Translation," *Traditio* 37 (1981): 396–411. Dumont's introduction to the new translation of the *Mirror of Charity* in Cistercian Publications (see Abbreviations, p. xiii above) also provides a good introduction to Aelred's theology.

David N. Bell, *An Index of Authors and Works in Cistercian Libraries in Great Britain* (Kalamazoo: CP, 1992), gives an overview of the spread of Aelredian works in monastic libraries (18–19).

For the buildings and layout of Rievaulx and other Cistercian houses in Britain, I have made use of the helpful Department of the Environment guides, e.g., *Rievaulx Abbey, Yorkshire,* by Charles Peers (London: Her Majesty's Stationery Office, 1967, 1975). The well-kept sites of Rievaulx, Fountains, Byland, Furness, Melrose, and many other Cistercian houses in England, Wales, and Scotland are for the most part open to the public all year round, according to the hours of light. These places, more so even than most of the original Cistercian sites in France (scarred by the Revolution and today often privately owned), provide an overwhelming impression of Cistercian ideals and ambitions. Even today, almost all the Cistercian sites remain far out in the countryside and can be reached easily only by car. But on a summer evening, after the bus parties and family picnics have left,

Yorkshire sites, especially Rievaulx, evoke the spiritual life they once fostered.

1. Ends and Beginnings

The standard biography of Edward the Confessor is Frank Barlow, *Edward the Confessor* (Berkeley and Los Angeles: University of California Press, 1970). See also the invaluable collection of Barlow's articles in *The Norman Conquest and Beyond* (London: Hambledon Press, 1983). There are many accounts of this period. Those I have used include: Peter Hunter Blair, *An Introduction to Anglo-Saxon England* (Cambridge: University Press, 1956, 1970); R. L. G. Ritchie, *The Normans in Scotland* (Edinburgh: University Press, 1954); A. A. M. Duncan, *Scotland: The Making of the Kingdom: The Edinburgh History of Scotland* 1 (Edinburgh: Oliver and Boyd, 1978).

My translation of the *Anglo-Saxon Chronicle* is from *English Historical Documents 1042–1189*, ed. David C. Douglas and George W. Greenaway (New York: Oxford University Press, 1953), 149–52.

For English and Scottish saints, such as the two Waldefs, I have obtained much helpful bibliographical information from David Hugh Farmer's thumbnail biographies in *The Oxford Dictionary of Saints* (Oxford: Clarendon Press, 1978).

The quotation from Southern's essay is found in his collection *Medieval Humanism and Other Studies* (Oxford: Basil Blackwell, 1970), 137. The *Life of Saint Waldef* is contained in the *Acta Sanctorum* (AS), vol. 1 (1733), under August 3, pp. 249–78. The passage is on p. 250.

For Orderic Vitalis, see Marjorie Chibnall, *The Ecclesiastical History* IV, Books 7 and 8, Oxford Medieval Texts (Oxford: Clarendon Press, 1974). For background, see Chibnall's useful epilogue to her translation of all of Orderic in the Oxford Medieval Texts series: *The World of Orderic Vitalis* (Oxford: Clarendon Press, 1984).

For Canterbury and Eadmer, see Southern's books on Anselm: *Saint Anselm and His Biographer* (Cambridge: University Press, 1963) and *Saint Anselm: A Portrait in a Landscape* (Cambridge: Cambridge University Press, 1990). Eadmer's *Life of Saint Anselm*, ed. R. W. Southern, Oxford Medieval Texts (Oxford: Clarendon Press, 1972), provides an excellent contrast to Walter Daniel's account of Aelred, even though Eadmer wrote a half-century earlier.

For Aelred and national identity, there are two fascinating articles that provide much food for thought: Rosalind Ransford, "A Kind of Noah's Ark: Aelred of Rievaulx and National Identity," *Religion and National Identity*, ed. Stuart Mews (Oxford: Ecclesiastical History Society and Basil Blackwell, 1982), 119–35, and David Walker, "Cultural Survival in an Age of Conquest," *Welsh Society and Nationhood:*

Historical Essays Presented to Glanmor Williams, ed. R. R. Davies, Ralph A. Griffiths, Ienan Gwynedd Jones, and Kenneth D. Morgan (Cardiff, 1984), 35–50, esp. 41–46.

For Christina, see C. H. Talbot's edition, *The Life of Christina of Markyate: A Twelfth Century Recluse,* Oxford Medieval Texts (Clarendon Press, 1959, 1987). For a treatment of the historical milieu, Sharon K. Elkins, *Holy Women of Twelfth-Century England* (Chapel Hill and London: University of North Carolina Press, 1988), esp. 27–37.

The turning point in a reevaluation of the Anglo-Saxon church came with R. R. Darlington's "Ecclesiastical Reform in the Late Old English Period," *English Historical Review* 51 (1936): 385–428. As Dorothy Whitelock wrote in *The Beginnings of English Society,* Pelican History of England 2 (Harmondsworth: Pelican, 1952, 1964), 245, this article "exposed the fallacy that the eleventh-century English church was decadent." Thanks to the emphasis on the pragmatism of William the Conqueror and his archbishop Lanfranc as found, for example, in the work of David C. Douglas, the Anglo-Saxon church by comparison looks almost ethereal. See his *William the Conqueror* (Berkeley and Los Angeles: University of California Press, 1964), 317: "For William, as for his contemporaries, the conception of Christendom was neither a pious aspiration nor a threat to national independence. It was a factor of practical politics." I am not sure if I can accept this extreme pragmatism: for William's archbishop, Lanfranc, Christianity was more than politics. I do not find a great distance between Anglo-Saxon church life and its Norman continuation. See the more balanced view of Margaret Gibson, who concludes her *Lanfranc of Bec* (Oxford: Oxford University Press, 1978), 193, with the remark that Lanfranc was a "pragmatic and traditional bishop," but "at home, he was a superior resplendent in the praises of his monks, whom we ourselves see walking away through the cloister, with his hood up."

2. The Bodies of Saints

For Bede, see the Penguin Classic, *A History of the English Church and People,* trans. Leo Sherley-Price (Harmondsworth, 1965 and later). For Bede's "Life of Cuthbert," see *The Age of Bede,* trans J. F. Webb (Harmondsworth: Penguin Classics, 1965, 1986).

See James Raine, ed., *The Priory of Hexham* 1, Surtees Society 44 (Durham, 1864), li–lxxvi, for the attachment of Aelred and his family to Hexham. For Durham, Bernard Meehan, "Outsiders, Insiders, and Property in Durham around 1100," *Church, Society and Politics,* ed. Derek Baker (Oxford: Ecclesiastical History Society and Basil Blackwell, 1975), 45–58.

For the architecture of Durham, T. G. Jackson, *Byzantine and Romanesque Architecture* 1 (Cambridge: Cambridge University Press, 1913), 4. A picture of the cathedral serves as the frontispiece in H. G. Koenigsberger's popular textbook, *Medieval Europe 400–1500* (New York: Longman, 1987), with the comment: "Durham was certainly meant to represent the might and magnificence of the new Norman monarchy and its Church in the north of England."

I can find very little since the time of Raine and the formidable Surtees Society concerning Aelred's *On the Saints of Hexham* (see Abbreviations). I have chosen to refer to this work in detail, for I think Aelred's concerns here emphasize a part of his mental universe that usually is ignored or considered only in passing.

For the impact of the church reform in England, see the important article by C. N. L. Brooke, "Gregorian Reform in Action: Clerical Marriage in England 1050–1200," most easily available in Sylvia Thrupp, ed., *Change in Medieval Society: Europe North of the Alps 1050–1500* (New York: Appleton-Century-Crofts, 1964), 49–71. Christopher Brooke's results were later integrated into his synthesis, *The Medieval Idea of Marriage* (Oxford and New York: Oxford University Press, 1989, 1991).

Prior Richard of Hexham's *History of the Church of Durham* is contained in James Raine's *Priory of Durham*, 8–62, cited above. The passage quoted is on p. 53.

Aelred Squire, *Aelred of Rievaulx: A Study*, 11: "If there were tensions and unedifying episodes during his earliest years, it is probable that many of these would be lost on Aelred as a small boy."

3. An Absent Mother

An excellent translation of Augustine's *Confessions* is by R. S. Pine-Coffin in the Penguin Classics series (Harmondsworth, 1961 and later). I have considered more closely Aelred's debt to Augustine in my article "Sexual Identity and Awareness in Aelred of Rievaulx," forthcoming in the *American Benedictine Review* 45 (1994). The best recent biography of Augustine remains Peter Brown, *Augustine of Hippo* (London: Faber and Faber, 1967 and later).

For Eadmer's *Life of Anselm*, see above, under Ch. 2 bibliography. Guibert of Nogent's bizarre autobiography appeared in a revised translation in 1970 and is now in the invaluable series known as MART (Medieval Academy Reprints for Teaching) 15: John F. Benton, *Self and Society in Medieval France: The Memoirs of Abbot Guibert of Nogent* (Toronto: University of Toronto Press, 1984). Benton's remark on mothers is found in an important collection of articles, *Renaissance and Renewal in the Twelfth Century*, ed. Robert L. Benson, Giles Constable, and Carol D. Lanham (Oxford: Clarendon Press, 1982), 294. Benton, who died in 1988, exercised immense personal influence on many American medieval historians, including myself. A tremendous source of inspiration, he never completed a book. Thankfully his colleague from Harvard Thomas N. Bisson has now edited a collection of Benton's most significant articles, *Culture, Power and Personality in Medieval France* (London and Rio Grande, Ohio: Hambledon Press, 1991).

William of Saint Thierry wrote about Bernard's infancy and childhood in the first book of the *Vita Prima*, the twelfth-century Life of Bernard, PL 185:227–28. This is available in a good English translation by the Cistercian monk Martinus Cawley as *Bernard of Clairvaux: Early Biographies*, vol. 1 by William of St. Thierry (Guadalupe Translations. P.O. Box 97, Lafayette, OR 97127).

Marsha Dutton's article "The Conversion and Vocation of Aelred of Rievaulx: A Historical Hypothesis" is found in *England in the Twelfth Century*, ed. Daniel Williams (London: Boydell Press, 1990), 31–49. I am frequently in disagreement with Professor Dutton's arguments here and in other articles, but at the same time I find her presentation both stimulating and provocative.

The passage from Anselm's "Prayer to St. Mary (3)" is taken from Benedicta Ward's excellent translation, *The Prayers and Meditations of St. Anselm*, Penguin Classics (Harmondsworth: Penguin, 1973, 1986), 121.

For Saint Anselm's nephew, Anselm abbot of Bury, see R. W. Southern, "The English Origins of the Miracles of the Virgin," *Medieval and Renaissance Studies* 4 (1958): 176–216, esp. 90–91, 198–200.

For the nun of Watton, see the central study by Giles Constable, "Aelred of Rievaulx and the Nun of Watton: An Episode in the Early History of the Gilbertine Order," *Medieval Women*, ed. Derek Baker (Oxford: Ecclesiastical History Society and Basil Blackwell, 1978), 205–26.

For an interpretation of the *Rule of Life for a Recluse* that is quite different from mine, see Stephan Borgehammar, "The Ideal of the Recluse in Aelred's *De Institutione Inclusarum*," *In Quest of the Kingdom: Ten Papers on Medieval Monastic Spirituality*, ed. Alf Härdelin (Stockholm: Almquist & Wiksell International, 1991), 177–202.

For the image of mother in Cistercian writers, see Caroline Walker Bynum's landmark study, *Jesus as Mother: Studies in the Spirituality of the High Middle Ages* (Berkeley and Los Angeles: University of California Press, 1982). An earlier and abbreviated version of this study is "Maternal Imagery in Twelfth-Century Cistercian Writings," *Noble Piety and Reformed Monasticism*, Studies in Medieval Cistercian History 7, ed. E. Rozanne Elder (Kalamazoo: CP, 1981), 68–80.

4. School Friends and Court Intimacies

For the controversy over the York election and Aelred's role, see David Knowles, "The Case of St William of York," *The Historian and Character and Other Essays* (Cambridge: University Press, 1963), 76–97. The relevant letters of Saint Bernard are translated in Bruno Scott James, *The Letters of St. Bernard of Clairvaux* (London: Burns Oates, 1953), with a summary pp. 259–61. The letter quoted here is no. 188 in James, but no. 347 in the standard Latin edition of Bernard's letters, ed. Jean Leclercq and Henri Rochais, *S. Bernardi Opera*, vol. 8: *Epistolae* (Rome: Editiones Cistercienses, 1977), 290.

For Ethelred, abbot of Dunkeld and earl of Fife, see A. A. M. Duncan, *Scotland: The Making of the Kingdom* (cited under ch. 2 bibliography), 127, 164.

The dedicatory letter of the *Life of Saint Brigid* is printed in Squire, *Collectanea* 22 (1960): 272–73. For *The Life of Saint Ninian*, see Wilhelm Levison, "An Eighth-century Poem on St. Ninian," *Antiquity* 14 (1940): 280–91, and Alan Orr Anderson, "Ninian and the Southern Picts," *Scottish Historical Review* 27 (1948): 25–47.

Baker's article on Waldef is "Legend and Reality: The Case of Waldef of Melrose," *Church, Society and Politics*, ed. Derek Baker (Oxford: Ecclesiastical History Society and Basil Blackwell, 1975), 59–82.

5. Valley of Bliss

A good general introduction to the history of monasticism in the West is C. H. Lawrence, *Medieval Monasticism* (London and New York: Longman, 1984). See esp. ch. 9, "The Cistercian Model," 146–66. An excellent collection of early Cistercian sources, concentrating on England and beautifully translated by Pauline Matarasso, is *The Cistercian World: Monastic Writings of the Twelfth Century* (Harmondsworth and New York: Penguin Classics, 1993).

The standard account of the early days of the Cistercian Order is contained in Louis Lekai, *The Cistercians: Ideals and Reality* (Kent, Ohio: Kent State University Press, 1977), 11–51. There remains much controversy about Cistercian origins and the intentions of the founders. The basic problem is that there is no agreement on the dating and interrelationships of the early texts. See, for example, Chrysogonus Waddell, "The *Exordium cistercii* and the *Summa cartae caritatis*: A Discussion Continued," *Cistercian Ideals and Reality*, ed. John R. Sommerfeldt (Kalamazoo: CP, 1978), 30–61. For a fascinating treatment of Aelred's life in terms of Cistercian observances, see, in the same volume, Douglas Roby, "Chimaera of the North: The Active Life of Aelred of Rievaulx," 152–69.

For the quotation from Marsha Dutton on Aelred and Walter Daniel, see the article mentioned in the bibliography for ch. 4, p. 47.

This chapter's version of Cistercian changes in the twelfth century is based on some of my earlier studies, few of which are easily available in America. But see some of the more general remarks in my *The Cistercians in Denmark: Attitudes, Roles and Functions in Medieval Society* (Kalamazoo: CP, 1982). See also James France, *The Cistercians in Scandinavia* (Kalamazoo: CP, 1992) for an excellent account of the development of the Order in one part of Europe. Likewise Constance Brittain Bouchard, *Holy Entrepreneurs: Cistercians, Knights, and Economic Exchange in Twelfth-Century Burgundy* (Ithaca and London: Cornell University Press, 1991). Though she does not deal with England, Professor Bouchard describes a development in many ways close to the English Cistercian one.

6. Worst Habit and Best Friend

The classic study on the literary element in lamentation is Peter von Moos, *Consolatio: Studien zur mittelalterlichen Trostliteratur,* Münstersche Mittelalter Schriften 3 (Munich: Wilhelm Fink Verlag, 1971). For Bernard and Aelred, see my "Monks and Tears: A Twelfth-Century Change," *The Difficult Saint* (Kalamazoo: CP, 1991), 133–51, esp. 140–46. In this article I considered Lawrence (or Laurence) of Durham and his *Consolation on the Death of a Friend* from the 1140s, the same period as Aelred's lament for his dead friend. So far as I know, no researcher so far has asked which of the two, Lawrence or Aelred, influenced the other. But once again we see a link between Cistercian Rievaulx and Benedictine Durham through Aelred.

For the building program at Rievaulx, I have used the Department of the Environment's handbook mentioned above, in the general section. For Melrose, J. S. Richardson and Marguerite Wood, *Melrose Abbey, Roxburghshire* (Edinburgh: Her Majesty's Stationery Office, 1949, 1962). General information on the Cistercian houses can be gleaned from David Knowles and R. N. Hadcock, *Medieval Religious Houses, England and Wales* (London, 1953). For the growth and problems of the English houses, see Bennett D. Hill, *English Cistercian Monasteries and Their Patrons in the Twelfth Century* (Urbana: University of Illinois Press, 1968). There is, to my knowledge, no study of Rievaulx that corresponds to the helpful work by Joan Wardrop, *Fountains Abbey and Its Benefactors 1132–1300* (Kalamazoo: CP, 1987). For Cistercian monasteries in the British Isles, see Roger Stalley, *The Cistercian Monasteries of Ireland* (London and New Haven: Yale University Press, 1987), as well as E. C. Norton and W. D. Park, ed., *Cistercian Art and Architecture in the British Isles* (Cambridge, 1986).

James Hogg, whose specialty is the Carthusians, has provided a delightful presentation of Rievaulx and other Cistercian houses in his series, *The Yorkshire Cistercian Heritage* (Salzburg English and American Studies, available from Edwin Mellen Press, Lewiston, New York). Rievaulx, Jervaulx, and Byland are found in vol. 2, from 1978. An introduction is promised as vol. 1 in 1994.

7. The Politics of Peace

For the period of the Anarchy, as it is called, the classic treatment is Austin Lane Poole, *From Domesday Book to Magna Carta 1087–1216* (Oxford: Clarendon Press, 1951, 1966), 131–66, and for Scotland, 265–75. For a very rich and positive portrait of David I of Scotland (1124–53), see chapter 9 in G. W. S. Barrow, *Feudal Britain* (London: Edward Arnold, 1956, 1971), 134–45. More detailed is Barrow's article, "Scottish Rulers and the Religious Orders 1070–1153," *Transactions of the Royal Historical Society*, 5th series, vol. 3 (London, 1953), 77–100.

Derek Baker, "Ailred of Rievaulx and Walter Espec," *Haskins Society Journal* 1 (1989): 93, argues for an earlier dating than the one 1154–57 usually assigned and promises "a full-length study, edition and translation" of the *Battle of the Standard*. Here I hope he will provide further information concerning dating. I have also made use of John Bliese, "The Battle Rhetoric of Aelred of Rievaulx," 99–107, in the same collection, and Aelred Glidden, "Aelred the Historian: The Account of the Battle of the Standard," *Erudition at God's Service*, ed. John R. Sommerfeldt (Kalamazoo: CP, 1987), 175–84. Glidden is excellent concerning the dependence of Aelred on Henry of Huntingdon's *Chronicle*, and especially the alterations Aelred made in order to protect the reputation of King David of Scotland.

The quote from Aelred Squire is p. 92 in his *Aelred of Rievaulx: A Study* (see general bibliography above). Squire's analysis of the *Genealogy* in his chapter "Knights and Kings" is sensitive and thoughtful.

For Theobald of Canterbury, see W. L. Warren, *Henry II* (Berkeley: University of California Press, 1977), 442. The hagiography of Edward by Osbert of Clare was edited by a young French historian who later became famous because of his work on feudalism and founded the Annales school of history in Paris, Marc Bloch: "La Vie de S. Édouard Le Confesseur," *Analecta Bollandiana* 41 (1923): 5–131.

The modern description of the Scottish church is from G. W. S. Barrow, *Feudal Britain*, 140 (see above in this section).

For Waldef, see Derek Baker's article (ch. 4 bibliography). The Kirkham agreement is contained in *Cartularium Abbathiae de Rievalle*, James Raine, ed., Surtees Society 88 (Durham, 1889), 108–9.

8. Making Love's Mirror

For Waldef's crisis see AS, August, vol. 1, pp. 257–58, and Powicke's summary in his introduction to WD, pp. lxxiv–lxxv.

For Augustine's temptations and the chase, see the magnificent tenth book of his *Confessions*, section 35 (as in the Penguin Classic, above in bibliography for ch. 4). For the *Lives of the Fathers* in terms of separation from all human bonds, see my *Friendship and Community: The Monastic Experience* (Kalamazoo: CP, 1988), "The Eastern Consensus," 32–34. For texts, Benedicta Ward, *The Sayings of the Desert Fathers* (London and Oxford: Mowbrays, 1975), as Abba Alonios, 30: "If a man does not say in his heart, in the world there is only myself and God, he will not gain peace."

The Cantor quote on Knowles is from *Inventing the Middle Ages* (New York: William Morrow and Co., 1991), 312.

For *The Life of Saint Anselm*, see ch. 1 bibliography. The Osbern episode is described in ch. 10, pp. 16–20. Southern in his new version of *Saint Anselm* did not respond to my view of Osbern first indicated in an article from 1974 and in my *Friendship and Community*, even though he listed the book in his general bibliography.

9. Abbot Hated and Loved

For lay brother revolts, see James S. Donnelly, *The Decline of the Medieval Cistercian Laybrotherhood*, History Series 3 (New York: Fordham University Studies, 1949).

A good translation of Sulpicius's *Life of Saint Martin of Tours* is F. R. Hoare, *The Western Fathers* (London: Sheed and Ward, 1954, 1980), 3–44. For bibliography, see D. H. Farmer, *The Oxford Dictionary of Saints* (Oxford: University Press, 1978), 266. There are many excellent observations on Sulpicius, Martin, and his cult, in Peter Brown, *The Cult of the Saints: Its Rise and Function in Latin Christianity* (Chicago: University of Chicago Press, 1981).

A complementary approach to my interpretation of Walter Daniel is available in Thomas J. Heffernan, *Sacred Biography: Saints and Their Biographers in the Middle Ages* (New York and Oxford: Oxford University Press, 1988), ch. 3, "Sanctity in the Cloister: Walter Daniel's *Vita Sancti Aelredi* and Rhetoric," 72–122. This is an intelligent and learned analysis of the literary background for Walter's portrait. My objection is that this treatment, which moves forward and backward over the whole of the Middle Ages, lacks the necessary historical orientation that could have bound these themes together. Heffernan brilliantly uncovers layer after layer of perception in Walter Daniel's use of imagery and language taken from Sulpicius, but his "deconstruction" of Walter leaves the reader unsure whether we can use Walter at all to know who Aelred was. I think that Walter's Aelred is close to the Aelred who emerges from his own writings. Once aware of Walter's rhetorical form, we can indeed make use of him in order to enrich our understanding of Aelred's life and person.

For *Jesus as Mother*, see bibliography for ch. 3, at the end. For Psalm 12, I used the translation of Paulist Press, *The Psalms: A New Translation* (New York/Ramsey, 1983).

All Bernard's *Sermons on the Song of Songs*, published in CP (CF 4, 7, 31, 40) are available in translation. The standard Latin version is Jean Leclercq, Henri Rochais, and C. H. Talbot, *Opera Bernardi* 1–2 (Rome: Editiones Cistercienses, 1957–58).

10. Living Friendships

For Cassian on friendship, see my *Friendship and Community*, 77–85. Aelred was probably aware of Cassian's many strictures on sexual behavior for the monk. Two recent articles provide a sensitive and sensible treatment of the subject: Terrence Kardong, "John Cassian's Teaching on Perfect Chastity," *American Benedictine Review* 30 (1979): 249–63, and Kenneth Russell, "Cassian on a Delicate Subject," *Cistercian Studies Quarterly* 27 (1992): 1–12.

Some recent work that shows a new awareness of Aelred's view of marriage and friendship includes Brian Bethune, "Personality and Spirituality: Aelred of Rievaulx and Human Relationships," *Cistercian Studies* 20 (1985): 98–112, and Katherine M. TePas, "Spiritual Friendship in Aelred of Rievaulx and Mutual Sanctification in Marriage," *Cistercian Studies Quarterly* 27 (1992): 63–76, 153–65. As with Marsha Dutton, Katherine TePas is a scholar whose work on Aelred I find most stimulating but with whom I am not always in agreement. When Professor TePas (p. 75) cites Aelred's description in Am Sp, 1.57–58, of Adam and Eve's friendship of equality, I do not see him as dealing with this bond also as a marriage. Most of the time, I think Aelred avoids the subject of marriage. I find a parallel between his view of friendship and other twelfth-century theologians' view of marriage. But I do not see Aelred as concerning himself in more than a superficial manner with the question of the meaning of marriage as a sacrament.

The *Vita* (Life) of Robert of Newminster was edited by P. Grosjean, "Vita S. Roberti Novi Monasterii abbatis," *Analecta Bollandiana* 56 (1936): 334–60. For some remarks on the Cistercian pattern of biography, see my "Monastic and Episcopal Biography in the Thirteenth Century," *Analecta Cisterciensia* 39 (Rome, 1983): 195–230, esp. pp. 214–16.

Godric of Finchale's biography by Reginald of Durham is so full of adventure and charm that it inspired a novel by Frederick Buechner, *Godric* (San Francisco: Harper & Row, 1983). For the various stages of the composition of Godric's biography, see the Preface and Appendix to *Godric* (Surtees Society, 1845), viii–xx. This rich and informative biography deserves more attention.

11. A Body in Pain and in Beauty

For spiritual guidance in a modern context, see Kenneth Leech, *Soul Friend: The Practice of Christian Spirituality* (San Francisco: Harper & Row, 1980).

See Thomas Heffernan (in this bibliography for ch. 9) for a close reading of Walter's account of the dying Aelred. Heffernan's literary analysis provides a strong contrast to my attempt to determine what Aelred actually was experiencing. But I agree with Heffernan in seeing the importance of the literary background to Walter's account.

Perhaps the best recent treatment of Hildegard is Barbara Newman, *Sister of Wisdom: St. Hildegard's Theology of the Feminine* (Berkeley and Los Angeles: University of California Press, 1987).

For the twelfth-century's new attention to literal description, see Antonia Gransden, "Realistic Observation in Twelfth-Century England," *Speculum* 47 (1972): 29–51.

During the 1980s, the American cult of the body perhaps contributed to a growing awareness of the body in medieval literature. Some of the studies on the subject I find obscure and pretentious, while the work of Caroline Walker Bynum remains a beacon for me: *Holy Feast and Holy Fast: The Religious Significance of Food to Medieval Women* (Berkeley and Los Angeles: University of California Press, 1987), esp. ch. 9 "Woman as Body and as Food," 260–76. Also her *Fragmentation and Redemption: Essays on Gender and the Human Body in Medieval Religion* (New York: Zone Books, 1991). Bynum was harshly attacked for her approach by Kathleen Biddick in the April 1993 *Speculum*, an issue wholly dedicated to the subject of medieval women. I find Biddick's deconstructionist approach crude and dangerous, for she rejects the idea that medieval people can convey to us the content of their own awareness. If this were true, then it would be practically impossible to write about medieval people.

For the Villers abbots, see my "The Cistercians and the Transformation of Monastic Friendship," *Analecta Cisterciensia* 37 (1981): 1–61, esp. 34–36. For sweetness, see Edith Scholl, "The Sweetness of the Lord," *Cistercian Studies Quarterly* 27 (1992): 359–66.

Victor and Edith Turner treat the question of liminality in their *Image and Pilgrimage in Christian Culture* (Oxford: Blackwell, 1978), 249–50.

12. After Aelred

Gilbert's lament can be found in PL 184:216–18 and is translated by Lawrence C. Braceland in the CF series, no. 26, *Gilbert of Hoyland: Sermons on the Song of Songs 3* (Kalamazoo: CP, 1979), 495–96. For Powicke's comments, see WD, pp. xxxii–xxxiii. Bernard's lament is translated by Kilian Walsh in *On the Song of Songs II*, CF 7 (Kalamazoo: CP, 1976), 60–73.

For Jocelin of Furness on Aelred (AS, August, vol. 1, p. 257) I use the translation in Powicke, WD, p. xxxiii.

Stacpoole's comment is in his article "The Public Face of Aelred," *Downside Review* (1967): 183–99, p. 198.

For the warning about runaways from Rievaulx, I have translated from *Cartularium Abbathiae de Rievalle*, Surtees Society 83 (Durham: Andrews & Co., 1889), no. 261, p. 194. The mention of acts of violence against the monastery's possessions is no. 262, pp. 194–95.

The Esrum privilege is taken from *Codex Esromensis: Esrom Klosters Brevbog*, ed. O. Nielsen (Copenhagen: Selskabet for Udgivelse af Kilder til Dansk Historie, 1880–81 and 1973), no. 2, p. 6.

For one Cistercian response to the sense of a loss of zeal and attractiveness after the first generations, see my article "An Introduction to the *Exordium Magnum Cisterciense*," *Cistercian Studies Quarterly* 27 (1992): 277–98.

For Walter Map, *Courtiers' Trifles* (Cymmrodonon Record Series, 1923) dist. i, ch. 24, p. 45. C. N. L. Brooke and R. A. B. Mynors revised the M. R. James translation in the Oxford Medieval Texts series (Oxford: Clarendon Press, 1983).

Matthew of Rievaulx's poem is from André Wilmart, "Les mélanges de Mathieu Préchantre de Rievaulx au début du xiiie siècle," *Revue Benedictine* 32 (1940): 15–84, p. 55.

The epitomes of Aelred's work are published in CCCM 1, with references to articles that treat them in more detail. See my section "Derivative Expressions of Spiritual Friendship," *Friendship and Community*, 341–52.

The passages from William of Newburgh are taken from Joseph Stevenson, *The Church Historians of England* IV.2 (London, 1856), p. 397 (Prefatory Epistle), p. 472 (Godric: Bk. 2, ch. 20), p. 444 (Accession of Henry II: Bk. 2, ch. 1), and p. 421 (Gilbert of Sempringham: Bk. 1, ch. 17). For a treatment of William as a historian, see Nancy F. Partner, *Serious Entertainments: The Writing of History in*

Twelfth-Century England (Chicago and London: University of Chicago Press, 1977), 51–140. The Gilbertines and their development toward greater strictness are treated by Sharon K. Elkins, *Holy Women of Twelfth-Century England* (Chapel Hill and London: University of North Carolina Press, 1988), esp. 105–38.

For Aelred's "canonization," see Paul Grosjean, "La prétendue canonisation d'Aelred de Rievaulx par Célestin III," *Analecta Bollandiana* 78 (1960): 124–29. Brother John Baptist Porter at New Clairvaux monastery in Vina, California, has kindly informed me that in Northumbria today (northeastern England), the feast of Saint Aelred is kept by the local church.

13. Approaches to Aelred

For Gertrude the Great, see *The Herald of God's Loving-Kindness, Books One and Two*, CF 35, trans. Alexandra Barratt (Kalamazoo: CP, 1991).

The Rule of Saint Benedict is available in numerous editions. See Joan Chittister's translation (New York: Crossroad, 1992). For Bernard of Clairvaux, the literature is endless. An introduction to Bernard can be found in my *The Difficult Saint: Bernard of Clairvaux and His Tradition* (Kalamazoo: CP, 1991), 17–42.

John Boswell, *Christianity, Social Tolerance and Homosexuality* (Chicago: University of Chicago Press, 1980), is densely argued and difficult to read. More accessible is his essay "Homosexuality and Religious Life: A Historical Approach," in Jeannine Gramick, ed., *Homosexuality in the Priesthood and the Religious Life* (New York: Crossroad, 1989), 3–20. For a balanced criticism of Boswell's thesis, see Michael M. Sheehan's review article in *Journal of Ecclesiastical History* 33 (1982): 438–46.

For my work on friendship, see *Friendship and Community: The Monastic Experience* (Kalamazoo: CP, 1988), as well as numerous articles cited there. A summary of my conclusions can be found in "Looking Back on Friendship: Medieval Experience and Modern Context," *Cistercian Studies* (Trappist, Kentucky) 21 (1986): 123–42. For criticism, see Aelred Squire, "Friendship and Community: A Review Article," *Cistercian Studies* 24 (1989): 160–79, especially the final pages, dealing with Aelred.

Southern's remark on Aelred is contained in *Saint Anselm and His Biographer* (Cambridge: Cambridge University Press, 1963), 75, while in the much altered and expanded *Saint Anselm: A Portrait in a Landscape* (Cambridge: Cambridge University Press, 1990), Southern (p. 157) put an even greater distance between Anselm and Aelred, for he found in Anselm: "nothing at all of the pleasant sentimentalizing of Aelred of Rievaulx and his Cistercian friends, who a hundred years later lived at the other end of the great divide created by the romantic revolution."

Maurice Powicke's first work on Aelred, "Ailred of Rievaulx and His Biographer Walter Daniel" appeared in the *Bulletin of the John Rylands Library* 6 (1921–22).

C. H. Talbot's *Sermones Inediti B. Aelredi Abbatis Rievallensis* (Rome: Series Scriptorum S. Ordinis Cisterciensis, 1952) will be largely replaced by the new critical edition in CCCM 2.

Derek Baker's articles include: "Legend and Reality: The Case of Waldef of Melrose," *Church, Society and Politics*, ed. Derek Baker (Oxford: Ecclesiastical History Society and Basil Blackwell, 1975), 59–82; "A Nursery of Saints: St. Margaret of Scotland Reconsidered," in *Medieval Women*, ed. Derek Baker (Oxford: Ecclesiastical History Society and Blackwell, 1978), 119–42; "Ailred of Rievaulx and Walter Espec," *Haskins Society Journal: Studies in Medieval History* 1 (London: Hambledon Press, 1989), 91–98.

Some of Marsha Dutton's publications concerned with Aelred are: "Christ Our Mother: Aelred's Iconography for Contemplative Union," *Goad and Nail*, Studies in Medieval Cistercian History 10, ed. E. Rozanne Elder (CP, 1985), 21–45; "Eat, Drink, and Be Merry: The Eucharistic Spirituality of the Cistercian Fathers," *Erudition at God's Service*, Studies in Medieval Cistercian History 11, ed. John R. Sommerfeldt (CP, 1987), 1–32; "Intimacy and Imitation: The Humanity of Christ in Cistercian Spirituality," ibid., 33–70.

See Adèle Fiske, *Friends and Friendship in the Monastic Tradition* CIDOC Cuaderno 51 (Cuernavaca, Mexico: CIDOC, 1970). The chapter on Aelred was originally published in the journal *Cîteaux* 13 (1962): 5–17 and 97–132. Also Pedro M. Gasparotto, *La amistad cristiana según Aelredo de Rievaulx* (México: Universidad Pontificia de México, 1987).

Father Kevin Long of Saint Thomas More College in Western Australia is completing a Ph.D. thesis on friendship as depicted in Aelred's historical works. I look forward to his further work on Aelred.

Norman Cantor's *Inventing the Middle Ages: The Lives, Works and Ideas of the Great Medievalists of the Twentieth Century* (New York: William Morrow and Co., 1991) came into my hands in the spring of 1992 and has been a source of inspiration in the writing of this book. See my review of Cantor in "The Bulletin of Monastic Spirituality," *Cistercian Studies Quarterly* 27 (1992): 85–87.

Thomas Merton's manuscript on Aelred is published in five installments as "Saint Aelred of Rievaulx and the Cistercians," in *Cistercian Studies* (Trappist, Kentucky), 1985–89. This is the same journal now published at New Clairvaux Abbey in Vina, California, and known as

Cistercian Studies Quarterly, ed. John-Baptist Porter. Its "Bulletin of Monastic Spirituality" is an invaluable source of information about new studies and source publications for the history of monasticism and spirituality.

Afterword: Aelred in Our Time

The seminary recollection is from an anonymous writer who has called himself "Father Aelred," in his article "Without Shame," in Jeannine Gramick, ed., *Homosexuality in the Priesthood and the Religious Life* (New York: Crossroad, 1989), 171.

For a view of Aelred as "astonishingly relevant to the modern age," see Columban Heaney, "Aelred of Rievaulx: His Relevance to the Post-Vatican II Age," *The Cistercian Spirit: A Symposium In Memory of Thomas Merton,* ed. M. Basil Pennington (Washington, D.C.: CP, 1973), 166–89. Much different in approach, but still important for understanding the 1970s reevaluation of Aelred, is Kenneth C. Russell, "Aelred: The Gay Abbot of Rievaulx," *Studia Mystica* (Sacramento, Calif.) 5 (1982): 51–64.

Matthew Kelty's "The Land I Love In" is contained in Jeannine Gramick's collection, as above, 145–50. His description of Gethsemani is contained in his review of Robert Nugent and Jeannine Gramick, *Building Bridges: Gay and Lesbian Reality in the Catholic Church,* p. 79 in "Bulletin of Monastic Spirituality," to be found in *Cistercian Studies Quarterly* 27 (1992).

For a reply to the Vatican's recent declarations involving gay people, see "Human Dignity and the Common Good: A Response of New Ways Ministry to the Vatican Document on Lesbian and Gay Rights," reprinted in *Communication* 16 (P.O. Box 60125, Chicago IL 60660): 3–5.

índex